BLACK AND WHITE
TALES OF THE TEXAS HIGHWAY PATROL

Black and White
Tales of the Texas Highway Patrol
By Ben H. English

Front Cover Photo Credit: Ed Sanow (1999)

Copyright 2022 by Ben H. English
Cover copyright 2022 by Creative Texts Publishers, LLC
"Creative Texts" and "Creative Texts Publishers LLC" are registered trademarks of Creative Texts Publishers, LLC
All Rights Reserved

This book or parts thereof may not be reproduced in any form, stored in a retrieval system, or transmitted in any form by any means—electronic, mechanical, photocopy, recording, or otherwise—without prior written permission of the publisher, except as provided by United States of America copyright law.

Published by Creative Texts Publishers, LLC
PO Box 50
Barto, PA 19504
www.creativetexts.com

ISBN: 978-1-64738-058-8

BLACK AND WHITE:
TALES OF THE TEXAS HIGHWAY PATROL

By
Ben H. English

To Linda, a wonderful woman who much encouraged my writing early on, and who was so concerned about my wellbeing while working on this book. She passed the day before this manuscript was finished. God speed Linda, and thank you for being in my life.

"Whoever fights monsters should see to it that in the process he does not become a monster. And when you look into the abyss, the abyss also looks at you."

--Friedrich Nietzsche

TABLE OF CONTENTS

PROLOGUE i
A86 GRADUATION: OCTOBER 10, 1986 1
THE FIRST CITATION 3
DON'T DESPAIR, JESUS CARES 6
JESS AND THE EL CAMINO 12
NOT UNTIL WE CAN SHOOT BACK! 16
THE MEMORY THIEF 19
THE HAIRE FATALITY 23
WILLIE DALE TAYLOR 28
WHEN SOMEONE CHEATS DEATH 37
WARD CHRISTIAN 40
THE CURSE OF CHRISTINE 43
WHEN A LADY FALLS OFF THE WAGON 52
"I DON'T CARE IF YOU'RE WYATT EARP…" 58
THE BIG BAIL OUT 62
MR. ENGLISH, THERE'S A RIOT OUTSIDE! 67
CARLOS WARREN 70
STUCK IN LIVE OAK CREEK 76
SUICIDE BY FREIGHTLINER 81
SOOTHSAYING AND BUZZARD CONTROL DEPARTMENT 88
NO ONE SHOULD HAVE SURVIVED 93
WHOM THE HELLHOUNDS MOCK 98
A CUSTODIAL SUICIDE 108
JUST BAD LUCK IN WEST TEXAS 115
TROY HOGUE 120
MISSED IT BY THAT MUCH 125
AN EVIL AMONG US 132
TERRY MILLER 141

MY FASTEST PURSUIT 146
IN THE HIGHEST TRADITION… 151
KURT KNAPP 157
HURRICANE RITA 163
CARL W. MAYFIELD 189
MY LAST FATAL.. 199
FRED FIERRO... 209
PAT SIROIS 214
RETIREMENT, OR SOMETHING LIKE THAT 221
EPILOGUE: REFLECTIONS UPON LESSONS AND IRONIES 225

ACKNOWLEDGEMENTS

In these pages you will find the names of many peace officers who affected my life for the better, men and women who stood with me through the thick and the thin, and sometimes in extreme circumstance.

But no book of ordinary size could ever account for all those others I met during my career, who also shared a part of their life with me and from whom I received guidance, wisdom, friendship and sometimes a bit of humor when most needed.

Some helped me by reading certain parts of this manuscript in which they were involved, or who had special knowledge of the people and events described.

Some have been some of my most avid supporters, back when I carried a gun and a badge as well as in my writing career.

Many have since retired, as I did, while others still continue to serve their community, county, state and nation, and do so with courage and integrity.

Too many in the following list are no longer with us.

Each name brings forth a certain memory and spark to my spirit when thought about, and I could never adequately thank them for doing so. They are listed in alphabetical order, as I could never do this in any other way.

And though I am certain I have inadvertently left someone off such a long list, I still hope with all my heart that you know who you are.

For with all my innumerable blessings in this world, you can count yourself among them.

May God bless you and yours,

Ben H. English,
Alpine, Texas

R.A. Andrews, Frank Anguiano, Cliff Babbitt, R. B. Babbitt, Bob Bailey, Justin Baker, Erwin Ballarta, Chris Becker, Curtis Becker, Susan Bell, Junior Bilano, Bear Borrego, Debra Brown, Dale Burger, Ed Burris, Robert Bybee, Jerry Byrne, Ricky Campos, Richard Campbell, Elaine Lannom Capers, Glenda Capps, Monte Carroll, Hector Cantu, Rod Chalmers, Leon Choate, Donnie Collins, Cody Cory, Archie Crenwelge, Cory Crumrine, Rory Crumrine, Ryan Dalton, Alton Davis, Hector De La Garza, Victor De La Garza, Carlos De La Rosa, Roger Dixon, Ronny Dodson, David Duncan, Dave Durant and Lyndon English.

Bob Falkner, Richard Fernandez, Shane Fenton, Fred Fierro, Tony Fierro, Joe Fincher, Ray Francis, George Frazier, Rusty Frazier, Scotty Frazier, Brent Gesch, Ruben Galindo, Frank Galvan, Jimmy Gillit, Kim Gillit, Don Graham,

Dan Griffith, Aldo Gonzales, Jose Gutierrez, Alvin Hale, Les Hale, Nick Hanna, Bobby Harris, Cliff Harris, Melinda Harris, Ron Hawthorne, Ron Hernandez, Royce Hightower, Ed House, Bryn Humphrey, Joe Hunt, Skipper Hunt, Don Jackson, Larry Jackson, Bruce James, Todd Jennings, Mike Johnson and Dee Jordan.

Buster Lamb, John Land, Freddy Leija, Burleigh Locklar, Otis Locklar, Brooks Long, Roger Looka, Pete Lozano, Ben Macias, Jess Malone, Earl 'Tooter' Malone, Paula Westmoreland Maness, William H. 'Bill' Marsh, Lino Martinez, Tommy Matthews, Jack McCrea, David McIntyre, Billy Mills, David Morgan, Terry Neal, Royce Newton, Danny Nunez, Keith Olive, Norbert Oritz, Stan Paschall, Alex Papoutsas, Ken Pittman, Susan Poole, Kent Pullig and Kurt Pullig.

Glen Redmon, Rito Renteria, Truman Richey, Gary Rogers, Neil Roney, Tyler Roy, Todd Ross, Mark Sassman, Ron Shaw, Bendee Smith, Ron Snow, Regina English Sutton, Roy Glenn Sutton, Jimmy Talamantez, Pablo Talamantez, Emilio Tambunga, Johnny Tambunga, William Thomas, Mike Thomson, Steve Torres, Richard Treece, Doug Triplett, Tom Usery, Joey Van Gundy, Carmen Villanueva, Kenny Wadsworth, Dan Walker, Scott Warren, Stan Waters, Joe David West, Elda Whitten, L. D. Whitton, Carl C. Williams, Bruce Wilson, Jim Wilson, Tommy Wooten and Kevin Wright.

PROLOGUE

Of all the books I have written so far, and of all those I still plan to write, this was the one I really didn't want to. But not because these stories do not need telling, and not because I was ever, even for a single second, ashamed of who I was and what I stood for.

That last remark also goes for every man and woman mentioned in these pages. Not one was or is perfect, a result of our shared corruptible human nature that too often gets the better of us.

A word to the reader at this early junction. If you cannot or will not grasp the fact that a human being, or an organization, should not be judged out of its own time frame and in the totality of exigencies, then please close these pages and move on. Your wished-for utopia does not exist, at least not on this plane of existence.

These men and women were as flawed as any other in God's Creation, but still managed to rise above their natural provocations and shortcomings to be truly exemplary human beings. They fought their own fears, prejudices, angers, and presentiments every moment of every day because of that badge on their chest, and a sworn oath they considered sacred.

Are there bad officers? Of course there are. Power tends to corrupt and authority in the wrong hands does irreparable damage to the foundations of justice. Their names will not be in this book, though references will be made to this sorriest sort of charlatans and traitors to the worthiest of causes.

Yes, we have our bad apples and work hard to see them plucked from our midst. But remember this, any organization of people in public service is but a reflection of the society they serve. What that society creates, rightly or wrongly, is what fills the ranks of that organization; often by well-intentioned but poorly thought out recruiting procedures, vainglorious goals and outright quotas by legislative or judicial fiat.

Yet even at that, those same ranks swell to this day with people of outstanding moral, ethical and even heroic character. The ones who are the true believers and who behave in accordance to those beliefs, even when it comes to sacrificing their own welfare or lives.

My own life has been a collection of immeasurable blessings in every way. One of the greatest was in standing shoulder to shoulder with such people, knowing that I was in the company of the best that our society, and humanity as a whole, could produce.

It was an honor to do so, and is why I did not want to write this book. Because it hurts so much inside when I realize that so many are no longer with us, gone now to that next plane of existence where hopefully that aforementioned perfection can be found.

And at times, and especially in writing this book, I yearn for their presence again so deeply.

These are their stories, told as best as I know how. During those years I kept my tally books, memorandums, weeklies, offense reports and other paraphernalia from my career in large plastic containers, along with teletypes, newspaper articles and assorted correspondence.

The details of the following incidents and occurrences are as accurate as I can recall and/or verify. The finished content was double-checked by others who also remembered.

I owe those who gave their all at least that much.

We all do.

A86 GRADUATION: OCTOBER 10, 1986

That was our class, 'A86.' The designation meant the first class of the calendar year of the Texas Department of Public Safety All Service Recruit Training School, though hardly anyone ever had the time or inclination to go through such a mouthful in its totality.

Rather it was referred to by one and all as 'Recruit School,' often enough with the three-digit designator to signify the exact class. Everyone wants to think their particular recruit school was the toughest, and a good number of arguments have been known to erupt over such a claim.

Ours was no exception, and our counselors and training staff did all they could to prove that assumption true. Each of our counselors were sergeants in the Texas Highway Patrol, experienced men not to be trifled with. If memory serves me correctly our assigned platoon sergeant, Charles Carey, had been in the highway patrol since 1957. That statement alone shows the wealth of professional knowledge we were exposed to.

Sgt. Bob Collins and Sgt. Brad Parker had each been on for at least ten years, and commanded the other two platoons. Over the years, then the decades, our paths would cross and recross and to this day, I still hear from them occasionally. Each time I do, I smile to myself. A gent could do far worse than working for any of these men, or in having the pleasure to consider them as friends.

Then there was Albert 'Mad Dog' Rodriguez, our recruit school coordinator and physical training instructor, among other things. 'Mad Dog' was a nickname bestowed upon him by we recruits, but it was with respect and even a certain affection.

His was another path in life I met up with occasionally over the years, including when he did a great service for my family while in the performance of his duties. He would likely say he was just doing his job, and calling them as he saw them. Nevertheless, I was personally grateful it was him doing so, especially considering the circumstance.

Finally, there was Chief Firearms Instructor Reeves Jungkind. Renowned as not only a firearms instructor but also a multi-championship competitor and master gunsmith specializing in the Colt Python, his name was synonymous with generations of DPS recruits who stepped up to the academy firing line.

Usually, soft spoken and a gentleman of the first order, that range was still his fiefdom and woe to anyone who crossed the imposed boundary of safety and good sense. To this day, I cannot pick up a Python without recalling him.

These were the primary actors who took a beginning class of over 120 individuals and within seventeen weeks had whittled them down to a graduating 83 in number, deemed fit to be commissioned officers in one of the finest law enforcement agencies in the world, the Texas Department of Public Safety.

Since then many have asked which was tougher, Marine boot camp or DPS Academy. In some ways it is like comparing apples and oranges, I was seventeen and as green as they came while in boot camp. Attending the academy ten years later, I had a better understanding of the world around me and had sipped at the cup of both shining revelation as well as bitter experience.

In boot camp, if you decided to hop the fence the MPs were sure to sooner or later catch up and drag you back for proper punishment. At the academy, you were told near constantly that if you did not like the current environment, you were always free to walk away.

The lack of intellectual capacity was one that could wash you out of DPS Academy just as quickly as the physical challenges. In the Marine Corps, if you could put two and two together and come up somewhere around three and six, you were good to go.

The greatest gulf of all was in what was expected from us upon graduation. As a commissioned peace officer you had the legal authority to take a citizen's time, money, freedom or their very lives. That was a sobering thought to anyone with a modicum of conscience and sense of justice, and every one of the men mentioned above made certain we kept this foremost in our minds.

Upon entering service with a badge and a gun, and now possessing that authority, others of the same cut would be in our supervisory ranks to keep us thinking those very same thoughts.

In summation, I can say that Marine Corps boot camp and DPS Recruit Academy were both rife with difficulties that the individual could either fail in or surmount. Each took your measure and on occasion demanded even more. Both were experiences that I am grateful for, but I doubt if I would ever want to experience either again.

When the moment came, I walked across the stage, received my certification and headed for Ozona as a rookie highway patrolman. It was my first choice in both service as well as location, so I must have done something right.

THE FIRST CITATION

Trooper Willie Dale Taylor was assigned as my field training officer, and I likely could not have been blessed with a better one. A highway patrolman who first came to the department back in 1962, he always seemed to have a knowing half grin on his face and the twinkle of liveliness in his eye.

He also had a great deal of patience in most things including overeager rookies out to prove themselves, such as myself. Habitually polite and easy going, I learned career serving lessons from him for the decades to follow. Willie Dale taught me to be considerate and respectful to everyone I came into contact with while wearing that uniform.

But he also taught me to be ready to go from zero to a hundred in the blink of an eye, if the situation called for doing so. The trick was in knowing exactly when and how, and I realized quickly enough that his many years on the road had made him a master of the art. The same went for anything else we encountered in our daily patrol duties.

Within a month or so Willie Dale had me on the radio, driving the patrol car, working the radar unit and most everything else. He even had me making traffic contacts when a warning would suffice for the observed violation.

In the week leading into Thanksgiving, he told me to be ready to start issuing hard copies, more properly known as citations and what the public referred to as 'tickets.' Feeling secure under his expert supervision and even a little cocky due to my rapid advancements in training, I found myself looking forward to doing so.

After all, what could possibly go wrong over a simple traffic citation?

It was the 20th of November and we were patrolling near the Pandale Overpass when that opportunity came. I do not remember the make or color of the car, but it was a late model four door with Massachusetts tags traveling east.

I visually estimated the speed at around 70 MPH, as we were trained to do in utilizing the radar unit to confirm. The black box Decatur, velcroed to the dash of our Ford, sounded the audio tracking and told the story: 70 MPH in a 55 MPH speed zone.

We have a winner!

Putting my head and eyes on a swivel, I checked for any possible cross traffic and swung our '84 Crown Victoria around to get her pointed the right direction. Then I laid into that 351 V8 for all it had, and off we went.

We didn't get the car stopped until it started slowing for the exit to Ozona, even with a downhill run. Though comfortable and well-made, those years of

Crown Vics were beyond pitiful in straight line performance and accelerated much like a three-legged turtle.

But with red and blue emergency lamps blazing stop them we did, and I stepped out of the unit briskly with clipboard in hand. Willie Dale did the same, positioning himself so that he could observe everything that was about to transpire.

I could see there were two occupants inside the car, apparently women. Stepping up to the left rear quarter of the vehicle, I identified myself and asked the driver to step out.

The initial contact went well enough, the middle-aged woman was informed why she had been stopped and was asked if there was an emergency for speeding. After determining there was not any, I informed her that she would be issued a traffic citation for 70 miles per hour in a 55 zone.

This is where things started to fall apart.

She squinted at me suspiciously, one eye cocked with her matching painted eyebrow arching upward. "A traffic citation? Do you mean you are giving me a speeding ticket?"

"Uh, yes ma'am. I'm afraid so."

It took about a nano second for that to sink in, and that painted eyebrow to climb all the way to the top of her head.

The result was a real Fourth of July fireworks display of words, and none of them were very nice. She began in general fashion, starting with the state of Texas as a whole and informing me that she watched 'Dallas,' and knew how things worked down here. Then she narrowed it down to Texas cops in particular and our speed traps, along with being on the take.

Meanwhile I was attempting to fill in the appropriate boxes on the still unfamiliar citation form, checking for spelling, accuracy, penmanship and everything else as she continued to rake me from bow to stern and back again. Then she was on to me personally, including class, rank and pedigree.

I cut my eye over to Willie Dale, who was leaning on the front passenger fender of the Ford, arms folded with the look of pure merriment on his face.

'No cavalry coming from that direction' I thought to myself, as I continued to try to concentrate on the form. I was nearly half way through.

Then it got worse, much worse.

The front passenger door of her vehicle swung open abruptly, and an obviously agitated elderly woman began heading our way.

With a walker.

It was her mother.

They paired up on either side and now I had it going in stereo.

I snuck another quick glance over to Willie Dale, in vain hope of being rescued from this unseemly situation.

He was now near shaking with glee, trying to keep from laughing out loud.

Meanwhile, both had taken up the scent that if there was any way around this godforsaken state with its crooked cops, hellish empty spaces and J.R. Ewings running the show, they would never set foot in Texas again.

I thought about the courtesy road maps in the back seat of our patrol car and was sorely tempted to pull one out, introducing them to an alternate route through our neighboring states of New Mexico, Oklahoma and Arkansas.

Heck, I was about ready to chip in for the extra gas.

Somehow I finished without saying a word. I had her sign the promise to appear, offered up a silent prayer of thanks that she didn't start in on me about that, and gave the woman a courtesy letter from the local justice of the peace.

I was never so glad to see anybody drive away in my entire life. Almost wanted to give them a friendly Jed Clampett wave like in *The Beverly Hillbillies*, but decided against it.

They just might misinterpret it as a hand signal to come back.

I turned around just in time to see Willie Dale completely lose it, guffawing and slapping his thigh as his last bit of professional resolve left him completely. He was still laughing uproariously when we climbed back into the Ford, pinching the bridge of his nose as the tears of mirth began to flow.

Between the laughter he managed to say, "I started to jump in, but it was just too funny to watch!"

I smiled somewhat sickly, not knowing what else to do.

"Cheer up, Ben" he said happily. "If this is the worst thing that happens to you while on the road, you'll be real lucky!"

I never gave those words much thought then, but they have come back to haunt me time and again.

And the lessons continued…

DON'T DESPAIR, JESUS CARES

Two months after graduating from recruit school, Willie Dale and I were patrolling west of Ozona on Interstate 10. I was in the lead, meaning that during the shift I did the driving and served as contact officer. Willie Dale was referred, riding shotgun and watching me during those contacts to make certain I didn't do anything too stupid.

We were working our way back from Iraan, which sits just west of the Pecos River about ten miles north of the interstate. During those years a Ford dealership was located in that community and was in the process of closing down.

Willie Dale and I shared an affinity for fast cars, and he had heard of a brand new black 1987 Mustang GT on showroom display. Thinking there may be a deal to be had for one of us, we eased across the river to take a look and have lunch.

Rolling along in our Crown Vic, we were talking about the car and just life in general. Looking in his rear-view mirror, (the referred man often had his own rear view mirror on the windshield for better situational awareness) he said something like "Well, ain't that a coincidence."

I checked my own mirror and noted a charcoal gray Mustang GT coming up behind us, very similar in appearance to the one we had gone to see in Iraan. As the car closed in we could see a single occupant, a black male with an afro haircut. When he eased past he never so much as glanced at us, keeping both hands on the steering wheel and looking straight ahead.

The traffic flow was slow that afternoon, and both Willie Dale and I were curious about the driver's behavior. The car was displaying a California tag so I ran it through DPS Ozona. I remember thinking the Mustang did not have the third brake light in the rear spoiler, so it must have been a 1985 model with the four-barrel Holley.

DPS Communications came back with a return, that license plate was supposed to be on a 1980 Oldsmobile.

Now there were several valid reasons for this to happen. The plate could be entered wrong, the owner could have several vehicles and gotten the license plates mixed up or someone could have switched plates without the owner realizing it.

In short, you don't go around screwing a .357 Magnum into the side of someone's ear over a registration mix up.

But it was a traffic violation and needed checking into.

Willie Dale confirmed the plate and gave DPS Ozona our location as I engaged the overheads to pull the Mustang over. The driver responded almost immediately, coming to a stop on the improved shoulder. But as he did so, he started fumbling around with something behind his seat.

I think that was the point when our idle curiosity was taken over by danger signals.

Both of us were pulling on door handles and putting boots on the ground the moment our patrol car came to a stop. Willie Dale's normal jocularity and easy-going ways vanished, and he was now wearing his game face.

I was playing off his body language and though I was still green, after seven years in the Marines and of a habitually suspicious nature I wasn't that green. Neither of us went anywhere near the doors of that Mustang, electing to stay at our respective rear corners to the gray pony car.

The driver was holding his California driver license out the open window, but doing so in an unusually forced manner.

'Kind of like bait on the end of a hook,' I thought to myself.

Keeping my position, I verbally identified myself and asked the driver to step out with his license and registration. I wanted to see the story behind that license plate on a piece of official California DMV paper.

"What's the trouble, officer?" he responded politely, but making no effort whatsoever to get out of the car. Something else caught my attention, I could not see where his right hand was.

None of this was adding up and the little guy in the back of my head was running between my ears back and forth, shouting the alarm. I repeated my introduction and asked him again to step out, getting in turn the very same response. Though I could not be certain, that right hand appeared clenched on his chest.

Three times I repeated myself, and on the final attempt everything went into overdrive all at once. In a blur his hand holding the license disappeared, and simultaneously he grabbed the wheel and the shifter, revved the engine and dropped the clutch.

It was a nigh perfect drag strip launch, that 5.0 didn't bog and he didn't smoke the tires too much. As the old racing saying used to go, "color him gone."

And in one of those odd ways usually accompanied by odd circumstance, I made a mental note and filed it away for future reference. *'Whoever this guy is, he can drive.'*

Meanwhile my left hand had developed a mind of its own, dropping to my Model 28 and popping the snap on the holster as soon as the Mustang launched. It stayed there on the grip, but I did not draw.

I glanced over at Willie Dale, he was mirror image of me with one hand on the grip of his .357, crouched down slightly and ready to draw and fire.

He looked at me, eyes hard and full of fire.

"C'mon!" he yelled and both of us sprinted to the Ford, jumping inside.

Willie Dale grabbed the radio mike and let DPS Communications know we had a pursuit in progress. I manually grabbed the lowest gear I could find and put my foot in that variable venturi carburetor. In response the Ford moaned like an out-of-whack Hoover vacuum cleaner, and began easing leisurely forward.

Did I mention that you could time that Crown Vic's acceleration with a sun dial? The race had only started and we were already almost out of it.

We watched helplessly as that dark gray Mustang GT accelerated for the horizon, blending in with the likewise colored pavement. I kept whipping and spurring that confounded Crown Vic for all it was worth. Willie Dale was giving speed and location over the radio, and requesting a roadblock be set up by the Crockett County Sheriff's Office.

And then that Mustang was not only gone, but had flat disappeared.

"Watch the cuts," Willie Dale urged, "He may try to turn around west."

It was good advice; this section of Interstate 10 went through a series of canyons that ultimately fed into the Pecos River. Numerous cuts channeled through hundreds of feet of rock for the interstate right of way, making for numerous hiding holes and areas difficult to observe.

I kept pushing that Ford until my right foot almost developed a cramp from mashing the gas pedal. True to form, the 351 powered land yacht topped out at its traditional 106 MPH.

From there on it was more like *Driving Miss Daisy* than any kind of a real pursuit.

Minutes later we came upon Sheriff Billy Mills and some of his deputies who set up a roadblock at the Pandale Overpass. Bringing our incoming black and white to a smoking, skidding, dust strewn halt, we learned that no gray Mustangs had come their way.

Willie Dale cussed a bit as we were both thinking the same thing. Somewhere, somehow, that driver had managed to double back without us seeing him do so.

I turned around to the west, setting sail in the slowest boat in the fleet. Destination unknown, location of suspect unknown. All we did know was that we had a fairly solid guarantee of another run at 106 miles an hour.

At about that juncture our shortwave radio crackled to life. It was Jess Malone, THP Iraan, and he had found our missing miscreant.

Jess later related that he was traveling on the overpass for Texas Highway 349, just west of the Pecos River, when he observed a dark gray Mustang GT shoot off the exit ramp from the interstate and barrel northward, heading for Iraan.

By habit, he triggered the rear antenna for his radar unit. The Mustang was already running 115 MPH and accelerating rapidly.

BLACK AND WHITE

Jess cleared the overpass and spun around, lining up his black and white Dodge Diplomat and advising everyone listening in as to what he had. Two trailing Pecos County Sheriff's units began setting up roadblocks between the fleeing Mustang and Iraan.

Texas Highway 349 is not as conducive to driving wide open as easily as Interstate 10, and there are several sweeping curves along this section of two lane blacktop. Jess's Dodge could accelerate and top out both quicker and faster than our '84 Crown Vic, and had better brakes and suspension. Plus Jess knew that highway and could have probably driven it in his sleep.

Being a veteran Texas Highway Patrolman, he probably had.

As the chaotic chase rocketed up Texas 349, the driver of the gray Mustang blew both roadblocks in short order, still traveling north. Deputy Ward Christian, a good man and a good officer who would die in the line of duty less than four years later, managed to pull his Browning Hi Power before the driver got clean away.

The sheriff of Pecos County, Bruce Wilson, took a rather dim view of cars hurtling along at 140 MPH while busting road blocks and endangering the motoring public. His rules about shooting at cars, like many other sheriffs of that time, were quite a bit more liberal than related Texas DPS policies and procedures.

Ward knew this and acted accordingly, sending several 9mm rounds while aiming at the rear of the Mustang.

But like Willie Dale later joked, "That Mustang was traveling so fast that when those bullets caught up with it, they started panting like an overheated bloodhound and fell on the ground."

And the pursuit continued on.

Speaking of bloodhounds, Jess Malone still had the Mustang barely in sight and was not about to give any more ground. Help came when the driver, careening into the middle of Iraan, missed the highway junction leading out of town and became lost temporarily in a residential section. By the time the suspect corrected his mistake, Jess was hard on him again and nipping at his heels.

Still on Highway 349 and headed north to a tee intersection with US Highway 67, the Mustang GT began pulling away from Jess's Diplomat. It is wide open country through there, and the roadway is as straight as an arrow for miles. No real driver skill needed to be involved, other than holding on tight and keeping your foot planted on the floorboard.

But it was all about to come to a head at that three way intersection between McCamey and Rankin.

Upton County Sheriff's Office, Upton County Constable's Office and Texas Parks and Wildlife set up a third roadblock that the desperate driver would try to blow through, but three was the magic number.

As the Mustang approached the spot where Texas 349 dead-ended into US 67, it was obvious the driver had no intention of stopping. He only slowed down enough to launch across an adjoining railroad track and try navigating the three way intersection on to US 67 North.

Shots were fired as the pony car blasted through the road block, losing a bit of control as it barreled into the road junction and through a barbed wire fence. Yet somehow the driver was able to get the Mustang straightened out, and began accelerating again parallel to the fence line while still in the pasture.

At that very same moment a late arriving TPWD Ramcharger rolled into the scene from the south, saw what was happening and tried to pace the fleeing Mustang GT. With the Mustang still in open pasture and the Dodge Ramcharger on highway pavement, the little gray car began to out accelerate the Game Warden unit.

That is, until the Mustang high centered on a long abandoned rear axle hidden in tall grass.

The impact stopped the little car cold and the driver bailed out. He began running for a nearby trailer house, armed with a snub-nosed Charter Arms revolver chambered in .38 Special. While doing so, he snapped off two quick shots at the pursuing officers.

That was his final and greatest mistake of all, because he basically brought a five-shot revolver to a twelve-gauge shotgun fight, shotguns loaded with rifled slugs and buckshot.

He managed to stay alive just long enough to make it to the hospital, but died on the ER table.

A day or so later Willie Dale and I drove to Rankin to visit with the sheriff there concerning what happened, and to examine the spot where a life of bad choices came to a violent end. In the interim we learned the suspect, a felon and five-time loser who had spent years in different state penitentiaries, had stolen the car from a dealership in Oakland, California.

A car salesman went along with the suspect, who said he wanted to test drive the like-new Mustang GT. About five blocks later, the felon stuck that Charter Arms revolver in the man's ribs and told him to get out. Without argument, the salesman complied.

Smart man.

In the meantime, we had figured this guy had covered some seventy-nine miles while averaging about 120 MPH, including the time spent being lost in Iraan before finding a way out.

That is fast in anybody's book.

While at the scene I walked out the Mustang's final hundred yards, observing where the Traction Lok rear end spun both rear tires each time the dead man upshifted.

Backtracking to where he went through the fence line, I observed something else: one of those small metal signs that local businesses and civic groups used to like to put up. It was lying face down in the dirt, and when I kicked the sign over it read, 'DON'T DESPAIR, JESUS CARES.'

It occurred to me this truncated but prescient statement was one of the last things that fellow saw while still on this earth. I found myself wondering if the message might have had any effect on him.

I also wondered what his other hand, as well as that snub nosed .38, were up to while I was trying to coax him out of that car. And why I did not take another step forward past that Mustang's rear quarter.

Probably life altering decisions on all counts…

JESS AND THE EL CAMINO

Jess Malone has been retired for some years now after ultimately becoming a Texas Ranger. In all his duties and capacities, he has served the Lone Star state both ably and well.

But before he pinned on the ranger's badge made from a Mexican cinco peso, he was the highway patrolman in Iraan. When I use the word *'the,'* I do not mean the only one physically as he was usually training rookies such as myself. Yet Jess was the one who stayed around, the one who everybody thought of when you heard 'THP Iraan.'

This was understandable as the Pecos Canyon country was his home ground. His parents lived in Ozona and his uncle, Earl 'Tooter' Malone, was a constable for Pecos County in Sheffield. Tooter Malone was another peace officer I could always count upon no matter the situation, and who taught me more than I actually realized at the time.

During those years Jess had a penchant for getting involved in one fracas or another, and often enough that involved running someone or something into Crockett County. Either that, or I just happened to be doing the same from the opposite direction.

In either event we spent a goodly amount of time coming to help the other, and I was always glad to know that Jess was prowling about nearby. Or as in this particular case, herding along trouble like some sort of late Twentieth Century drover behind the wheel of his black and white metal pony.

I don't remember how I first found out what Jess was up to this particular day, but I was not much surprised. He had jumped out a late model Chevrolet El Camino that had been reported stolen in Van Horn, and the suspect in the vehicle was just not giving it up.

I do remember that other Crockett County units began to respond, specifically Deputy Harvey Hill. You could spot Harvey's unit from a good distance away on most occasions, as he was the only officer I ever knew that had chromed steer horns mounted like a hood ornament.

Never did figure that one out, but more on the concept later.

Anyway, whatever was handy around Ozona was headed west to help Jess, and I just happened to be leading the parade.

I was in a hand-me-down 1986 Dodge Diplomat and had just cleared the Interstate split near mile marker 340, when I saw them coming. Jess was driving a new Mustang 5.0 patrol unit and trailing that El Camino from close behind.

This wasn't a case of a real high-speed pursuit, the guy was not running much more than 70 MPH, though Jess reported the vehicle would speed up and slow down at different intervals. The biggest problem was its very erratic side to side maneuvering, swerving in and out of both lanes as well as the improved shoulder, and nearly colliding with other traffic.

As the Mustang and the El Camino did their delicate blacktop ballet, I turned around and drifted along behind, waiting for Jess to tell me what he wanted done. Meanwhile he was warning responding units via two way about the driver being really unpredictable, and was either drunk, high or crazy.

About that time the second Ozona unit arrived in near spectacular fashion. Harvey Hill came charging down from Lancaster cutoff, his overhead lights blazing in full glory and with a full head of steam on.

He was also coming westbound at us while traveling in the east bound lanes, running hellbent for election with the evident intention of jousting with that El Camino head on.

Kind of gives new meaning to those chrome steer horns, don't it?

Jess was immediately on the car to car frequency, telling Harvey to get out of the way as the driver of the El Camino was nuts. Harvey veered off, turned around and fell into line behind me.

After the El Camino ran yet another civilian vehicle off the road, Jess decided that he had finally had enough. If memory serves me correctly, he had been in contact with this vehicle since somewhere near Bakersfield. That is a long way while in very close proximity with someone with seemingly no care for anyone's welfare, including his own and while at the helm of a two ton lethal weapon.

Jess unlimbered his Department-issued Remington 870, with a serious intention of trying to take a tire off the suspect vehicle.

Now picture this scene in your mind. Jess is a single man unit in a patrol car with a manual transmission and was trying to drive, work the radio, handle that pump action shotgun and keep from getting run over all at the same time.

And he was doing a pretty good job of it! I could see clumps of pavement jump around the right rear tire of the Chevrolet each time he fired, but there was no visible deflation.

Since I was left-handed and my unit had an automatic transmission, I felt sure I could take that right rear tire off with my magnum revolver. I eased in closer and radioed Jess to let me have a go at it, but he did not answer.

Knowing he had heard me, I backed off again as he continued to try to deflate the tire.

As we neared the rest area for east bound traffic, the El Camino suddenly veered to the exit ramp. I suppose that fellow was getting really tired of Jess, that black and white Mustang and the incoming loads of triple ought buckshot. By now he probably wasn't real happy about even being in the state of Texas.

Jess followed him in, hot on his heels.

I chose to stay on the interstate, because he seemed to take a line through that parking area that would put him back on the main highway. But true to form, the driver changed his tack again and headed straight for the only vehicle there, an occupied motor home.

At that point the only thing on my mind was to stop that Chevrolet from getting to whoever was inside the RV, and that included ramming. After all, the Diplomat was a hand-me-down and the right front fender on that black and white had 'El Camino' written all over it.

I turned the wheel, blowing through the dividing dirt partition and sighted upon the El Camino with that Dodge's hood ornament. Evidently my sudden change of course caught the driver's attention and he angled away from the RV, coming to a stop near the fence line with Jess still all over him.

At the same instant, a man who would come to be a real friend entered the fray. His name was Danny Rhea, and he was the newly promoted Texas Ranger for Ozona. Danny had heard the radio traffic while in his office, and hit the road in his issued Caprice with gravel flying.

The Chevrolet Caprice was a very popular car at that time, but Danny's was easy enough to spot from all others. His car was white but with a tan vinyl roof, I never saw another one like it. A special unit for a very special man.

Later, Danny recalled how he tried to force every last bit of power out of that undersized 305 small block, trying to get to where the action was. He arrived just in time to see the RV, a huge cloud of blinding dust and my Dodge Diplomat flying out of that cloud with all four wheels off the ground.

Thinking back, he chuckled drily and remarked: "Suddenly I wasn't so anxious to get there anymore."

Meanwhile the El Camino skidded to a stop near the fence line, the driver bailing out and crossing into the stone studded, cedar and mesquite infested pasture. Jess did likewise, clambering out with his twelve gauge and giving chase.

Coming in from a different angle, I hit the brakes hard and rode her in until the Dodge quit moving. Then I was out my own door and trying to catch up on foot. I had stopped a bit further down and now needed to make up time and distance, as both men's paths were leading away from my current position.

Sprinting toward the fence line, I realized there was a spot where I could hurdle over. As I came closer and saw how the ground rose up on my side, I *knew* that I could hurdle that fence. Gathering myself up, I hit the point of no return and lunged up and over.

Except that about halfway through my star performance, I realized this was no UIL sanctioned track meet.

You see I was carrying a little extra ballast including my issued revolver, my back up revolver, my Sam Brown with all accessories including handcuffs and speed loaders, as well as my front body armor. Not to mention being in full winter uniform and trying to launch in a pair of black Justin ropers.

Still, I would have made it if not for that darned top strand of barbed wire.

My left boot toe hung and I turned a half somersault, landing near full on my back just beyond the fence. Rolling with the momentum I came up running, hollering encouragement for Jess to catch him.

The suspect had turned up a thin dry wash, Jess shrinking the distance with that 870 held at port arms. Just as Jess pulled up close behind, the guy glanced quickly over his shoulder and started fumbling with the front of his trousers.

It did not look good at all and since Jess was within striking range, he swatted the fellow with the butt of that shotgun, attempting to knock him down.

The guy stumbled but regained his footing, still trying to do something with his belt buckle area.

This time Jess reared back with the wood stock of that Remington and let fly. The impact sent the suspect sprawling, and when he stopped skidding amid the dirt and rocks Jess was on top, the muzzle of that shotgun pressed hard against the back of the suspect's head.

After getting the guy handcuffed and patted down, we did an inventory of the stolen El Camino while Harvey hauled the arrestee to the Crockett County Jail. During the course of the inventory Jess explained that he had heard me on the radio, about taking a shot at that tire with my magnum.

Then shaking his head, Jess good-naturedly but firmly pointed out that I was still embroiled in a prior shooting investigation, and did not need to add anything else to my tally right now.

He could better stand the heat if someone in the chain of command had a problem with 'shooting at cars' in this particular instance.

Good ol' Jess.

But no matter how long or hard I polished the toe of that left boot; you could still see where I hung that strand of barbed wire...

NOT UNTIL WE CAN SHOOT BACK!

During my decades in the Texas Highway Patrol, weapons qualification occurred twice a year in each sergeant area across the state. You qualified with your duty handgun every six months, and the issued shotgun and rifle once a year.

At that time, we were still carrying .357 Magnum revolvers, mostly the Smith and Wesson Model 28 Highway Patrolman as well as the Smith & Wesson 586 Distinguished Combat Magnum. There was also a smattering of Colt .357 Troopers carried by uniformed female personnel, due to the slightly smaller grip frame.

The Department rifle was the Ruger Mini-14 in .223, the Ruger having replaced our older Winchester .30-30s prior to my graduating the academy. Our shotguns were Remington 870 riot guns, though an occasional far older Remington 31 was still on the inventory. I know, because I had one issued to my patrol unit.

When loaded with our duty 000 Buckshot or rifled slug, that steel buttplated gun could kill on both ends. With the possible exception of a Winchester '94 carbine I once had in .44 magnum that exhibited headspacing problems, that shotgun kicked harder than anything else I ever shouldered. I'm telling you folks; it would bring tears to your eyes.

Our qualifications were set up during our monthly area meetings, and it gave us the opportunity to all get together and visit in a more relaxed environment, other than while investigating a bad wreck or during an all-night manhunt, or like emergency.

Now a certain amount of tomfoolery occurred during many of those meetings. Highway patrolmen like few things better than a good joke, especially when it involves someone other than themselves.

This tends to carry over to range qualifications, such as when a new man comes in and during a string of fire everyone blasts away at his target. Then the sergeant comes over, examines the tattered remains, and begins yelling about what in the blue blazes happened.

There were also times when a couple of the younger jokers decided to turn the tables on an older troop and toss a couple of rounds on his target, especially when he had a really good run going. Years later Kurt Knapp and Cody Cory were the big instigators we had for this, and it was usually my target.

But one thing remained inviolate in all this, and that was safety. Every manjack of us wanted to keep the exact same number of holes that we were born with. As an old friend of mine used to say during my Marine Corps days:

"It ain't the bullet with your name written on it that you worry about, it's those addressed 'To Whom It May Concern.'"

However, every now and then someone comes along, usually a rookie, that for one reason or another does not give proper respect and attention to a loaded gun. Whether due to a temporary brain burr, being nervous or a real case of the stupid, they have that sickening surprise of a moment that sets everyone else's heart racing in response.

After an immediate jolt of adrenalin all present conduct a hasty equipment check, focusing on that same issued number of holes. If anyone should ever doubt the existence of an All Mighty, one only needs to be aware of the silent prayers of thanks offered up when this happens, and no one is hurt.

This was one of those days.

I will not mention the trooper's name, as my intention in this book is to not embarrass someone. Yet this was not the first time involving a negligent discharge with this individual, prior he had done so with an issued revolver. The worst part about these incidents was in the person's reaction.

Each time he would trigger a wayward round, he would start laughing like it was some sort of joke. Maybe because of the embarrassment, maybe because it was the only thing he could think of or maybe he found some sort of offbeat humor in it all. Whatever the reason, I still wonder if he ever realized that no one else was laughing.

Or even tried to give the mere hint of a smile.

We were at the range south of Sonora, Don Van Zandt was one of our area firearms instructors and was in charge of the process. Don had joined the DPS back in 1968, so he had better than twenty years on at that time.

I admired Don, he seemed to have a rare knack of being able to change with the times and still get the job done. That was a hard thing to do in this line of work, yet on the day I retired Don was still in the harness, still going strong and making certain the Department got its money's worth. He would continue to do so for almost another ten years, ultimately retiring with a half century of service.

Don Van Zandt would also bust a gut or blow a motor to get to you if you needed help, which was always good in my book.

Willie Dale and I were through qualifying and standing off to the side, visiting with some other hands when a shotgun loaded with triple ought went off. Every one of us had heard enough guns fired to know when a tin overhead rattled like that, something was definitely wrong.

By instinct we bolted for the opposite side of the target shed, as it was the biggest and closest shelter at hand. Once safely behind cover, we peeked around the corner to re-evaluate the situation.

Don was still on the firing line, standing behind that yahoo with a smoking Remington 870 in his hands. Sunshine was coming through a gaping new hole in that tin roof, the result of what a load of buckshot does when concentrated at near point-blank range. Van Zandt was a tobacco man, and at this point in time looked like he might have swallowed his entire chew.

Stepping forward, he snatched the Remington away as that inane giggling began anew. With obvious disgust, Don cleared the weapon and turned to our congregation gathered behind the target shed, saying it was safe to come out now.

But Willie Dale, still eyeballing the situation from the corner of the shed, remained thoroughly unconvinced.

"Like hell!" he retorted in a loud voice. "Not until we can shoot back!"

And I think he was only about half facetious when he said it, too.

THP Area 4B07 in 1988. From left to right: Trooper Tom Usery, Trooper Norbert Ortiz, Captain W. D. 'Bill' Marsh, Trooper Reuben Terrones, Major Kenneth Bertling, Trooper Ben H. English, Trooper Donald Van Zandt, Corporal W. D. Taylor, Trooper Buster Lamb, Trooper Richard Barton, Trooper L. D. Whitton and Sergeant Glen Redmon.

THE MEMORY THIEF

In the early part of my career, the officers coming on shift would often meet someplace to chew the fat and share where they were thinking of patrolling, or what they might be doing other than normal patrol work.

When you have so few men on duty for a 3,000 square mile county, with a seventy some odd mile stretch of interstate, it just made sense to do so. Those gents sitting with you would likely be the only help you would have available, when something blew up in your face. He might be a good hour away, but you knew he was coming just as hard as he could. And you'd do the same for him.

On this particular afternoon, I was blessed to be working the same basic shift as Rod Chalmers and Shane Fenton. Rod was our state game warden and Shane a deputy sheriff at the time.

Ultimately Rod would promote to lieutenant and move to Austin, where he became widely known as an instructor on their academy staff. For his part, Shane would become sheriff for Crockett County and serve two terms in that capacity.

We were in the dining area at the truck stop when the call came in, man with a gun at the rest area west of Ozona. The reports were saying he was screaming at people and threatening to shoot.

All three of us hit the front door of that truck stop at a dead run, scrambling to make it to our individual patrol units. It was almost thirty miles to the rest area, which already meant at least fifteen minutes in response time. That makes for far too many minutes adding up when the call is a man with a gun.

Within a mile or so I was in the lead and pulling away, Rod was in a TPWD issued Dodge Ramcharger and Shane in a near new 1990 Ford LTD Crown Victoria, their so-called 'Police Interceptor.' It was more powerful than the 1984 model I had started out with, but my Dodge Diplomat could always take him on the big end.

And today, we were all pushing on the big end for all that it was worth.

Working my way through traffic, I tried to be as smooth as possible and not let my foot go near the brake pedal. The other one was planted firmly on the floor and I was doing my best to will that little 318 four barrel into giving me another hundred RPMs. Shane and Rod were falling further and further behind.

Fifteen minutes later I was on that brake pedal and attempting to rein in as I hit the exit ramp into the rest area. The suspect was easy enough to pick out, he was the guy waving around the Browning Auto 5 beside a late model half ton pickup, driver's door open.

And yeah, he was screaming at the top of his lungs to anybody parked in the vicinity.

The black and white Diplomat came to a shuddering, tire melting halt, stopping about fifty yards short of the suspect's vehicle. I turned my front wheels full right to give me a bit more protection and grabbed my Department issued Mini-14, which I kept secured in the front passenger seat with the safety belt.

Chambering a round, I plastered myself behind the door frame and the spotlamp. If that Browning was loaded with buckshot or a slug, he could make my life really miserable. Or worse.

Putting the sights on his chest, I used my best command voice to get him to put down the shotgun, repeating myself over and again with a few seconds pause in between. Now he was hollering at me in return, and our time together was quickly devolving into a shouting match.

As he ranted on the muzzle of the Browning swung crazily in every direction. In response, I etched a red line in my mind that if he deliberately pointed the gun at me, I would drop him.

All the slack in the Mini-14's trigger was already taken up.

Then I finally heard clearly what he was screaming about. He was yelling that someone in that parking area had taken his wife. We continued our back and forth, he wailing about his wife being taken and me shouting back to put the gun down so I could help find her.

I hear Shane pull up beside me, his door opening and the distinct sound of a rifle round being chambered. Shortly thereafter, I hear Rod do the same on the opposite side. I never glance to either, I know who they are already and have no doubt they will do what needs done.

Every bit of my concentration is still focused on the armed subject, and the muzzle of that shotgun. I am still trying to get him to drop the Browning without having to do so the hard way.

The seconds tick by, life and death riding each fraction of a movement on a faraway timepiece, measuring for the records of eternity.

Then I notice the scantest flicker of indecision on his part. His voice is not as strident and enraged, and the muzzle of that twelve gauge starts to droop a bit. He is starting to hear what I have been trying to tell him.

In return, I begin lowering my own tone and volume. Speaking slowly, emphatically while trying to reach into the guy's mind to find that toggle switch marked 'reason.'

Help me, God.

The muzzle of the shotgun lowers slowly to point at the pavement. The elderly man turns away and quietly places the Browning on the seat of his pickup truck, buttstock toward us. At my instruction, he moves away from the vehicle and faces the other direction.

BLACK AND WHITE

Making sure his hands are empty, I put the Ruger down and start moving forward. As I do so Shane and Rod fan out to the sides, keeping him covered and me out of any possible crossfire.

Soon enough, I have him secured, as he continues to declare that someone has kidnapped his wife. At this juncture I realize there is something wrong with him.

Something seriously wrong.

Shane and Rod begin talking to him, trying to calm him as they look for some sort of identification. I step over to the pickup truck to clear the shotgun. Grabbing the charging handle I jerk the bolt back, expecting a load to eject out of the chamber.

But the chamber is empty. Quickly, I turn the gun upside down and check the magazine tube.

Also empty.

That is when a sickening sensation swept through my body like few times before in my life, settling down where I live deep within myself. My thoughts went to my rifle sights centered on the man's chest, and of all the trigger slack gathered up on that Mini-14. If he had as much as flinched wrong…

The sickening sensation intensified and I could feel my features paling.

And then I gathered it all up, put it away and locked that particular door in my mind.

The old man continued to repeat that someone had taken his wife, and that he would be completely lost without her. He was in tears and emotionally distraught, and it was obvious he truly believed what he was saying.

But the more he talked, the more confused he became.

Gently and with genuine compassion, Shane placed the elderly gentleman in his patrol unit and started for town. Rod stayed around and helped me inventory the vehicle.

A bit later we found out there was a nationwide alert to locate the man. Talking with the originating agency and the family, we learned he had been living with his daughter in the Tyler area.

Two days before, he said he was going to the local Dairy Queen for an ice cream cone, about six blocks away. Next thing anybody knew he was nearly five hundred miles southwest, at an interstate highway rest area waving a Browning Auto 5 shotgun around.

His wife of many decades had passed away some five years before.

Throughout the rest of my time while working Interstate 10, I would have several brushes with what I began to think upon as 'The Memory Thief.' Billy Mills, sheriff of Crockett County for over thirty years and friend to my family for more than that, used to say that every crazy person on earth must have either a road map or a phone number to Ozona, Texas.

But these people aren't 'crazy' by any normal meaning of the word. In actuality, they are victims of the most heartbreaking theft of all: their memories. For what would any of us be without our recollections of the past? Of friends, family, events, and the special remembrances of our lives?

When I was in grade school, I read a short story by Edward Everett Hale entitled *The Man Without A Country*. The tale left a lasting impression on me and I never forgot the moral to the story.

Yet how far more sad, pitiful and lost would any man be without his personal memories?

I came to despise that one I called The Memory Thief, for he is must be the most insidious villain of all. He causes us to do things that later we look back upon and shudder, still fearful as to what might have been.

In my career there were several instances where I was forced to use a gun. There were many others when I would have been legally justified in doing so, but chose not to.

When I think back to this spring afternoon and that poor old man suffering from the horrid curse of The Memory Thief, I want to fall down on my knees and thank the Good Lord I didn't.

THE HAIRE FATALITY

Any loss of human life is a tragedy in some manner, because for any of us life is the greatest gift of all. When that loss occurs, so many hearts and lives of others are also affected. It is much like a spiderweb of cracks in shattered safety glass, traveling away in every direction from the point of impact, changing and colliding in so many unpredictable ways. So many loved ones left grieving, so many promises left unfulfilled, so many questions left unanswered.

There are times when all of this comes upon one's self in torrents, and possibly no more so than for peace officers in a small community. We are at the scene, at the hospital, at the funeral, inside the interview room, we conduct the investigations and file the necessary reports.

We break the news to the survivors, and inevitably walk away feeling we have failed them in some way with our pitifully insufficient words, or awkward behavior.

We are the ones who have to make the arrests and take someone to jail, to the courtroom and sometimes escort the convicted to prison. A few times, you might be called upon to witness an ensuing execution.

Through it all you live with the circumstance and the horror, strung out over days, weeks, months, or even years and decades. In the back of your mind, often subconsciously, you wonder how long this process must take. Then one day the memory slips away from you, or at least it feels that way. That is until something triggers those very same sensations and you are right back where you started so long ago.

When I opened the sealed investigation packet to this case, these same feelings and sensations swept over me yet again.

It is difficult enough when you are able to hold tragedy at arm's length, and distance yourself somewhat from what occurred and what will occur. But that same sort of sorrow becomes nearly overwhelming when it concerns people that you know. Young people with their entire lives before them; the pride of parents, families, neighbors, small town schools and your community as a whole.

Those are the ones that stick closest to you, for all your remaining days.

It was a late Saturday night or early Sunday morn, depending on how one measured upon the hour. That was when the phone rang and I knew it was bad news, as no one calls during those hours unless they have some. Besides, I was the trooper on call and the two just seemed to go hand in hand.

The voice on the other end was Bob Falkner's, the most experienced PCO (Police Communications Operator) we had in Ozona and who was there when the station opened in 1973. He not only worked for the DPS but was also fire chief for the local volunteer department, and would hold that position for decades to come. There are some who naturally give more, and then a precious few who donate so much more than that. Bob Falkner was that sort of man.

Ever the professional, Bob relayed to me what he was sure of and I knew then it was really bad. Throwing on my uniform as quickly as I could, I stepped into the wet, frigid night, trying to be as quiet as possible to not disturb Cathy or our sleeping baby boy.

That hardly ever seemed to work out as well as intended.

The location was east of Ozona and then south about two miles on a paved county lane known as Taylor Box Road. The weather seemed to ally itself in setting the dismal scene, spitting freezing rain and sleet as my Dodge rolled along. Deputy Shane Fenton was on the scene and reporting there was a fatality.

Later in the investigation I learned that two of the occupants had walked from where the wreck occurred, up to the truck stop along the interstate to find help. When Shane arrived, they kept saying they could not find one of the others who was with them.

The young girl's name was Christine Haire, all of seventeen years old. In the rapidly growing icy angst inside his gut, the deputy already knew where she was.

He transported the two back to the scene where two others, a boy and a girl, continued to vainly search for the missing occupant. Shane got out of his unit with his flashlight and looked under the engine area. The teenager had been thrown out of the car when it began rolling, and was pinned underneath.

The deputy forced himself underneath and close enough to check for a pulse. There wasn't any, and her body was cold to the touch.

The surviving occupants were crying near hysterically and begging Shane to do something. He warned them to stay away from the car and that help was enroute to take care of Chris. Shane was born and raised in Ozona, and had watched every one of those kids grow up.

And now, when they needed him most, he could only try to keep them from making matters worse in the dark and the cold, and wait for that help to arrive. His personal crucible of helplessness and despair is the worst sensation that any peace officer can ever bear. For him, it was a heartbreaking nightmare come to life.

I saw it all on his face when I pulled up to the accident scene.

Once the ambulance arrived, we loaded the surviving occupants not only into it but also Shane's unit to get them to the hospital. While there, a mandatory blood sample was drawn from the driver.

That drinking was involved was obvious, beer cans were scattered about the vehicle and it literally reeked with the odor of alcohol. Later in statements taken from the surviving occupants, it was learned that all had been drinking prior to the wreck.

Yet in an irony among so many, a blood sample taken from the deceased girl revealed she was the only one who had not been drinking.

More so, the survivors would state the deceased did not seem particularly at ease in riding around with the others, suggesting more than once that she and the other girl be taken back to their pickup truck.

These are the sort of cold, cheerless facts that a man carries with him, in an investigation that brought so much sadness to so many.

The wreck occurred on a paved county road with a posted speed limit of 55 MPH, but in a left-hand curve where a yellow warning sign advised all who entered to slow down to twenty-five.

This was not the first time I had worked an accident at this spot, nor would it be the last. I even had a pursuit end at this location because of that curve. Years later, after yet another fatality, it was reconfigured to allow for a much safer entrance and exit.

The car, a maroon 1990 Plymouth Laser two door, had entered the bend at a calculated 52.1 MPH. The young driver, later determined to be DWI, panicked and stood hard on the brakes as he tried to swerve left. The vehicle skidded off the road in a pronounced understeer, meaning the nose kept trying to go straight.

Leaving the pavement, the Plymouth went off about a three foot embankment as it went through a fence line, becoming airborne in the process. Landing in the pasture on its nose, the car began cartwheeling across. The deceased, along with the other two rear seat occupants, were ejected as none of them had their safety belts on.

Chris was thrown in the same direction as the rolling Plymouth, and when the maroon Laser came to rest on all four wheels it landed on her body, crushing her with the engine and transaxle.

In either panic or premonition, the last thing anyone heard from Chris was when she screamed "I'm going to die!"

And she did.

Brian Morrow arrived with the duty wrecker. Like Shane, Brian had graduated school in Ozona and was not that much older than those involved in the wreck. With all the care and respect that we could muster, Chris's body was removed from under the car.

By now it was nearly dawn and a cold, nasty winter morning was beginning to settle like a thick blanket of despair in a pall of unanswered what ifs. It was as if the souls of tragedies before had all gathered in the clouds, crying over lost dreams and lives cut too short.

We sat in Shane's patrol car, trying to shake the chill and perhaps share in silence the awfulness of the receding night, one that none of us wanted to say anything about. Then came another call of another accident with multiple injuries, some fifty miles away in Val Verde County.

Yet we were the nearest units to the reported location.

I don't remember the reason why but we were all still in Shane's unit, I think it was because the other trooper coming on day shift needed my car. In any event, we decided to stay together until we could arrive on scene and ascertain the particulars. Reports were spotty and other units were trying to respond from Del Rio.

But we would get there long before they could.

We were all dog tired. I had gotten about an hour's worth of sleep and Shane had none at all, both of us were already emotionally and physically done. Maybe that was one of the reasons we decided to stick together.

Shane opened the big Ford up with me riding shotgun, and Brian in the back. He pushed the Crown Vic as fast as he dared and still arrive in one piece, as it was soaking wet and the roadway was slick.

About eight miles north of the abandoned community of Juno, we came upon a light green Ford extended cab rolled over in a pasture to the east side of the highway. What was left of a camper shell laid nearby, and numerous people were wandering around in a daze.

It did not take long to ascertain that a coyote had been taking a load of illegals north and lost control, overturning the truck and throwing at least ten individuals out of the vehicle. Unhurt himself the human trafficker fled the scene, leaving his human cargo to fend for themselves.

He did not stop even long enough to see if any of them were hurt.

Still in shock, one of the group led us to an old man lying beneath a cedar tree. He was at least seventy-five.

And in every breath he took, it rattled in his lungs as if it was his last.

We had an ambulance coming, but Shane ran back to his unit to try to get out a broadcast about our situation. He also wanted to send out the word concerning the fleeing coyote.

I don't know who wanted that piece of human garbage more, me or Shane.

But Shane's communications efforts were in vain. South of the county line and at our present location, we were in a dead zone.

So, we waited beside that old man, doing what we could to make him comfortable until the volunteer ambulance crew could get there. The soft drizzle continued to fall, the wind picked up and it got even colder.

When the ambulance arrived, we loaded the old man up and they started back for Ozona. Praise be to God, they made it to the clinic soon enough and he did not die.

From there forward we had plenty of help. Border Patrol, Val Verde Sheriff's Office and some of my compatriots stationed in Del Rio showed up and we turned it all over to them.

BLACK AND WHITE

These officers realized we already had plenty to handle on our side of the county line. Likely they had been in the same situation as we were now, once upon a time.

The ensuing investigation took over a month for me to complete. Every one of the young people involved lived within a six-block radius of my home. I knew every one of them personally, and their parents.

The task widened; other young people were interviewed who had something to do with that tragic night. I also knew them as well as their families.

After the last letter in the last word of the last paragraph was checked and rechecked, charges were filed against the driver. He was arrested for Involuntary Manslaughter-DWI, a Third Degree Felony.

I took no pleasure in doing so. But there are times when all of us must do something that we really don't want to do. Being a peace officer, especially in a small, tightly knit community, makes one face those kinds of decisions more often than most.

You just pray that you are doing the right thing.

Decades later a similar circumstance arose, involving local young people and a DWI-related fatality. This accident was also in Val Verde County, on the dirt road that leads to Pandale. And this time, I was the first on the scene with no radio contact.

Again I knew all the young people involved as well as their families. In fact, I was searching for the vehicle they were in because we had a citizen's report of reckless driving. I just could not find them.

That is, until I found them the hard way.

And though many years had passed in the interim, it was still too soon for me.

WILLIE DALE TAYLOR

On the Saturday afternoon of May 19th, 1990, Death came calling for a fellow peace officer and Texas Highway Patrolman.

This was not the first time such had happened since my joining the DPS. We had already lost Ranger Stanley Guffey in a hostage rescue of a two-year-old girl in Brady, and THP Sgt. William Kunhle along with Trooper Ralph Zerda died in a horrific crash outside of San Antonio.

The two had stopped an intoxicated driver, when their patrol car was struck from the rear by another DWI behind the wheel of a semi-truck tractor.

However, this time was different for myself as well as my fellow area troopers, for this time it was someone we all knew well. Our friend and mentor Willie Dale Taylor was killed at about 2:20 pm on Interstate 10 west of Ozona. Now a corporal, he had been a highway patrolman since 1962 and was the 66th DPS officer to die in the line of duty.

Those are the facts, the kind of facts that you often find on a wall or in a memorial passage. Yet even as I write this all these years later, the emotion wells up inside. I know I am not alone in feeling this way, when others read these words.

Because there was so much more to Willie Dale than some facts and statistics, and this was the biggest reason in forcing myself to write this book.

I was in Austin that day on a special detail, President George H. W. Bush was giving the commencement speech for the latest University of Texas graduating class. We were tasked with outer perimeter security and were standing on the line, looking good but really not doing much of anything.

With me was L. D. Whitton, a fellow classmate from the academy who was now stationed in Sonora. L. D. was a hand in any sort of situation, a whiz with a short gun and the kind of man who'd fight a tornado with a feather. We had already been through a lot together, in both the best and worst of times.

We were about to deal with a great deal more of the latter.

It was around 3 pm that afternoon, L.D. and I had become separated due to different postings. I was standing in a security line on the west side when I was approached by an unnamed lieutenant. He walked up to me and asked:

"Do you know a Willie Dale Taylor?"

"Yes sir," I replied. "He's our corporal in Ozona."

"Well, not anymore. He was killed about thirty minutes ago."

Then the lieutenant walked away while I stood there slack-jawed at the news. My mind went two directions at once, one from the shock of it all and the other as to why I absolutely despised certain butter bar lieutenants while in the Marine Corps.

BLACK AND WHITE

There was no effort to pull either L. D. or myself off our positions and send us home. Not that I really expected it to happen, I had visited earlier in the day with a rookie who said his wife was having a baby that morning. This did not matter one whit to his chain-of-command, and his home station was a lot further from Austin than Ozona was.

About another hour and a half went by before they rotated us off the line for a break. When that happened, I went looking for a pay phone. A part of me still could not believe the news, and would not accept it without some sort of confirmation.

After finding one, I placed a collect call to my wife Cathy at our home. In the short time that we had, Cathy confirmed that Willie Dale had been killed in a car wreck just west of the Pandale overpass, his Mustang patrol unit struck from the rear by a commercial truck.

Then came the real shocker. Cathy and my sister-in-law, Laurie English, later to be elected district attorney, were traveling to Fort Lancaster for the Frontier Days festivities when they came upon the scene. The dust was still settling from the impact and Cathy scrambled out of her Trans Am to see if she could help.

She found Willie Dale lying face down, in front of his demolished Mustang. The truck had literally ran over the top of the unit, breaking Willie Dale's safety belt and propelling him out of the little car's interior. It was Cathy who drove to the DPS office in Ozona, and told PCO Frank Galvan and Communications Supervisor R. B. Babbitt what had occurred.

R. B. and Willie Dale were the best of friends, and it was Frank's first day behind the console.

Cathy went on to relate that after leaving the office she drove to Willie Dale's residence, where she sat with his wife Jean until Tommy Matthews arrived to help. Tommy had been one of Willie Dale's rookies before my time and was now stationed in San Angelo.

To this day I give thanks that Tommy was able to get there when he did. You see, my wife was five months pregnant with our second son. She was mentally dealing with what she had seen on the interstate just a few hours before, and he was a Godsend when he walked through that door.

And then my break time was up and I was back on the job again.

That was where I stayed until our detail was relieved at around nine o'clock that night. I don't remember if L. D. and I had the chance to talk beforehand, as I was working mainly on autopilot with many thoughts a long way from Austin, Texas. But we certainly did when we loaded on the bus to take us back to the DPS Headquarters.

Before doing so the brass, most likely that same lieutenant, made it absolutely clear that we were to stay at the academy dormitory for the night. Under no circumstances were we to drive back to our home stations.

I am not much for colorful language, but distinctly recall thinking at that point *'You'll play hell keeping me from it.'*

During the bus ride to the academy L. D., who had likely already figured out my intentions, asked me what I was going to do.

I told him.

"They'll hang your ass if they find out!" he retorted.

"Let 'em," I replied.

Upon stepping off the bus I grabbed my gear in our room and headed for the stairs, L. D. shaking his head in exasperation. Cautiously I made my way out to the parking lot, tossed my bags in my black and white and fired that Dodge up.

In less than three hours I was sitting in our driveway in Ozona. Cathy was awake and waiting on me, and we talked until the sun was full up next morning.

To this day and after all of our years together, if there was one memory I could erase from my wife's mind it would be what she saw that afternoon. For a long time afterward, Cathy said when she closed her eyes, she could see me laying there instead of Willie Dale.

The next few days were a blur of activity, ugly but necessary tasks that absolutely had to be done whether one wanted to or not. In that vein I think that Glen Redmon, our area sergeant, had it worst of all.

Glen was a long-time road troop before becoming a supervisor and had experienced many things during those years. He had been good friends with Sammy Long, who years before was brutally murdered on a traffic stop near Rankin. Decades later and with both of us retired, we were present when a stretch of US Highway 67 was officially renamed in Trooper Long's memory.

But now, he was dealing with Willie Dale's death.

Plus, he was trying to run his sergeant area, and handle all the daily tasks that come with such a demanding assignment. He was also fully engaged in a myriad of reports, inquiries, notifications, and applications for benefits in regards to what had happened.

At no time, day or night, do I think he had one waking moment's respite from the memory of Willie Dale. Nor do I think he had much when trying to sleep, either. Yet he handled this great strain, taking as much as possible upon himself to give the rest of us the breather he so badly needed.

On the afternoon following the funeral, he called us together and told us to go home to our families. That we had done all that we could, and if anything happened a unit would be sent from a neighboring sergeant area. While sitting there listening, my mind began forming the premonition of what he planned to do while we were with our families.

And as usual he was going to go it alone. However, in this one instance, I just could not let that happen.

BLACK AND WHITE

So, I went to the house and changed into a worn-out pair of cutoffs, an old t-shirt and some tennis shoes. Taking a bucket and some scrub brushes, I tossed them in the back of my Firebird and drove to the wrecking yard.

In a few minutes Glen showed up, dressed about exactly as I was and carrying his own bucket. He stopped and looked at me.

"What are you doing here?" he asked.

"Same thing you are," I replied.

He did not say another word as we walked together into the secured room, where they had stored Willie Dale's patrol car. For the next two hours the two of us quietly scrubbed the remains of the Mustang clean, lost in our own individual thoughts.

I will not go into the particulars as to what we had to wash away.

Now that Willie Dale's unit was as ready as we could make it, a Department wrecker would come to provide transport to its own final resting place. Until then, the sanitized vehicle would remain hidden inside the room.

Upon returning home I changed out of my clothing. Then I went into the back yard, dug a shallow grave, placed the clothing, rags and brushes in the hole and incinerated them. Once everything that could be burned had been done so, the hole was filled back in.

As far as I know, that spot of ground has not been disturbed since. The bucket was cleaned up and thrown away.

Next morning, I was in full uniform again and back on duty. As was my habit when beginning a shift, I drove to the office to study the read sheet and visit with the duty communications operator.

While there, I stepped into Sergeant Redmon's office. Those piles of reports, inquiries, benefits, notifications, and applications scattered across his desk were far fewer. What remained was neatly arranged and awaiting further disposition.

Neither of us said anything about the afternoon before.

Glen leaned back in his chair and looked up, an expression of deep sadness and even a bit of uncertainty was present.

"Ben, what do I do now?" he asked.

The question caught me off guard, as did the look on his face. I suppose it was akin to when you see a family patriarch in the same state of mind, and for the first time. Something was happening that you often enough can't discern immediately, but it was something important.

"I think you've done all you could, Sarge. Now it's time to grieve."

He sighed heavily, nodding his head.

It was only after climbing in my patrol car that I realized what had just happened. Sergeant Glen Redmon no longer saw Ben English as just another rookie, he estimated me now as an experienced road troop.

And at that point in my life with all that had recently happened, a humbling feeling swept through which brought me near to tears. I sat there for a few seconds to regain my composure, started up my black and white and went on patrol.

Like the proverbial pebble tossed into a still pond, the reverberations to this senseless tragedy traveled on into the following months and years. Jean Taylor, Willie Dale's wife, ultimately remarried and moved away from Ozona.

Both of Willie Dale's daughters, Lori and Pamela, married fellow highway patrolmen. Pamela's husband, Tommy Scales, was stationed in Ozona some years later.

Those same ripples in the pond affected my own family, too. Everyone voiced their appreciation in how Cathy had handled the ordeal. I distinctly remember R. B. Babbitt saying; "Your wife was a real trooper that afternoon, Ben. You have every reason to be proud of her."

But that appreciation came at a real cost. Cathy was five months pregnant with our second son, Ethan L'Amour, and Willie Dale was the first dead man she had ever seen. Ethan tried to come early, too early and Cathy spent the next month in bed at her parents' home in Christoval. Ozona was eighty-four miles from the hospital in San Angelo, and the doctor did not want to chance it.

Ultimately everything turned out well for both her and Ethan. However, those dreadful memories and the ensuing strain put her health at risk, as well as that of our unborn child. Unfortunately, this would not be the last time the needs of my family were adversely affected by the needs of my chosen profession.

For anyone reading these lines who has a family and is contemplating a career in law enforcement, remember this. When you put that badge on, your family becomes part of everything that follows. No matter how you try to figure or attempt to rationalize the situation, you are putting them at extra risk. Physically, mentally, emotionally and yes, spiritually.

You volunteered for that risk while they could only follow along with the program. So be ready and always keep your options in mind, because finding another job is much easier than finding another family.

Not a month later, Texas Department of Highways supervisor George Ybarra had a marker made and placed along the fence line where Willie Dale died. George was an extraordinary human being in his own right, and long after his retirement continued to serve the community of Ozona in various ways. Though George has long since passed on, I will always remember him for his humanity and dedication to others.

Time continued on and I had my own rookies to train. Many would follow, along with the thousands of recruits I came into contact with when assigned as an instructor at DPS Academy. What Willie Dale taught me I tried to pass along to them.

Things like be as nice to others as you can possibly be, until it is no longer possible to be nice.

Or try to remember that most folks you stop aren't really bad, they just might be having a bad day and the last thing they needed was being stopped by the darned ol' highway patrol.

Or that you can train a monkey to write a ticket. It's everything else that comes along with the badge that makes the difference between being a monkey and a Texas Highway Patrolman.

Or you never really know how badly you want to be a highway patrolman until you make a stop in the middle of the night, some thirty miles from town. There are four guys inside the car, and at least one needs to go to jail. But he, or they, don't want to.

And finally watch that traffic, watch that traffic, watch that traffic! Traffic will kill you quicker than any bullet will. Yet Willie Dale died that very same way, in a one out of a million scenario where everything went wrong in the matter of a very few seconds.

The irony of the last one would sometimes be like a voice from the grave for me. On occasions I could almost hear him when I was on a traffic contact, or parked along the road. Invariably I would check to see what was coming up behind, and there were times when it was a very good thing that I did so.

Meanwhile, those same ripples continued outward and onward.

Some six- and one-half years following his death, an official stone memorial was dedicated to Willie Dale's memory at the DPS Office in Ozona. This was in large part because of one man's campaign to do so, and that man's name was Richard Metcalf.

Mr. Metcalf was once stopped by one of my academy classmates, Carlos Warren, and was impressed with Carlos' behavior and professionalism. So much so that after Carlos was murdered one night while on patrol, Richard Metcalf had a monument emplaced were Carlos died. This was when he learned that no one had memorialized other DPS officers killed in the line of duty.

Richard Metcalf had found his personal crusade.

When Willie Dale's monument was placed in front of the office, I was given the assignment of speaking to the assembled crowd. In reality, that honor belonged to Tommy Matthews far more than me. I said as much to Carl Mayfield, my sergeant at the time. But Carl said the decision had already been made by the higher ups and I was now the area corporal, the same rank and position that Willie Dale held when killed.

Standing at the podium in front of so many of his friends, family and others who came to show their respect, I felt an intense sense of personal responsibility. Willie Dale was gone, and all that some in the crowd would ever know about him would be in the words I had to say.

In those few minutes, I tried to condense a full and well-lived life that truly mattered. Someone who made a difference each and every day he went to work, and saw and did things that so many others simply could not imagine. The last paragraphs spoken were these:

"*Charles Kingsley once wrote, 'The men whom I have seen succeed have always been cheerful and hopeful, who went about their business with a smile on their faces, and took the changes and chances of this mortal life like men.'*

I believe that no quotation could ever ring more true than when one thinks of Willie Dale Taylor. He was a man who enriched my life, and as I look out today at the faces of friends and family, I see that same thought reflected in your eyes. I miss him, we all do.

May God rest his soul."

I have no doubt that someone else could have done a better job, but that was the best I knew how.

The ripples continued to go about their business. Each time I had a new rookie, I took them to the spot where Willie Dale died and said a bit about him. Then I would lead them through the brush to where George Ybarra erected that first marker, all those years ago.

And before I really comprehended how much time had slipped by in between, I was retiring. It was a blessing that Willie Dale never had, and one for which I was very grateful. I just wish he could have enjoyed his own.

My doing so brought many changes, including Cathy and I deciding to relocate to the Big Bend area. Those sirens of the desert had been calling near continually, and she understood the pull they had on me. After living in Ozona for nearly thirty years, I started the lengthy process of moving back home.

That included getting our old home in Ozona ready to sell, and quite a bit of driving back and forth to accomplish this. One day Ryan Dalton, my last rookie, called and asked if he could borrow me for a few hours. Unlike so many others who passed through in Texas tan, Ryan had decided to stay in Crockett County. He married a local girl and together they started a family.

Climbing into his black and white Tahoe, I marveled at the surrounding array of gear and gadgetry. I had only been retired for a few years, yet so much had changed. Ryan was no longer a rookie, he was a veteran troop in his own right and was now a firearms instructor, same as I was once upon a time.

We visited about any and all things, and of course about the many changes in the Department. Turning on to the entrance ramp for Interstate10 West, Ryan said "Years ago you took me the marker for Corporal Taylor, I want you to show me again so I can remember for sure."

BLACK AND WHITE

We drove out to the scene and parked his unit to the side of the pavement. Making our way through the mesquite and cedar, we walked to where the marker resided.

Ryan asked some questions as to what had exactly happened, now a quarter of a century ago. I answered them as best I could, standing with one foot in the present while memories took me into the past, and where my other foot was still firmly planted.

Then we were back in the Chevrolet and soon enough he was driving away from my old house.

I watched him do so, my mind crowded with so many thoughts. Ryan Dalton was a good man, and one with the kind of integrity that few others possess. The torch had been passed and I was confident in the hand that took it from mine.

I was proud of my old rookie, and somewhere out there I knew that Willie Dale was too.

And those ripples from that single pebble cast into the still pond continue on…

*Corporal W. D. Taylor, Texas Highway Patrol
End of Watch May 19th, 1990*

WHEN SOMEONE CHEATS DEATH

Two days after we buried Willie Dale, I was called to a bad wreck just north of Ozona. It was only about half an hour before starting my day shift, so I was out the front door and had my Dodge Diplomat rolling in the span of a few minutes.

Halfway to the scene, DPS Communications updated me as to the severity of the crash. It was another fatality. I remember beating on the steering wheel of the patrol car in frustration and bitterness, and saying to myself repeatedly, "This is too soon, too soon." As far as I was concerned, the month of May was a total wash and I was ready for it to be over.

But I had a job to do, and I was the guy with the gun and the badge. When I pulled up to the scene, I had my game face on and ready to go to work.

Around me was a cataclysm of emotions, confusion and concern; everyone wanting to do the right thing while at the same time feeling a little more alive, because it wasn't them the funeral home was coming for. An ambulance crew was already there and treating the injured, as well as a deputy sheriff helping with traffic.

The deputy identified two men standing nearby as witnesses. He had asked them to stay until I had a chance to visit with them.

During this era, there were a couple of full-sized mesquite trees growing on the west side of Texas Highway 163, as you entered the curve just north of town. From the day I arrived in Ozona nearly four years before I had predicted someday, someone would have a bad wreck there.

That day had come.

Preliminary examination revealed that a pale yellow 1976 Lincoln Mark IV had been traveling south on the roadway. For some unknown reason, the car suddenly veered to the right and off pavement, trying to correct itself before slamming into one of those large mesquite trees.

The ensuing impact was devastating, and the big Lincoln literally welded itself to the tree. Furthermore, the tremendous force generated had come from a direction that easily compromised the passenger compartment of the vehicle. When the Lincoln started to slide it had done so with the right rear swinging out, exposing a critical area between the right front wheel and the leading edge of the passenger door.

That is exactly where the tree trunk entered, plunging through frame and sheet metal as if the tree itself was the proverbial hot knife through the butter-colored skin of the car. The unsecured front passenger never had a chance. Tree, twisted steel and large splatters of blood combined together to occupy the seat where he had been sitting.

A slight aside to illustrate the severity of the impact, and why it was so severe. The Lincoln Mark IV was a heavy car in itself, but with four large adult males and all their gear inside, that car was weighing in at over three tons. When traveling down the road at highway speed, this kind of weight translates into a tremendous amount of momentum.

Many people think the larger and heavier a vehicle, the generally safer it is in a collision. For the most part I have found this to be true, especially when the collision involves another vehicle or object that can be moved.

But there is no movement when a vehicle impacts a full-sized tree, especially a mesquite with its large, complex root system. All the momentum that served as an ally is now an enemy, and the instantaneous dissipation of such enormous force was focused on one point when striking this mesquite.

Words alone cannot adequately describe the results of such a collision, you have to see it for yourself.

Once the ambulances cleared the scene, written statements were obtained from the two witnesses. Both said the Lincoln was traveling at about the legal speed limit, then veered suddenly off and slammed into the mesquite. One reported that as he met the car, the driver abruptly slumped over.

That was strange, both in the abruptness as well as when it occurred. People just don't slump over when meeting other vehicles on a two lane road.

Meanwhile, Sergeant Redmon arrived to assist. He didn't have to do that, there was a plentitude of tasks awaiting him at the office. But he did so anyway, and I was glad to have him.

Maybe he somehow sensed my maddened beating on the steering wheel of that Dodge.

When Glen saw the driver's name, a thoughtful look came to his eye. "Ben," he declared. "I think I know this guy. He was in the office just the other day."

And that's when things started to get weird.

Once I had done what I could at the scene, I drove to the hospital to check on the injured and to have blood drawn from the driver. After assessing the condition of the other occupants of the vehicle, I moved on to our station. Sergeant Redmon was already there, and helped me further by sending a message to San Angelo to notify next of kin.

I had settled in to begin the preliminary paperwork when Glen called me into his office. He handed me an accident report and declared; "I was right, I did know that name. The guy was in here ten days ago wanting a copy of this report."

Curious, I began scanning the details. The accident involved the same driver on the same road thirteen days before, only a mile from this second one and within five minutes of the same time. The vehicle was a green '81 Monte

Carlo and there were four occupants then, too. Of the three passengers, one of them was involved in both wrecks.

In the first accident, the Monte Carlo struck three horses belonging to a local rancher. Somehow, they had managed to get into the highway right-of-way and were in the car's lane when it came around a curve. There was no time to stop, and the Chevrolet slammed into all three animals.

A strange, almost revelatory feeling began gnawing at my gut. I had heard this story before. Continuing down I finally let my eyes drift to where the investigating officer was listed at the bottom of the page, though by now I already knew who it was.

His name was Willie Dale Taylor. This was the last wreck that Willie Dale worked before that fatal Saturday.

He had talked to me about the accident right after it happened, saying it was a miracle that no one was killed as one of the horses had come through the windshield. Nothing really beyond that, just one of those stories you share with someone who understands the true meaning of 'that was a close one.'

There was another notation of interest in the report. That gent who was a passenger in both vehicles? He was in the right front passenger seat of the Monte Carlo when that horse came through the windshield.

This morning he decided to sit in the right rear position. You could say that he cheated death twice.

But in some way beyond where mere fact and logic coexist, and where grim tallies are kept on a spreadsheet never seen by mortal eye, you might also say that two other men paid the ultimate price for his incredible feat.

The front seat passenger of the Lincoln and Corporal W. D. Taylor, Texas Highway Patrol.

WARD CHRISTIAN

During my career, the area where Interstate 10 crossed the Pecos River proved to be an epicenter for where I spent a good deal of my time.

This seemed particularly so during my early years in Ozona. My saved reports reveal a steady stream of lost travelers, stranded motorists, bad wrecks, manhunts, high speed pursuits, suicides, stolen vehicles, drug seizures, the mentally ill, missing persons and serial killers, along with the attending occasional John or Jane Doe.

In 1990 the Houston Chronicle published a feature article about this stretch of interstate, under the somewhat hyperbolic headline of 'Freeway From Hell.' As with many such reports by the mass media, the story was sensationalized by a journalist from a major metropolitan area who actually knew very little about the subject he was reporting on.

But the fact remained that an unusual number of criminal acts and outright weird occurrences happened along that interstate from Sutton to Pecos counties. If one were to take a compass and draw a twenty-mile radius where Interstate 10 crossed the Pecos River, a goodly percentage of these events would be encompassed within that circle.

Perhaps this had something to do with the perceived isolation. After all, it was 108 miles between Ozona and Fort Stockton with not much in between. The two small enclaves of Iraan and Sheffield sat some miles off the interstate to either side.

Such remoteness can frighten or embolden certain people to act in ways they might otherwise not. I suppose this all has root in human psychology and the inner construct of the individual, and who they really are when they think that no one else might be watching.

Another factor was the scant law enforcement resources available. When traveling to other more populous parts of the state, I was shocked to discover that different agencies hardly spoke to their fellows. They did not monitor the other department frequencies and preferred that each agency took care of their own and tended to their own business.

During a course in defensive tactics, I was assisting with at DPS Academy, we had instructors from different agencies across the state. While there, I learned this concept of 'minding our own business' often extended down to the individual officer when employed in the major cities.

More than one stated that no matter what might be happening in the immediate vicinity of their domicile, if the officer was not on duty they did not intervene. That included even when private citizens were clamoring for their assistance in some rather serious situations.

BLACK AND WHITE

This constituted quite a difference in philosophy from what I was used to. In West Texas you considered yourself on duty, to some extent, all the time. When someone called for help be they a citizen, neighbor or another officer, you responded without a second thought to a set number of work hours or official duty status.

When I picked up the mike and called for assistance, it did not matter to me if it came in the form of a police officer, a deputy sheriff, a border patrolman, a game warden, a constable, a fellow highway patrolman or a citizen of Good Samaritan quality. I was just glad to have them.

I also knew if they overheard one of my radio transmissions and my voice inflection did not sound quite right, they would near automatically begin drifting in my direction. For they had been out there alone many times themselves, when they weren't really sure of what they had and what might happen next.

One of those men was Ward Christian, a Pecos County deputy from Iraan. I mentioned before how Jess Malone and I always seemed to be running something across each other's county line. It was the same with Ward, as well as with other officers such as Don Jackson or Tooter Malone. But it was Ward and Jess who were there most often.

Ward was older than most the rest of us, and possessed a certain kindness and dignity in how he went about his business. He had also been a peace officer longer, and with that came a canny knowledge into human nature and the many failings of it.

He was also active in his civic responsibilities and especially so when concerning young people. Ward understood if you could reach them when they were young, you would likely have less problems as they grew older and so would they.

In short, Ward Christian cared.

But on Tuesday, May 29th of 1990, ten days after Willie Dale died, we lost Ward in a traffic accident west of Iraan. It was not one of those high speed, lights and siren blaring emergency runs that most might think of. Ward was only driving down the road while on patrol, when another vehicle came around a blind curve and went bumper to bumper with him.

Ward had no place to go and no time to get out of the way. Behind the wheel of the other vehicle was one of those young people he cared so much about.

At his funeral Ward's caring nature was reciprocated in full. Young people in abundance attended as well as some not so young anymore, illustrating that same care that Ward possessed for all.

An entire community in West Texas turned out to mourn for one of their own, and no peace officer could ever expect a better testimony as to how his life really mattered.

Rest in peace, Ward.

THE CURSE OF CHRISTINE

Men who spend much time in perilous pursuits often enough become attached to what most others consider an inanimate object. They talk about them as if they have their own personality, likes and dislikes, character flaws and mood swings.

That is why airplanes are given individual nicknames, and during past wars have not only nicknames but attending elaborate nose art, sometimes a bit on the risqué side. Ships live double lives under different monikers in the military, being christened with one with a ceremonial bottle of champagne and receiving another once at sea. Often enough, for one of those particular traits mentioned before.

Same goes for a gun or a knife, usually one that has drawn more than its fair share of blood.

Locomotives, large trucks, space modules, axes, land holdings and heavy equipment can also be members of this unnatural club.

And patrol cars? Oh, most certainly, and sometimes for all the wrong reasons.

Enter Christine, a hopefully long gone 1988 Dodge Diplomat with a continual black cloud overhead, and an even blacker mechanical heart within. We named her after the Stephen King horror movie concerning a certain diabolical '58 Plymouth Fury possessed by some sort of demon. Thirty years in age separated the two, but a diabolical old Mopar is still a diabolical old Mopar.

Much like the rest of my career in the highway patrol, we were shorthanded then. This meant we each had our own unit, save for the rookies fresh out of the academy and still being trained. During those times Christine would sit behind the area office both untrusted as well as unwanted, and probably plotting against us all.

But when our unit went down or we took one out of the sergeant area for a special assignment, Christine was brought into active duty.

You would approach her with keys in hand, putting on a brave front and telling yourself she was nothing more than sheet metal, glass and rubber. In turn she would glare back in open disdain, much like a very mean and drunk red headed woman, looking to mess somebody up. You tried to play nice because you knew that she could, if she took a notion. Yet in return she didn't care, she was going to try to mess you up anyway.

Stories of mischief and mayhem among the area troopers abounded about that car. Brave men would visibly wince when Glen Redmon delivered his sentence to the newly condemned: "Take that black and white Dodge parked out back," and he would toss you the keys.

Norbert Ortiz and his rookie had to use it one time and promptly blew a water hose. All those hoses had been replaced prior, save for the bypass between the intake and the water pump. Those hoses never blew, I have seen thirty-year-old Mopars with the same one as installed at the factory. Mind you, Christine was only two years old.

Guess what happened next?

That car had its own peculiar aura, you could spot it in a sea of other black and white Dodges. It squatted different, it looked different, it started different, if it would start at all.

One day Norbert spotted me completely across Interstate 10, and hollered on the radio.

"Why're you driving Christine?"

"Headed to San Antonio to pick up a prisoner."

"Really? (pause) I'll go light a candle at the church."

At one juncture Norbert was idly considering finding an exorcist. But he finally decided against the idea because, as in his own words, "It'd probably only make her mad."

One of her other little tricks was to run out of gas when the gauge still showed fuel. Sometimes it would be an eighth of a tank, a quarter of a tank, or as in some reports from hapless troopers, over a quarter of a tank.

You just never knew with Christine. Of course, you never knew a lot of things that might occur with that car.

Finally, there was the braking system. When you hit the brakes you never had the same pedal feel and response twice, and none of them felt really good. Lay into the anchor really hard, and for some crazy reason the windshield washer would start spraying.

This was really disconcerting during some high speed, high intensity work and you learned to hit the windshield wipers in a flash to clear your vision ahead. That is, if the windshield wipers worked.

That was when the ugly rumors got started about the car having one true calling in life, and that was to severely injure or kill any unwary highway patrolman within her immediate vicinity.

And that old Diplomat would just sit there, plotting and planning to scare the bejesus out of the uninformed or unwary.

In truth, I was one of the luckier of the unlucky hands having to drive her from time to time. I had my own Diplomat, a 1989 model, that proved not only as reliable as an anvil but by far the fastest Dodge Diplomat I ever crawled into. There are some who say I helped in making that possible, but there lies another story for another day.

Then, the fickle finger of fate drifted my direction. I was chosen to attend the Specialized Performance Driving Instructor School at College Station and Glen Redmon pronounced sentence on me:

"Take that Diplomat parked out back."

I arrived at College Station in one piece and began to breathe a little easier, maybe Christine was going to behave herself for once. That single ray of hope disappeared into the black cloud that always seemed to hover around her, the moment she planted the first Goodyear Eagle GT on the track.

It was kind of like trying to ride an outlaw bucking horse in a steeplechase, one with the unpredictability and uncanny intuition as Ol' Fooler in the classic modern cowboy film, *The Rounders*.

This was a demanding course, as any instructor course should be. Short straightaways, decreasing radius curves, chicanes, emergency lane changes, cone weaves, you even had to come to a complete stop within a certain number of inches and then run part of the course backwards, before coming to another emergency stop at the end.

You ran this course over and over, day and night, with and without 'rabbit' cars and occasionally the layout changed to keep you on your toes. And through it all, Christine was doing everything she could to make it tougher, and at the most inopportune times.

Remember everyone's complaint about the brakes?

Then there was the backing portion, if I managed to get the car stopped before plowing into the cones. To properly back the car and be able to see where you were going, the technique was to brace yourself as high as possible above your normal sitting position.

Right arm on the back of the front seat, left foot hard against the floorboard and left hand on the wheel, all three points providing leverage to keep elevated as you looked through the back window. But every time I'd try, the tilt steering would give way and slam into its lowest position. And you never really knew exactly when it was going to do this.

So there I was roaring around the track half blinded by wiper fluid, steering wheel in my lap and fighting the brake system from hell. Oh yeah, Christine was starting to cut out too. But you never knew exactly when or where this would occur.

This led me to overdriving the car, trying to make up for time being lost due to the unpredictability of available power. Like any other instructor course, there was a maximum lap time to qualify and I was dangerously close.

Later I was told that one of the chief instructors turned to the other during one of my performances and exclaimed, "You know, that Trooper English drives like a crazy woman slings s---!"

"Yeah," countered the other. "But he sure ain't getting anywhere very fast."

Then Bobby, the prior instructor, declared that no car could be that bad and elected to give Christine a try himself.

He lasted one lap before easing off the track and gingerly coming to a halt. A near chain smoker, he opened the car door and immediately lit a cigarette. Or more accurately, he tried to light a cigarette.

"That sonovab---- is trying to kill someone!" he finally announced after getting his first couple of puffs.

By the beginning of the third day, Christine was dropping cylinders and they weren't coming back. I had seven, then six, then five, and then only four before she gave it up completely and I coasted to a dead stop in the middle of the road course.

Any attempt to restart the engine proved futile, so we pushed Christine over to the side until the wrecker could come from the local Dodge house.

I had joked with my fellow students on the morning of the first day about Christine, and why she was named that. At first they scoffed, thinking it was another one of those highway patrol tall tales.

Now they were really starting to wonder, too.

We all watched warily as the wrecker driver hooked up and towed her away. No one waved a fond farewell as the rear end of Christine disappeared from view. One of the older troops took pity and allowed me the use of his 1990 Chevrolet Caprice for qualification. When my turn came, on the first pass I knocked nearly a half minute off my best run in Christine.

I received my instructor certification.

However now I had another problem, how was I going to get back to Ozona? Ours was a very small class and our home stations were scattered across the state. One of the guys who lived near Lubbock volunteered to drop me off, but it would be a substantial detour for him to do so.

And if I did that, someone was going to have to come all the way from the Ozona area to pick up Christine, once she was deemed fit to drive again.

Which was always relative in her case.

But again, everything having to do with that car was unpredictable and on Friday morning, we received word she was ready to go. Instead of having to travel all the way to Ozona, my Lubbock ride only had to take me to nearby Bryan. Yet he would not leave until he saw Christine rolling under her own power and me giving the thumbs up.

When I walked into the service area for the dealership, the manager met me with keys in hand.

"Try it," he advised.

The Diplomat cranked up immediately and settled down into a nice, even purr, hitting on all eight and tying each bundle. Christine never sounded better.

"What did you do?" I asked incredulously.

"I could lie to you" he responded, shaking his head. "But truth is we don't really know. Yesterday afternoon one of my mechanics decided to try one more time, and it started just like it did for you."

He shook his head again. "Never could figure out what was wrong, before or afterwards."

They refused to charge the Department for anything, even for the tow so I signed the release form and pointed that Pentastar hood ornament home. Christine continued to tick over like a finely made Swiss watch.

The trip remained uneventful until I was some miles west of Junction, Texas. Traveling down Interstate 10, I started receiving some garbled radio traffic from Randy Hall, one of our communications operators and a friend of the family.

He was calling my unit number repeatedly, trying to make contact with me. You work long enough with a man who provides a lifeline in occasional deep water, and you can tell by the tone of his voice when something is wrong.

I tried to respond but he could not hear me, and Randy continued to call out my unit number. Checking the gas gauge, I saw the needle on half a tank and we were only about forty miles out of Sonora, my next gas stop.

Sticking my foot into that Quadrajet four barrel, I switched over to the hammer lane and we commenced to passing traffic. Climbing above the Roosevelt area where we could finally hear each other clearly, I learned that Cathy had been rushed to the hospital in San Angelo. Ethan L'Amour was trying to come early.

Christine still registered about half a tank so I punched that Dodge up to 110 MPH, and let 'er roll. About three miles east of Sonora and with the gas gauge still showing a quarter of a tank, the engine lost power, fluttered and died, and I coasted to a stop.

I had no clue as to whether it was the same problem as before, or if that gas gauge was playing the same periodic game as it had on other troopers, or if it was something else. I tried a restart to no avail, said some choice words and picked up the mike to advise Randy of my situation.

Don Van Zandt came back immediately, saying that he was patrolling to the other side of Sonora and would bring some gas to me. This was the quickest, simplest possibility of all the options available, so I hung my hat on the idea and waited.

The weather closed in and I waited some more. Soon enough the sound of rain began sounding on the roof of the Dodge. Still no sign of Don.

I have often thought one of the saddest sights in the world is a highway patrolman alongside the road, broke down or out of gas. Cars went flying by and then braked hard by the dozen, realizing too late that the vehicle they just passed was actually a black and white.

It would have even proved a bit entertaining, if my mind was not upon what was happening with Cathy. That and thinking black thoughts about Christine, who likely cared not the least.

And still not a sign of Don Van Zandt, which was highly unusual for him. Finally, the radio crackled the life again and Don said he would be there in a minute.

True to his word, Don was pulling up soon enough and started putting in gas from a plastic container. As he did so, he explained the reason for his delay.

"Ben, you're not going to believe this. I already picked up the gas and was headed your direction when this drunk came out of no place, and nearly ran smooth over me. I finally got him stopped and had to find a deputy to transport, so I could get here."

He paused, looking more closely at the Diplomat. "Say," he added, "Isn't this Christine?"

Considering the root cause in this circumstance, I more than believed him. Started to say so in emphatic language too, but Norbert's words about making her mad came to mind. Right now, I needed this rolling piece of junk to do me one favor, and that was to get me to Ozona.

I thanked Don for his help and we saved the last of the gas to prime the carb. I hit the ignition switch and that small block V8 came to life again. Don, who did not trust Christine any more than anyone else, followed me to the nearest gas station to make sure I made it.

Drunk or no drunk.

I filled the tank and hit I-10 west, once more setting the needle on the 110 mark. Wheeling into the DPS office in Ozona, Randy Hall clued me in as to what he knew about Cathy's condition. Randy did me many a kindness in the years we worked together, but never more so than that evening.

Pulling into the driveway of our home, I hurried to the front door to pick up some clothes and change into civvies before starting for San Angelo. That was when I realized my house keys were on the same ring as those for my regular patrol unit, laying on the nightstand beside the bed.

I was faced with a decision: trust Christine to get me all the way to San Angelo, or break into my own home for the keys to something else.

I broke into my own home.

But as they so often say, "All's well that ends well." Ethan ultimately came into this world a month later and at the proper time, though Cathy had to stay with her parents. Due to everything that happened over the past several weeks, the doctor wanted her close to the hospital. So, I bached it in the interim, and I can't remember having to ever drive Christine again.

But she was still around, and still raising mechanical mayhem.

Not too much longer, Steve Torres arrived to take over the substation in Mertzon after Tom Usery left. Tom, one of the best officers I ever had the pleasure to work with and learn from, had resigned from the force to pursue a career as an attorney. He was one of those rare sort of gifted individuals who were exemplary in whatever they chose to involve themselves in, and this proved to be the case in law school.

Steve Torres was another cut above, and a wonderful human being who always seemed to have a smile and a positive spin for most any occurrence. In police work, you need a man like Steve around to help balance out the ugliness and negativity, and anyone who knew him would say the same.

But when Steve checked into the area, guess what patrol unit Glen Redmon assigned him?

My first memory of Steve Torres was him standing at the back of the Ozona office with Christine's hood open, peering questioningly inside. I introduced myself and we shook hands, and began talking while heading into the building.

He asked me if there was something wrong with that car.

Two notions dawned on me simultaneously. Steve wasn't using Christine temporarily due to dire circumstance, as was the area custom. She was going to be his issued unit, and Glen had told him nothing about her sordid past.

I stuck my head inside the sergeant's office.

"Sarge! You didn't give him Christine without warning him, did you?"

"Shutup, Ben English" was Glen's reply.

"But Sarge, that's terrible."

"I said shutup, Ben English." He reiterated, a tad more forcefully.

I shook my head in disbelief and told Steve some of the high, or more accurately, low points concerning his new patrol car. Glen glowered as I did so, the idea of assigning me night shifts forever dancing in his eyes.

Soon enough Steve started reporting on what we referred to only half-jokingly as 'The Curse of Christine.' Mostly the same old repertoire of gas gauge troubles, inexplicable leaks, drained batteries and that spooky braking system. But since Steve had to live with her on a daily basis, those weird incidents were a far more common occurrence.

One Tuesday morning Steve came in late for our area meeting, sheer consternation on his usually smiling face.

"Where've you been, Scoop?" someone hollered. 'Scoop' was his nickname among those who knew him, because his favorite line was "What's the scoop?" With this, he began to relate yet another personal tale of woe linked to his assigned unit.

Seems that he was enroute to Ozona and checked a speeder running 70 in a 55, heading the other direction. Engaging his emergency lamps, he turned around and gave chase to write a quick ticket before continuing on.

Problem was, Christine would only run 67 miles per hour. No matter what he did or how loud he yelled at her, that was her top speed for the day. He chased the violator for miles and miles, and then finally gave up in disgust.

Next morning he limped her over to the Dodge house in San Angelo, and she ran fine. The mechanics in the shop could not find a single thing wrong with that Dodge.

Coincidentally this occurred on US Highway 67, so we figured that Christine managed to get a highway sign mixed up with the posted limit. 67 MPH sounded like a nice, leisurely speed to go somewhere that morning.

And the next day? Why, that was a brand new day with brand new ideas!

The last time I can recall a story about Christine was when Steve and I attended in-service school together. It was winter time and New Year's was only a few days past.

And Christine's heater was not working.

So rather than spend Department money on having her fixed in San Angelo, Glen Redmon told Steve to take the car to Austin and have it repaired at DPS Shops. An ice-cold northerner was blowing when he left, and Steve was half frozen by the time he reached our academy.

Next morning, we dropped off Christine at the shop. While there I went in and visited with some of the mechanics I knew. We shared the same fascination with anything to do with cars, and they always had good information on what was happening at Fleet Operations. One was in a particularly jovial mood; the holidays had been very good to him and he was ready to get to work.

By Wednesday afternoon, Steve had received no progress report on the repairs so we went back during a classroom break. Walking into the building, we ran into that very same mechanic again.

However, he now appeared as the unhappiest of all and near beside himself in gloom. Slump shouldered and moving along listlessly, he paid no attention to me or much of anything else until I hailed him.

"Hey, what's wrong? You look awful!" I exclaimed.

"I feel awful" he replied ruefully, "I tell you, I'm at my wit's end." He held his two hands up, fingers taped by several band aids.

"There's a Dodge in there I've been working on since Monday morning. Should have been done that afternoon, but everything that could go wrong, has gone wrong. It's like something possessed!"

Then he walked on, mumbling something about a heater core as it all came into focus.

I walked into the main part of the shop and peered around the corner. Sure enough, there sat Christine about three stalls over and backed against the opposite wall. She was on a floor jack, doors open as was the hood with the front seat laying alongside, mixed in with most of her instrument panel and dash.

But she still had that same look to her grille, like she was thinking up something really special. I backed away quietly as to not attract her attention.

That was many years ago, and Christine has almost certainly gone on to where all bad cars with worse attitudes belong. Yet if she is still around someplace and if I ever see her again, I'll probably entertain the thought of buying her, if I can cheaply enough.

Then I'm going to fill her full of fresh sheep manure, set her on fire, and run her off the highest bluff that I can find in the state of Texas.

However, I am also certain that whatever little good sense I still possess will have me passing on that particular idea.

Like Norbert always said, it'd probably only make her mad…

WHEN A LADY FALLS OFF THE WAGON

Any intoxicated subject who gets behind the wheel of an automobile constitutes a threat not only to themselves, but everyone else around them. While usually this means alcohol abuse, it can also be drugs both illegal as well as prescribed, or most anything else that people can possibly use to escape reality.

When an officer is involved in the apprehension of such a subject, he is often engaged in one of the most potentially dangerous situations he can come across. You have a mostly unguided two-ton object traveling along at speed, often nominally controlled by someone in a highly charged emotional state, which is why they have allowed themselves to reach this point and why they often could care less about the result.

In short, it is much akin to someone standing on a street corner of Anytown, USA, pulling out a pistol, and shooting randomly in every direction.

During the early years of World War II my grandfather, H.C. Cash, was chief deputy for the sheriff's office in Uvalde County. One Christmas Eve, he stopped a drunk who had his entire family inside the car. Granddad was trying to talk the man into stepping out of the vehicle, when the subject suddenly popped the clutch and began driving off. Grandfather Cash jumped on the running board and was reaching in to grab the ignition key, when he slipped and fell away.

But not completely so. Somehow his Sam Brown strap, aptly referred to as a 'suicide strap' by old time officers, became entangled with a lower protrusion on the car. He was dragged several hundred yards before the drunk's hysterical wife could get her severely intoxicated husband to stop.

My grandfather was rushed to the hospital more dead than alive, a large amount of pea-sized gravel embedded in his body. Somehow, he managed to survive, though the doctor on duty would take no credit for saving him. "That was God's Hand, not mine' was all the surgeon said. Granddad carried a good deal of that gravel still in his body until the day he died.

When we buried him in November of 1964, I was just a small boy. But that story stayed with me as a cautionary tale through all my years while on patrol. I never handled any drunk lightly, nor looked upon the situation as some sort of routine.

Yett that did not mean that humor, as well as sincere thanks to the All Mighty, was not involved in some of these cases. There was also chance, fear and destruction mixed with booze, blood and the saddest stories of human frailties and attending tragedies imaginable.

BLACK AND WHITE

It was a Monday afternoon in December, a day that was often spent either writing reports or checking them, depending on the assignment. But I had finished early and was leisurely drifting along Interstate 10, a couple of miles east of Ozona.

As I neared an overpass, I noted a late model full-sized Oldsmobile four door parked along the west bound lanes. I also noticed what appeared to be a woman sitting in the driver's seat, leaning forward with her head resting on the steering wheel.

Whatever was going on was in no way normal, so I crossed the median and approached the white Delta 88 from the rear, running a check on the license plates as I rolled to a stop. The woman did not move.

Alarm bells started going off, and the little guy inside my head was on full alert. Condensation arose from the exhaust pipe of the Olds, telling me the car was still running. My approach was not a stealthy one, as she was pulled completely off the pavement and my Goodyear tires made plenty of noise in the adjoining gravel.

I radioed a quick blurb to Paula Maness, our duty PCO, to tell her I was checking out this vehicle and why. Opening the door on my black and white, I began to step out when there was a sudden flurry of activity inside the Delta 88.

The dark-haired woman sprung straight up in her seat and was just as quickly on the gas, spinning the rear tires and throwing rocks and road debris on both my unit as well as myself. A cloud of dust erupted as the car accelerated away, and into the path of another passing motorist.

The second motorist braked hard and swerved to the left to avoid collision, while I scrambled back to my Dodge. Once rolling with that four barrel carb in full song, I radioed Paula that I had a possible pursuit in progress. As we gathered speed, I also broadcasted the particulars to any available units listening in.

Ahead I watched helplessly as the big Oldsmobile weaved erratically from improved shoulder to improved shoulder. The car would speed up and then slow down again, allowing me the opportunity to catch up within about a half mile.

My Dodge was a 'slick top,' meaning my emergency lamps were all either in the grille or on the back deck area. The advantage to this arrangement was a faster unit due to the improved aerodynamics. The disadvantage was what I was experiencing now, as a light bar was much better in clearing traffic.

My siren was shrieking out a warning and I flipped on my headlamps, driver's side spotlight and four way flashers to give me all the visibility possible. My worst fear was the white Delta 88 would slam into an unsuspecting civilian vehicle. The momentum from that heavy, full-sized Olds at speed could easily cause a legitimately horrific crash.

That nearly happened just before the randomly piloted car reached the exit ramp for Ozona. The Oldsmobile was crowding the yellow line on the inside lane when it abruptly veered to the right, forcing a dark red sedan with several passengers off the pavement and into the barrow ditch. In my rear view mirror I saw the red car come to a sliding, sideways halt before a huge plume of dirt enveloped it.

The white four door began to take the off ramp, then whipped back to the interstate again. Now we were nearing a combination bridge, dual overpass and entrance ramp for west bound traffic, guardrails hard against the pavement on each side. I swallowed hard and crawled up on the steering wheel, trying to figure some options and literally praying that we would make it to the other end.

As I topped over the second bridge, I heard a radio response from one of the other on-duty troopers, saying he was coming to help. Sure enough, I saw his black and white Mustang 5.0 on the onramp with lights going and accelerating rapidly. Every time he would grab another gear, the front end of that Ford would lift from the torque of the straining V8.

However, that white Delta 88 was traveling still faster, and he was running out of lane for the entrance ramp.

"Give her room!" I yelled into the mike. "She'll run smooth over you!"

I don't know if it was my warning or a side view mirror full of Oldsmobile, but the Mustang braked hard and crowded the outside guard rail.

Then the heavy white four door filled the same space the little Ford had occupied just a split second before. From there it slowed down and came to a jerky, uneven stop to the right side of the roadway.

I began to breathe just a bit more easily.

Getting out of my unit, I positioned myself near the left rear corner of the vehicle and ordered the driver to step out, while the other trooper provided cover. We still did not know exactly what we had, and were as cautious as circumstances would permit.

The physical reaction of the woman gave every appearance of being dazed, uncertain and confused. I had to repeat myself several times to get her out of the vehicle. When she finally did, she was barefoot and promptly almost fell to the ground. To keep her from hurting herself, I moved forward to help the suspect to the rear of the car.

It was obvious the woman was heavily intoxicated and she literally reeked of the accompanying odor. I leaned her against the right rear fender of the Delta 88 while she senselessly mumbled out words not understood, oblivious as to why she had been stopped or likely what planet she was on.

I slowly turned her around and put on the handcuffs, then walked the woman over to my unit and placed her inside. The other trooper stayed with her while I examined the interior of her Olds.

BLACK AND WHITE

In the front floorboard were three bottles of DeKuyper Peppermint Schnapps. One was nearly empty while another only half full. Many times I heard highly experienced officers say the average woman could hold their liquor better than most any man, a summation backed by scientific fact. This lady was a prime example of this, as most any man would have been out cold.

Yet that did not mean she was exactly lucid, either. The officer who was watching her was the recipient of a sudden outburst of loud curses that would do a Marine drill instructor proud, followed just as quickly by hysterical sobbing and crying. I pointed to the bottles of schnapps and how much of the liquid was missing, he shook his head in open disbelief.

After inventorying her car and starting for the DPS office, it was my turn in the barrel. For those who might be interested, I have been witness to a plentitude of memorable cussings but never, ever in the fashion of how that woman cussed me. In the time it took us to get to the station and her out of the car, she called me everything in the book at least twice and maybe three times for good measure.

Once inside her mood changes went from venomous to remorseful to near unconsciousness, and then again to withering blasts of verbal fury. She said she had a sick brother, then a brother who was going to die and finally her brother was dead, and it was all my fault.

In the middle of one tirade Paula happened to wander in to use the copier, and she received broadside after broadside of spirited profanity from our unhappy guest. Later Paula confessed to me, "Ben, I have never heard anyone, man or woman, that could swear like that!"

I tried to conduct the standard DWI interview, but did not have much luck. Cursing, crying and confused, occasionally all at the same time, I could get little out of her other than she thought she was in Bandera and that it was eight o'clock at night. She did admit to drinking a little glass of peppermint schnapps.

Some glass.

The woman was now showing some difficulty in staying awake so I finally loaded her up and took her to the county jail. The duty jailor took one look and elected to put her in the drunk tank until she sobered up, before conducting the standard booking procedures.

He also got his own dose of a five-star, profanity laced, tongue lashing and would not let me leave until getting her in the cell and securing the door.

Chicken.

I could still hear her cursing from inside the jail as I drove away in my Dodge. Reckon that entire side of Ozona could, too.

On the way home I stopped by the wrecker service to examine the white Oldsmobile more closely. I had noted some undercarriage damage at the scene and thought I would make some field notes about the car.

The bottom of the vehicle was banged up with fresh scrapes and dents, as if it had been high centered. The left front tire had grass and dirt embedded between the tire and the rim, as if the vehicle was involved in a long side skid through a pasture. The right rear was nearly bald on one side and slowly losing air.

I don't know what happened to her and that Oldsmobile between Bandera and where I found her, but it must have been quite a ride. I made a mental note to keep an extra sharp lookout for any teletypes asking for information concerning a white car with an enraged woman behind the wheel.

As was my habit, the next morning I swung by the sheriff's office and found Emilio Tambunga as the jailor on duty. Emilio had been a drill instructor in the Marine Corps and we used to call him 'Old Stone Face,' as smiles were hard to come by with that fellow. But he was grinning in pure mirth now, as he had heard the story about the lady in the cell upstairs.

"I heard she gave you a real cussing," he opined.

"It was a rarity, that's for sure" I admitted. "She missed her calling, should have been on the drill field with you."

"She wants to speak with you again" he replied, grinning even more widely.

I sensed that even with that evil smile he was being sincere, and began wondering if I really wanted to do that.

"No, seriously, she wants to apologize to you" he said, as if reading my mind. 'Course, that's a specialty for any good Marine drill instructor, especially with those who don't have much going on upstairs to begin with.

Which kind of self-convicts me, don't it?

We went upstairs and Emilio gave us a bit of privacy so we could chat through the bars.

Never was any woman more different in every way, from one meeting to the next. What had been a raging, crying, cussing, hysterical and superbly soused human being was now a soft-spoken lady of culture, breeding and intellect.

She told me she realized any apology would have no bearing in a court of law, but wanted to apologize all the same. The woman went on to say that though she did not remember much, she did remember that I treated her with kindness and courtesy, both of which she estimated was undeserving due to her own behavior.

Then she told me what had happened prior to our paths crossing.

"I have been a recovering alcoholic for the past two years," the woman explained. "That is, until I caught my husband-to-be with someone else."

"I stopped at the first liquor store I could find, bought three bottles of peppermint schnapps, and started driving west," she continued. "I don't remember much of anything else, other than I really just wanted to die."

She turned her face away in embarrassment. "Evidently that is how you found me and I am glad you did. Guess I fell off the wagon, as they used to say."

The lady looked at me again. "Anyway, thank you for finding me before something worse happened. I am so sorry for all those dreadful things I said to you."

And you know what? I believed her.

That was over thirty years ago and much has happened since, and in the interim, I have handled a lot of drunks. But when someone asks to hear a funny DWI story, my thoughts usually go to her.

However, in reality her story was not so much humorous as a truly sad one, and I find myself wondering how life might have turned out for the lady who fell off the wagon.

She was special, no doubt about that and I wish her well to this day.

But she sure could cuss.

"I DON'T CARE IF YOU'RE WYATT EARP..."

It was New Year's Day on a Tuesday afternoon along Interstate 10, the weather was near gorgeous for the middle of winter and I was on the hunt for whatever might be found. Patrol work can be a whole lot like fishing, a certain amount of patience and no telling what you might hook on to.

I was about eleven miles west of Ozona, easing along into the late afternoon sun when that fishing pole began to jiggle. Coming east was a white late model Nissan 300ZX, and whoever was driving wasn't letting any grass grow underneath that car. This was when the federally mandated 55 MPH speed limit was still in effect, though most highway patrolmen in West Texas would hardly break out their ticket book for less than 70, unless other violations were noted.

But this particular citizen was throwing all caution to the wind. I visually estimated his speed at 85 MPH before confirming my guess on my black box Decatur radar. It read 87 miles an hour.

Flipping on my grille lamps, I began to cross the median. The Nissan was already giving it up, slowing down to pull over to the improved shoulder. As I rolled up behind the car, I ran the Arizona license plate and told Ozona DPS to give me the return 'in the blind,' meaning to transmit when the information was available without expecting me to reply.

When asked to step out of the vehicle, the driver complied readily enough and was courteous in both tone and behavior. He was a tall man, about six foot three and sparingly built with a distinguished, educated air to him. Nothing appeared to be out of the ordinary, when asked he said there was no emergency for his speed and I obtained his driver license to run a check.

But all that changed in the blink of an eye when our duty PCO, Royce Newton, advised the car was stolen. I have often been accused of being a fairly polite person, but also accused of being able to go from zero to a hundred in record time. This was one of those occasions.

The clipboard fell to the ground and I palmed a fistful of .357 Magnum, ordering the driver to turn away and put his hands behind his head. He was advised to make no sudden moves and to walk several steps to the side, away from the Nissan.

Then I told him to drop slowly to the ground on his stomach, and put his arms straight out with palms up.

"But I am a supreme court justice for the state of Arizona," he protested loudly.

"I don't care if you're Wyatt Earp from the OK Corral," I testily replied. "You do as I say." So down he went.

"Now," I continued, "if you are who you say you are, then you know why I'm doing this. And if you ain't, then you know even better." I backed away to my unit, opening the door and advising communications to run a confirmation.

Walking back over to where I had dropped the clipboard, I retrieved his Arizona driver license and ran it through DPS Ozona. The driver came back clean, no criminal record. Not even any traffic offenses.

Something wasn't adding up.

Since he was still on the ground, I did a cautionary pat down and found nothing pointing to the criminal side of life. Telling him to stay where he was and not to move a muscle, I also went through the 300ZX.

There were no weapons, fast food wrappers, drug residue, spilt beverages, dirt, trash or other telltale signs as you usually find in a stolen car. It was neat as a pin, well cared for with expensive luggage and a hanging bag with his name on it.

And still no confirmation on the stolen vehicle, reported as so by the Mesa, Arizona Police Department.

Strange.

I advised him he could change to a sitting position and he was grateful to do so. While waiting for the confirmation, I began quizzing the driver about the car, his trip and his background.

He maintained that he was indeed an Arizona Supreme Court Justice and was traveling to the Houston area to see relatives. He had purchased the Nissan about ten days ago, from a used car dealership in Phoenix. There was nothing, absolutely no holes whatsoever in his story.

My doubts grew about this being an actual stolen car.

When we hit the ten-minute mark with no confirmation, the driver was advised I had no reason to hold him, other than for speeding. But I did ask him to follow me to my office to get this cleared up. He was willing to do so, even somewhat anxious.

After what he had already been through, I'd probably be a little anxious myself.

A few minutes following our arrival, Royce passed me a teletype from the Mesa PD. They advised after further investigation it was determined the 300ZX had been repossessed a month or so before, and was reported stolen in error.

Then Royce added, "But it's still in the system."

I shot him a questioning look. When Royce was confused about something, he often would shrug his shoulders and cock his head. He did so now.

I reread the teletype and advised the presently established owner what had occurred. Then I added, "Sir, you are free to go. I'm not even going to issue a speeding citation; figure you've already been through enough."

"But the car is still listed as being stolen?" he queried.

"Yes sir. I don't know what's going on with your Mesa PD, but they're the ones who have to clear this out of the system."

"What would you do in my place, Trooper?"

I considered that since it was a holiday, everyone would be on patrol if at all possible. In the background I could hear L.D. Whitton working hard in Sutton County, running traffic.

"You hear that officer on the radio, sir?" I asked somewhat rhetorically. "We came out of the same academy class and he's a real go-getter. If he sees you go by in that kind of car and if he can, he'll check the license plate on it. When he does, you are liable to have round two of what just occurred."

"Now I can let him know about your situation and he'll let you pass on by," I continued. "But there is every kind of unit in the state of Texas working this evening. I won't be able to notify them all."

The man nodded in agreement.

"Again, you are free to go but if it was me, I'd hang around long enough to make certain that stolen car alert was cleared."

So, he did. We sat around and made small talk while Royce checked and rechecked every few minutes. The car was still in the system.

Finally, he came back to where we were, no longer confused but getting mad now.

"Ben, I even tried to call on the phone but they said it was a holiday and they were busy."

"Give me that phone number," I said.

When I called, they started the same routine with me, it being a holiday and they were shorthanded as well as too busy. Removing the warrant was just going to take a while.

"It's already taken a while" I retorted. "This needs to be out of the system."

"Look" said the voice on the line, sounding a mite snarky. "You don't seem to understand…"

"No," I interrupted. "You don't understand. The rightful owner of this car is…" and I read off his name. "He says he's a sitting justice on the Arizona Supreme Court. I think you'd be best served by getting this done as quickly as possible. Otherwise, I would not recommend ever meeting him in court."

Two minutes later the entry was cleared. We said our goodbyes and he thanked me for my help, as well as my attention to duty.

About three weeks later I received a letter in the mail. It was from the owner of the Nissan, thanking me again and asking that the letter be given to my chain of command as a sure enough atta-boy. The document described in detail what happened.

It was printed on the official letterhead for the Arizona Supreme Court, and with his personal signature.

I carried my prize with some ceremony into Glen Redmon's office, handing the paper over with a flourish. Glen read it and looked up at me, puffing on that habitual cigarette hanging out the corner of his mouth.

"I don't know what kind of magnet you got in your pocket, but I sure wish you'd lose it" was all he said.

I went back to work, grinning.

Glen A. Redmon, Sergeant, THP Ozona and Benjamin Levi English

THE BIG BAIL OUT

A few weeks later I was working day shift in the western part of Crockett County, and was training a rookie. The rookie was Ben Macias, a jailer for our local sheriff's office before deciding to join the DPS. I was one of those who encouraged him to do so, and was proud to have him in our area as well as in a patrol car with me.

The hour was nearing noon on another Monday, and we would soon turn and work our way back to Ozona. I never liked having my lunch during the twelve o'clock hour, because someone was usually having a fender bender someplace else. Lunch time can get hectic for drivers, even in a small town.

Besides my grandfather Ben English, Zavala County sheriff of many years before, said the mark of a good officer was to be when and where least expected. Not that I would ever claim to be as good an officer as he was, but his words made for sound advice. So I tried to be on patrol when both clock hands were pointing straight up.

We were nearing our turnaround point when the two way crackled to life on the Pecos County frequency. Sgt. John Ritter, THP Fort Stockton, had jumped out a stolen Dodge pickup and the ensuing pursuit was turning into a real melee. The chase was also headed right for Crockett County.

All thoughts of any sort of meal vanished and my foot pushed down the accelerator pedal, encouraging the Dodge to begin eating up pavement. Our adjoining counties were divided by the Pecos River, and the limited ways across provided natural chokepoints that could be utilized if the pursuit got that far.

And it had already gone a fair distance, starting only about ten miles east of Fort Stockton. Sgt. Ritter had been in his unmarked unit when he was passed by a brand-new brown Dodge Dakota truck. There were three dead giveaways to something being wrong; the license plate was unreadable, none of the three subjects matched the vehicle, and none of them were wearing a safety belt. Also, one of the hitchers was riding in the bed of the pickup.

John initiated a traffic stop and the pickup slowed while pulling over to the improved shoulder, rolling along for better than a mile before entering the main lanes again and accelerating to 97 MPH. That was likely about as fast as the little Dodge could go, and also the point where John Ritter knew he had a live one. The chase was on.

Though the Dakota was no match for any pursuit unit while on pavement, the driver of the stolen vehicle simply would not pull over. Driving far beyond his own limits as well as that of the truck's, he passed interstate traffic to the right as well as the left, driving on the improved shoulder and then in the median. Keep in mind there was still a hitchhiker in the bed of that Dodge, and he was trying to hold on to anything available to keep from being thrown out the vehicle.

This went on for thirty miles, the fleeing driver displaying no regard not only for his own life but those in the vehicle with him, not to mention every innocent civilian he came close to. Near the rest area fifty miles east of Fort Stockton, two Pecos County deputies attempted a rolling roadblock.

Any pursuit is a chancy thing in one way or another, but a rolling roadblock is one of the chancier things any officer can try. Basically, you are placing your patrol unit, as well as yourself, in front of someone who has already proven more than desperate enough to run other vehicles off the roadway.

The officer conducting this maneuver usually has no idea as to why the driver is running, or what he has already done to put himself in such a frame of mind. More so, you have no idea whatsoever as to what he is willing to do to keep running. During this maneuver the officer has his back literally to the suspect, a situation that no one would gladly put themselves into.

But the deputies did so all the same, risking their own lives in an attempt to keep someone from possibly killing somebody else.

At first the Dakota tried to drive between them. When that did not work, the fleeing vehicle suddenly veered from the interstate and onto the paralleling south service road, continuing east. As the truck neared the turnoff for US Highway 190 the driver lost control in the curve and slid off an embankment, and into the rough pasturage some twenty feet below.

How he kept from rolling that truck is still anyone's guess. But when he hit the bottom the two hapless, badly scared men with him decided they'd had enough. The passenger door flew open and the hitchhiker riding shotgun bailed out, followed by the other hitchhiker in the bed of the Dodge.

Now by himself but still completely undeterred from his mad course, the driver somehow maintained control of the Dakota while running through a grassy area beside the service road. Meanwhile, two of the pursuing units stopped to gather up the shaken hitchhikers and check them over for injuries.

Seeing that all lesser efforts had failed, other officers tried to take a tire off by firing multiple rounds from handguns as well as shotguns. Their gunfire had no effect, and the Dodge regained Interstate 10 via an entrance ramp located nearby.

On the pursuit went, with the subject behind the wheel of the Dakota becoming even more reckless and thus more dangerous to anyone in his path. After traveling another eight miles or so, he skidded off the interstate once more, cutting across the service road and traveling south into private ranchland.

The chase continued, sometimes on a caliche oilfield road and other times zig-zagging across the pasture. This went on for a good two miles before the driver decided to turn around and head back to the interstate.

Through all this Ben Macias and I were coming from the east at a blistering pace, charging across the interstate bridge and into Pecos County. I kept at it, now intent to place ourselves in a position to keep the stolen Dakota away from I-10, and the attending civilian traffic. By now we were so close you could see the cars and attending rising plumes of dust, as they turned around in the pasture.

That was when the sure and steady voice of Bruce Wilson, sheriff of Pecos County, came over the air. Too far away to lend any assistance, he was monitoring what was happening as his units called in updates during the pursuit. When he heard the brown pickup truck was headed back to the interstate, he made a decision for the welfare of all.

"Fellas, I don't want that vehicle back on that interstate" he said emphatically.

Hearing his sheriff and understanding his line of reasoning, Deputy Sheriff Bobby Harris pulled his .357 Magnum revolver and started shooting in earnest. On his last two rounds things started happening, including the Dodge finally coming to a stop and the driver stumbling out.

Ben Macias and I rolled up at about that exact moment, with thick clouds of dirt still hanging in the West Texas air. Exiting our unit, I could hear the driver screaming at the top of his lungs about having been shot and holding his right shoulder. Matter of fact, I suppose that everyone from Iraan to Sheffield could hear him, as he was yelling so loudly.

The officers present still had their guns trained on him, and justifiably so. Ultimately, I think it was Bobby Harris and I who finally approached him, once he dropped to his knees with his back turned to us. He continued to scream that he'd been shot.

I was leery too, as I could see no blood from any sort of wound. Yet the young driver was obviously in a great deal of pain and bordering on being hysterical. He was also so wound up that he was not following some of the verbal commands being given, which tended to ratchet up one's sense of expectation.

Once we had reached the suspect, Bobby went hands on to get him cuffed and Bobby was a big, powerful man. However, any fight left in our new prisoner was long gone, replaced with the frightful assumption that he had actually been shot.

I examined the shoulder area he had been holding with his other hand, as he continued to howl and carry on. There was not a drop of blood to be found anyplace. Full of consternation, I tore his tee shirt away for a better look.

BLACK AND WHITE

Underneath and turning every shade of red, blue and purple imaginable was the mother of all raspberries. Evidently one of the rounds Bobby fired went through the truck's sheet metal below the back window, passing through the top of the seat along the way.

Now mostly spent and mushroomed to nearly three quarters of an inch, the rapidly slowing bullet 'slapped' the driver's shoulder, leaving an ugly looking welt about an inch and a half across.

And yeah, it did look like it might smart a bit.

Once we were able to identify him, it turned out the driver was all of sixteen years old and had stolen the truck from a new car lot in Colorado. I don't know whatever happened to him, but I sure hope somewhere off in the future he realized just how lucky he was that day.

Along with the knowledge of luck like that not coming around very often.

After the excitement died down, Ben and I got ourselves back across the river and into our normal area of patrol. Later on, we went by the DPS office to visit with Randy Hall.

If you were looking for a laugh or a different perspective on life, especially in this business, Randy was your man of the hour. His father had been a sheriff when Randy was little, so he knew well this kind of life from early on. Of a quick and occasionally acidic wit, he was always up to something or playing a large hand in some sort of joke. He would have been just as much at home in a Dean Martin roast, as behind the microphone in our communications room.

"Hey!" he addressed us as we walked through the door. "Why are you two going to Pecos County to stir up s---?" he announced, pure devilment twinkling in his eye through a haze of cigarette smoke. "Can't you get enough of it around here?"

Ben Macias and I laughed, and Ben replied "Randy, I was just along for the ride. It was this guy" and pointed a thumb toward me.

"Yeah, I know and soon enough you'll be acting just like him." Randy took another pull from his cigarette. "But I did get a good one on ol' Redmon."

"How's that?" I asked.

"Well, he was having his noon meal when this started. So, when he walked in, he asked if anything had happened."

"Yeah?" I queried.

"I said not much, other than a pursuit in Pecos County. Cars run off the road, hitchhikers bailing out all over the place, dozens of shots fired, car crash, injuries, juveniles, ambulances and English is on the scene!"

Randy paused for effect, partly to take in another puff and partly to grin widely in sheer joy.

"You should have seen the look on his face, I thought he was going to chomp that cigarette in half!" he guffawed, slapping the console desk for good measure.

And we went on patrol again.

MR. ENGLISH, THERE'S A RIOT OUTSIDE!

During several of my years in Ozona, I served as the coach for the county 4-H smallbore rifle team. It was Rod Chalmers who talked me into volunteering, Rod was our game warden at that time and as good a man as I have known. He was also a fine officer, and would have been a top hand in any outfit.

Rod was also a more experienced officer than I, and wise to the ways of being a small-town lawman. That included doing sometimes unpopular tasks that could lead to conflict with certain locals, or even certain local officials. I remember well him telling me "They can't cuss you too much when they know you care about their kids."

It was sound, even sagely advice, and I kept it close to heart during all my remaining days in serving the state of Texas.

Anyway, Rod was heavily involved in the 4-H program and soon enough I was running the rifle team for our high school students. Had a fine time, too, we even went to state about the third year in.

But the most important and personally gratifying thing was the opportunity to work with these youngsters, and for they to see me as something more than just another uniform. This link established relationships, even kinship that lasts for a lifetime. Some of these kids later joined the military or became officers themselves. Every one made for a citizen to be proud of.

From the beginning, I wanted them to learn early on of the far more important things in this world than shooting a rifle well. A good deal of responsibility came with that skill, starting with being given the privilege. I expected good citizenship out of my young people; ethically and scholastically both on and off the firing line.

This included their grades in school. Each six weeks they brought me their report cards for inspection. For each 'A,' twenty points were added to their total rifle score, which in turn determined possible placement on our official competitive team. But for each 'C' ten points were removed and you were put on probation. If it was a failing grade, I refused to let them shoot until proof was shown they were back in the passing column.

Part of being on probation meant that if you weren't actually on the firing line during your relay, you were seated behind the firing line with a school book in your hand studying. And just to keep things on the up and up, I would step over unexpected-like and see exactly what they were doing and maybe ask a few questions on the subject.

That student had better know the answers, too.

One evening after dark we were inside the county barn practicing, one relay coming off the line while the other was readying to start. One of my probationers asked to go outside to retrieve some study material from his vehicle.

I said sure and returned my attention to the shooters on the firing line. Having put my hearing protection on, I was about to give the command to commence firing when that same student was in front of me again, and a little wild-eyed in demeanor.

I leaned forward and removed one muff, expecting some sort of excuse about forgetting to bring his school work to rifle practice.

It was anything but.

"Mr. English" he exclaimed, "there's a riot outside!"

I yelled for my team captain to make the line safe and started hustling for the door. Sure enough, once outside the building and shed of my headphones I could hear plenty of screaming, cussing and carrying on about a block away, at a local motel.

And by counting the number of heads in the gloom from those outside motel lights, there were more than enough to legally constitute a riot according to the Texas Penal Code.

I ran to my Trans Am and popped the trunk, retrieving my portable radio. My off-duty pistol and DPS identification were already on me. Then I charged to the sound of the guns, or rather the sound of several irate, angry voices.

Between the barn and the motel was an unimproved empty lot, later turned into an RV parking area. While running through the darkness and trying to negotiate the scattered rocks and brush, at the same time I was on the portable radio advising the sheriff's office of what I had, and of my location.

That combination of terrain, blackness and being at a dead run made my transmission sound a wee bit shaky, and the ensuing results were rapidly forthcoming.

Shane Fenton was the deputy on duty that night, and later I learned he nearly broke his neck trying to get out of the jail and to where I was. It never mattered much to Shane what the odds were or how ugly the situation, he was going to be there to back you up.

I had managed to clear the empty lot and to confront two ring leaders among all the shoving, yelling and occasional fist thrown. Identifying myself as I produced my badge holder, I advised everyone present to cease and desist. One of the ring leaders decided to call my bluff, except I wasn't bluffing and he went down for the count.

Already I could hear Shane coming, the familiar moan of his Crown Vic mixed with the blaring of his siren. Within seconds he was on the scene and we were sorting things out from there.

BLACK AND WHITE

After more help arrived, those who needed arrested were transferred to the county jail. Shane and I looked at each other and grinned, and he shook his head in mock disbelief.

That was when I started paying more attention to what had occurred around me. Parked discretely off to the sides of this large open area were dozens of cars and trucks, the occupants watching on silently. One by one people stepped out of those vehicles, and walked over to visit for a moment.

What each had to say was very much the same: we heard you calling for help on our scanner and came to see if you were okay. We weren't trying to get into your business, we only wanted to know if you needed help.

Now let me be clear on what was happening, and who these people were. Some I barely knew on a personal basis, some I had words with before that weren't particularly kind. Several I had stopped on traffic violations and a few issued citations to. One or two I had been forced to arrest.

But they all came to help when they thought I might be in trouble.

These were the people who for decades to come looked out not only for me, but for my wife and two growing sons when I was not around to do so. No peace officer could ever be more greatly honored, nor expect more out of his fellow citizens.

For what happened in those few minutes of a single, solitary night among so many others, I will always be grateful for.

Because I knew then I had found a home worth having.

CARLOS WARREN

Three days after the incident at the motel, I was standing in our communications shack with a teletype clutched in my hand. For a moment my mind went numb. I read the message again more carefully, though it had been absolutely clear in content.

Carlos Warren, one of my academy classmates, had been murdered east of Austin the night before. Moments before another trooper arrived to check on him, the unknown assailant(s) had fled the scene. However, a San Antonio police officer stopped a vehicle a few hours later that matched the general description, and ended up having to shoot the driver who pulled a gun. The suspect was in critical condition in an area hospital.

Carlos was a couple of years younger than I, and we first came to know each other while in our recruit class. He had been in the Army at Fort Bliss and still called El Paso home, which meant over a 1,200-mile round trip from DPS Academy in Austin. Most of us recruits were able to visit our families during the weekends, Carlos did not have that extra benefit.

During our academy training Carlos cracked a couple of ribs but pushed on regardless, that was how badly he wanted to be a DPS trooper. In the academy all recruits had to participate in at least three boxing matches, which tended to set the tone as one of the many reasons for recruits to stay or go. There have been instances when a recruit would flat refuse to fight, and would walk away from the program at that point.

Not Carlos, even while carrying those still healing ribs. I know this because I banged on them pretty good during one of those boxing matches in our gym. Both of us had been declared 'walking wounded,' I had fractured my sternum at about the same time as his ribs. There was no pity ever found at that academy, and both of us were briefed on each other's infirmities before the fight.

We wailed on each other unmercifully and with each of my shots to those ribs, I could see Carlos pale and wince. But he never gave in or gave up, and that was a major factor in determining who was worthy of wearing that trooper badge. Carlos was more than worthy, and I respected him for it.

At the time I believe Carlos was also a single man, which meant he was more susceptible to the rumored Texas-shaped dartboard that DPS Headquarters used to figure where new troopers would be stationed. He was assigned the Austin area and began making a hand.

And now he was dead.

The circumstances surrounding his murder became clearer as the investigation proceeded. Carlos had been pulling a late hour patrol east of

Austin on US Highway 71, and a little after 1 a.m. pulled into a rest area to check vehicles. While doing so, he unwittingly became part of a harebrained kidnapping scheme that was going south by the moment.

The perpetrators were three brothers, who believed a teenaged acquaintance had broken into their car to steal some $1200 worth of stereo equipment. Their solution? Take the alleged thief at gunpoint when he came home from work. They were sitting in their vehicle about to 'interrogate' him when Carlos happened upon the scene.

Inside the car and sitting in the driver's seat was David Madrigal, who was also in possession of a .380 caliber pistol. At about the time Madrigal pulled his pistol and pointed it at the alleged thief, Carlos drove up in his black and white. He illuminated the interior of their Toyota two door with his unit's spotlamp, and Madrigal quickly hid the pistol on his person.

David Madrigal then whispered to his brothers "to just be cool," as he was going to get them out of this.

Carlos approached the vehicle and engaged in a conversation with the occupants. Shining his flashlight around the interior and sensing that something was wrong, he asked Madrigal and the brother sitting up front to step out of the beige Toyota. Both began doing so very slowly.

For some reason Carlos started examining the exterior of the vehicle, and in doing so turned his back on David Madrigal.

In a flash Madrigal was out of the Toyota, firing the pistol numerous times. Three of his rounds struck Carlos in the back and my classmate crumpled to the pavement. Just as quickly, Madrigal was back in the car and starting the engine to flee the murder scene.

But somehow, with both lungs perforated and his spinal cord severed, Carlos managed to fire three rounds from his .357 Magnum revolver, striking the Toyota and deflating one of the front tires. Then the Toyota barreled into the blackness, leaving Carlos to die there alone only seconds afterwards. Those three rounds Carlos fired were instrumental in identifying the vehicle, as the bullets were matched to the rifling inside the barrel of his Smith & Wesson.

Think about the last half minute of his life; the shock, the surprise, the pain and the severity of his mortal wounds. Yet Carlos managed to still get those shots off and make them count. Just as he had done at the academy, he never gave up and he never gave in, until life itself was taken from his body.

Carlos Warren proved again why he was more than worthy to wear the badge of a Texas Highway Patrolman.

Meanwhile in the Toyota, one of the brothers was screaming repeatedly at Madrigal "What did you do that for?!!!"

Madrigal's reply? "Because I thought he was going to get us…"

Some two hours later, a rookie San Antonio police officer observed a beige Toyota two door cruise by, and that the driver did not have his seatbelt on. At this point in time, the driver was the sole occupant.

Immediately after the officer stopping the Toyota, the driver sprung from the car and began firing. But this time he wasn't shooting someone in the back and the officer returned fire, critically wounding his would be assailant. It was David Madrigal, and he was using the same .380 pistol he had murdered Carlos Warren with just hours before.

The following Monday, Carlos was buried in the Fort Bliss cemetery outside El Paso. He had made the long, six hundred-odd mile journey once again but this time it would be one way trip, and with an aching finality that could never be undone.

Days and then weeks passed, and David Madrigal recovered from his gunshot wounds. The case gathered against him was the result of a well-organized investigation that was devastating to the defense. A combined effort on the part of the Texas Rangers, Texas Highway Patrol, Travis County Sheriff's Office, Travis County constables, and the Austin as well as San Antonio police departments left no stone unturned.

Every bit of evidence was documented in minute detail. The ballistics matches from both Madrigal's .380 and the .357 issued to Carlos were irrefutable in what had occurred. Then, in a damning confession that showed the sheer callousness of his crime, Madrigal's own brothers turned against him in their testimony.

On Valentine's Day, the afternoon of February 14, 1992, after only a little more than an hour's deliberation, a Travis County jury found David Madrigal guilty of capital murder in the death of Trooper Carlos Warren.

There was no real surprise in the verdict. What was a surprise was the legal result: Madrigal was given a life sentence for murder, seventy years for attempted capital murder and twenty years for aggravated kidnapping.

To the average layman that might sound as if justice had been served, but those involved in the criminal justice system knew better. David Madrigal would be eligible for parole in fifteen years.

The key to this was the lack of two vital words detailing that life sentence, missing were "without parole." The jury determined that Madrigal was 'probably' no longer a continuing threat.

One only needs to read the aforementioned convictions to judge for themselves whether Madrigal still constituted a probable threat to society. In addition to and following his incarceration, David Madrigal was also involved in a fight with another prisoner in January 1997. According to prison officials at that time, he was suspected of being involved in an escape attempt linked to that free-for-all.

BLACK AND WHITE

Madrigal was denied parole in 2008 and in 2017, probably due to the continuing pressure from those who remembered Carlos. His murderer will be up for parole again in 2027. I hope there are enough of us left at that time to prevent Madrigal from ever being released. Afterwards, he can argue his case before a Higher Authority.

In all this senseless violence, brutality and lack of respect for innocent human life, one can also see good things that came from this tragic affair. On the linear scale between good versus ever-present evil, the good may not seem like much, but it does provide the essential outreach of hope we should all cling to.

Only days before Carlos was murdered, he made a traffic stop on a gentleman by the name of Richard Metcalf. The two visited beside the road and Mr. Metcalf was supremely impressed with the professionalism, courtesy and humanity the young trooper exhibited. When he heard the news of what happened, a great pain and sense of loss came upon him.

That pain was deep in his soul and it needed a release, even exorcisement. When Richard Metcalf discovered there was no monument or marker memorializing the deaths of some seventy-two DPS officers killed in the line of duty, he found his way to do so.

Out of his own pocket and on his own time, Richard Metcalf began having monuments erected on the spot where each of these men lost their lives. This included everything from picking up the 800 pound finished memorial in Rockdale to transporting to the fatal location, and then erecting the stone with his own two hands.

Carlos Warren was the first fallen DPS officer to receive one.

Richard Metcalf died in 1998, having set 56 such memorials across the state. His brother, Don Metcalf, continues the family tradition in this noble effort to memorialize those who gave their all for others.

Future changes in Texas criminal law, specifically in capital murder cases, occurred in the late 1990s. Sentencing and parole requirements became stiffer, no more fifteen years and eligible for parole as what Madrigal unjustly received. These days, you murder a peace officer in the state of Texas and it is either life without parole or a death sentence. Period.

The public outcry after hearing what happened to Carlos and other officers, and the ensuing lack of punishment, had a great deal to do with that change. With this mounting pressure from the citizens whom these men had served, our state legislature acted accordingly.

On March 21, 2013, the stone marker emplaced by Richard Metcalf in Carlos's memory was relocated off US Highway 71. A solemn rededication accompanied this action and another one of my old classmates, Stephen Bynum, played Taps as part of the ceremony.

I found that fitting.

Finally in March of 2019, the stretch of road where Carlos died was designated as the Trooper Carlos Ray Warren Memorial Highway by the Texas state legislature.

It is now thirty years later since Carlos was murdered, and our society is reeling in the midst of a rage of senseless violence against peace officers previously unheard of in my lifetime.

The cold-blooded, calculated murder of Carlos Warren should remind us of the kind of price paid in protecting society, and how that debt accrues every single day.

It is up to us, as that society, to protect and care for those who selflessly protect and care for us. For to do otherwise means the end of that society, and the way of life and constitutional freedoms that each of us cherish so much.

BLACK AND WHITE

*Trooper Carlos Ray Warren, Texas Highway Patrol
End of Watch March 5th, 1991*

STUCK IN LIVE OAK CREEK

It was a cloudy Sunday evening and I was swinging a wide loop across the western reaches of Crockett County, which made for a wide loop indeed. This particular route was a favorite of mine for the end of the weekend, and allowed me to patrol some stretches of my assigned area not normally tended to.

I would wander out of Ozona at the beginning of my shift, traveling on Texas Highway 137 and showing the flag to all the Midland-Odessa to San Antonio traffic that favored this route.

Then west across US Highway 190 to do likewise for the Fort Bliss to Fort Hood crowd, before heading south on a county road that paralleled Live Oak Creek. This allowed me to pop up undetected on Interstate 10 about thirty miles west of Ozona, and nab a high roller or two who might have thought the coast was clear.

The name of this route was Live Oak Creek Road, and though it extended all the way to what was once US Highway 290 west of Fort Lancaster, the paved part ended at the interstate. This made it even more suitable for my purposes, as it was a good enough road to catch an unwary speeder at times, as well as a DWI once or twice.

While prowling down Live Oak I came across Rex Fenton, who upon meeting my unit flagged me over to the side. Rex was Shane's father and had been a deputy sheriff for Billy Mills in years past, and had a reputation as a tough character. He was also a good man and one to have on your side when it counted.

He pulled up beside me and rolled his window down.

"What's a Texas highway patrolman doing out here?" he asked half-jokingly.

"Trying to catch sure enough desperados like you, Rex." I quipped.

"English, there ain't no safe place around here when you're on patrol!" he then smiled, peering out from under the brim of his straw hat. "Keep it up, you're making a hand."

Those few words meant more to me than if the director of the DPS had said them.

But there was no other traffic that day, and as I neared the interstate I discovered why. About a mile and a half shy of my destination was a low water crossing. Unbeknownst to me the creek had gone on a tear a few days ago, and that low water crossing was a four star mess. Most of the water had gone on, but in doing so left a morass of sand, mud and gravel where the crossing was situated.

BLACK AND WHITE

Staring out the Diplomat's windshield, I shook my head as the old adage of the best laid plans of mice and men came to mind. I would have to back track ten plus miles to US Highway 190, and decide from there what needed done next.

I had already put the gear selector in reverse and was starting to back away when my CB radio crackled. It was a truck driver, talking about a woman in a white mini-van who had suddenly swapped lanes in front of him and stopped on the improved shoulder. At first he was peeved, but started being concerned when she hit her four way flashers as his rig swept past.

Partially due to having to cross the creek at a ninety-degree angle, the county road paralleled the interstate for nearly half the remaining distance. From where my unit sat I could actually see the white minivan, though not very well due to the interstate's elevated lanes.

Other drivers were now reporting in, saying that she had some sort of problem and that all the doors were open on the passenger side. This was still the era where many truck drivers considered themselves professionals, and a certain code of chivalry still ran in their veins.

More so, many were family men who knew what could happen to a woman alone and unawares on that road, especially along a stretch where it was thirty miles to Ozona and eighty more to Fort Stockton.

So did I, and I got paid to take care of such matters. Keeping an eye on the mini-van, I stepped out of the Dodge to examine the crossing more carefully. It was forty miles to detour through Iraan, but if I could get my unit across this mess in front of me…

The CB traffic continued and the shared concern was rising. She was parked on the west bound side, which meant the drivers were leery to stop with a full load as it was a good-sized climb from there up to Red Ball Cut. That cut was supposedly the deepest for the entire length of Interstate 10, to give you an idea of what they faced when launching from a dead stop.

Finally one of them used that time honored remark that set my wheels in motion: "Where's a cop when you really need one?"

'You just wait a few minutes, fella,' I thought to myself. 'Have a got a surprise for you.'

A quick reconnoiter of the crossing revealed the worst part of my challenge was on my side, to the other was mostly puddles of water and a thin covering of drying mud over the roughened concrete surface.

I eyed a mostly dry-appearing sandbar on my end, extending out to nearly half way across. If I could hit that sandbar with my left wheels while moving at a good clip, and if it didn't collapse underneath me while doing so, my momentum should carry the day.

Or something like that.

I got back in the car, the CB radio still giving a moment-by-moment update of what was happening with the minivan. The guessing game went the gamut from a flat tire to an overheated vehicle to a blown motor.

Backing up to get a good, smooth approach, I launched forward.

The entire car was on that sandbar when the left side gave way. I was stuck to it like the proverbial pest to fresh flypaper.

Getting out of the Dodge again, it did not take me long to find out that I was going nowhere anytime soon. Coming to that sad resolution, I reached over for the mike to advise Ozona Communications about getting a Pecos County unit headed her direction.

At that same second, the CB came to life again.

"She's rolling!" someone announced.

I looked to the south and sure enough she was, the four ways flickering off as the minivan built speed.

"I think I got it figured out," chimed in another. "She was changing a baby diaper!"

Now why couldn't he have said that a minute or so earlier?

Oh, well. I wished her luck and turned to the task of unsticking myself.

One of the problems in doing so was those years of Dodge patrol cars did not come with a Sure Grip rear end, meaning both wheels did not pull evenly when on different surfaces. And of course, Goodyear Eagle GTs were never designed to have much traction in off-road situations.

With my portable tire jack and folding military e-tool out of the trunk, along with some nearby rocks scattered about, I lifted both rear tires high enough to pile the rocks underneath. This had to be done one wheel at a time and soon enough I had mud, sand and flecks of gravel all over me, too.

I was rewarded with little more than a lot of tire spin and absolutely no movement. It surely was turning into one of those days. Meanwhile that cloudy day had darkened considerably, as the far off boom of thunder began to echo down the canyon.

What was I saying about this being one of those days?

Three times I lifted the rear end up, one side at a time and placed rocks under the tires. Three times and I managed to move that black and white exactly a fraction of an inch, and not an ooch more. This chore was going to be a little tougher than first estimated.

Resigning myself to a more involved engineering plan, I jacked up not only the rear end this time but also the front, filling the void under each tire with flat rock. Then I began carrying in flat rock from all directions, building two individual tracks just wide enough for the tires to roll upon.

The cloud cover became really dark and a wind picked up from out of the north. I could smell the coming moisture before large drops of rain began to fall. Not only was I filthy dirty and half soaked in sweat, it now looked like I was fixing to be drenched, too.

I plodded on with my master plan, placing the flat rocks all the way to the far end of the sand bar. It was raining fairly steadily now, enough for me to be happy when I crawled in my Diplomat to start it up.

The 318 V8 came to life and I placed the transmission in second gear, so that I could crawl forward at a snail's pace, bereft of any tire spinning or sudden lurches. The Dodge began to ease forward and we were off like a herd of turtles.

But we were moving and that was all that mattered at this point. The rain was holding steady and I wanted out of that creek bed, as the heavy stuff was coming in from the north where the watershed lay. With infinite care I steered along the twin paths of rock, keeping my foot off the gas as well as away from the brake.

A few seconds later we were off the sandbar and tippy-toeing through the patches of water and wet gravel on the other side, then up the concrete ramp and back to pavement.

Ah, the sweet smell of victory! Or in this case, the odorous smell of a wet uniform that was dry cleaned regularly. I opened the driver's door into the rain and muck to pick up my jack and e-tool. When I got to the sandbar I had to stop and look, and even grin a bit in mild wonderment.

Imprinted on the ground was a mirror image of the undercarriage of that Dodge, complete with gas tank, exhaust system, rear axle and the front K-member. No wonder the car would not budge until all four wheels had been elevated.

Grabbing my tools, I made for the patrol unit and tossed everything in the trunk and drove straight for Ozona. There were no more thoughts of any normal patrol work until I had cleaned myself up, as well as the patrol unit. We were both a sight to see.

My first stop was the office. I needed to make certain there was nothing of importance going on, before I went home to take care of business. R. B. Babbitt, the communications supervisor for Ozona, was filling in for one of his people who asked for some time off. R. B. had been around a while and along with Bob Falkner, had helped open the DPS Ozona office. He was a good man too, and took good care of his people. His son, Cliff, carried on the family name first as a highway patrolman and later a lieutenant in Motor Vehicle Theft.

When I stepped through the door R.B. looked up and the expression on his face went from shades of puzzlement, to shock, to genuine mirth in rapid fashion. Then he started chuckling followed by laughter that set his entire body shaking.

"What happened to you?" he guffawed, removing his glasses to wipe away the tears forming in his eyes.

I told him my story of weariness and woe in truncated form. He listened intently, grinning with glee as my tale unfolded and started laughing again.

"And it never occurred to you to call for assistance?" his voice boomed in merriment.

"Nope, I got myself into it and was duty bound to get myself out" was my reply.

"Yeah," he responded. "You'd rather have floated down to the Pecos River than admit you needed help!"

"Yep."

R. B. chuckled once more and said, "Keep at it Ben, you'll make a hand yet."

I grinned and he waved me off. Going out the door, it occurred to me that two men whom I had a good deal of respect for had said I was making a hand.

And that made the day not so bad after all.

SUICIDE BY FREIGHTLINER

In my years on this earth as well as working the road, I saw the many faces of death many times. By strict definition that meant dozens upon dozens of traffic fatalities alone, as during that era Crockett County was calculated as the fifth deadliest stretch of interstate in the nation, by miles traveled. Plus the dozens upon dozens of others that I assisted fellow troopers with.

Added were also the unattended deaths, the welfare checks and searches that went bad, the killings, the house fires and the suicides. There were at least a half dozen suicides that I can think of offhand, including the loss of a friend as well as a fellow officer. As a general rule these are the saddest tragedies of all, because often enough suicide is a permanent solution for what is usually a temporary problem.

Of all the human tragedies that befall our fellow man, this act of despair and self-destruction is the most insidiously heartbreaking. We do not understand why such a thing occurs, nor do we really want to. For that would mean having to comprehend the feelings and emotions of someone who would willingly take the greatest individual gift of all; their own lives.

A certain percentage of these investigated first fell under the category of a traffic fatality, but the little guy in the back of one's head said different. That is when the investigative part of your mind is put to task in having to provide the evidence to let the truth come forth, though the truth can be so hurtful to so many others.

This proved to be one of those investigations, even when I knew it was a suicide before ever rolling upon the scene.

The hot afternoon was turning into a very warm evening in late July, I was pulling an evening shift and was in the office handling reports. Randy Hall was working the radio, and looked in to advise that Shane Fenton might need some help with a male subject at the bus stop. I shoved the dreaded death of a thousand papercuts away from me and hit the road running.

Over the radio Shane updated me to the situation, saying the subject in question had fled the scene on foot when informed a sheriff's deputy was enroute. That information was followed up by a physical description, a white male around thirty years of age, brown hair and about five foot seven. I kept my eyes moving while driving but did not see anyone, and pulled up to the bus stop approximately two minutes later.

About the time I was stepping out of my unit, Raymond P. 'Bear' Borrego, constable for Crockett County, came over the air and advised that he had a subject matching the description located behind the old Firestone store. He was taking him to the hospital.

Bear Borrego was another one of those good officers that I had the pleasure to work with, and as I write this, he is still serving in the capacity of constable there. In those many years we went through a lot together and I was always glad to have him around. That estimation included now.

Shane and I met him at the Ozona clinic. Since Shane was the lead officer, Bear and I stood by as he began questioning the subject who was obviously very ill. Beyond that, he appeared to be on some sort of controlled substance which did not help matters much. The subject was sweating profusely, his color was bad and his pupils were dilated, and he was just about as nervous as they come.

When interviewed the man stated he was feeling sick, had a bad cough and was suffering from the shakes. Shane asked if he was on anything and the subject responded as if insulted, saying emphatically that he was an alcoholic but had never touched drugs in his life.

However a check on his criminal record revealed otherwise. In the San Francisco area alone he had two arrests for vandalism, two for resisting arrest, one for arson and one for selling drugs.

That was enough for me to stick around until his situation was resolved. The guy was acting plenty nervous and gave every indication of being emotionally distraught, and not completely in control of himself.

While our mystery man was being examined by the clinical staff, Shane pulled me to the side and explained what he knew so far. Our subject had been put off a bus going to Houston due to his turbulent behavior. He had told the Greyhound driver that he was having trouble breathing and wanted to throw up, and needed to go to the nearest hospital to have his stomach pumped.

The driver had a mobile phone and advised the sheriff's office of the situation as he was pulling into town. Once stopped he helped the sick man off the bus, telling him a deputy was enroute to get him to the hospital as quickly as possible.

Upon hearing a sheriff's officer was coming to help, the subject yelled excitedly; "Hell no! I'm not going anyplace with any deputy," and took off running.

When the bus driver was asked what might be the reason for such a response, he stated a passenger advised the subject had ingested fifteen grams of cocaine at the Border Patrol checkpoint outside Van Horn. Evidently the sick passenger panicked when the officers supposedly brought a drug dog on the bus.

Meanwhile, Doctor Marcus Sims arrived at the clinic and was examining our subject, and showing every indicator of growing concern as he did so. Though the man had calmed down some by now and said he was feeling better, Marcus caught our attention as he put on a second pair of rubber gloves over those already on his hands. Then he told the subject that he had a fever of 104 degrees and apparently some fluid on his lungs.

This was during the height of the HIV/AIDS epidemic, and this fellow was exhibiting several of the more observable indicators. By federal mandate Marcus could not tell us the subject was infected, even if we were forced into close contact with him.

But he didn't have to. When you deal with a man long enough and learn to trust him, you know something isn't right by watching his actions. Marcus Sims would be our community doctor for decades to come and in some very serious situations, and I had respect for the man. He was one of those who did not see an assigned number or just another problem when you came in, he saw you as a human being. Marcus cared; he cared for the community, the clinic, his chosen profession and the citizenry of our small, somewhat isolated town.

He also cared for us, his local peace officers and first responders. If I could advise any young person beginning their career as a medical doctor, I would tell them to find a mentor like Doctor Marcus Sims.

When Marcus put on that second pair of gloves Shane, Bear and I glanced knowingly at each other. All three of us had caught on to what he was saying, without him uttering a single word.

Marcus turned his full attention back to his patient, saying he needed to go to San Angelo and to the regional hospital there. The doctor advised he was a very sick man, with true compassion in every syllable that he spoke.

Like I said Marcus Sims cared, and he cared about everyone entrusted to him.

But the fevered subject demurred, saying all he wanted to do was get on the next bus to Houston. Marcus slowly shook his head in dismay and gave a shot and some medications to the man, stating he needed to seek out medical attention as soon as possible upon arrival.

After Marcus did what he could, Shane approached and asked if the man wanted to wait at the county jail for the next bus, as it would be another three and a half hours. The deputy went on to explain the stay would be strictly voluntary, the man would not be under arrest and free to go at any time.

The subject was adamant in his refusal. Shane then volunteered to transport the seriously ill man back to the bus stop, rather than have him walk. Finally, the deputy asked the transient to stay there and not be wandering around.

I looped back to the office and quickly finished my necessary reports. As it was getting close to suppertime, I elected to patrol close to town until taking my meal break. A few minutes later, the CB radio in the Diplomat crackled with excited voices.

"Hey! Are you all right, driver?" asked someone.

"Yeah," came a shaky reply. "Break-break for any highway patrol, I just had a guy jump into the grille of my truck!"

Several things happened at that moment, including the thought of a hot meal anytime soon going away. I answered the call and the truckdriver gave out his location. Hitting the lights and siren, I put my foot in that four-barrel carb and gave the Dodge plenty of rein.

At the same time I grabbed the mike to my two way, advising DPS Ozona of the situation and to roll an ambulance. After doing so, I switched to the SO frequency to call Shane but he was already ahead of me.

"4211, I heard you on my CB. Will meet you there."

Within a minute of fast driving, I was on the brakes at the reported location, with Shane hard behind. What we found was best described as ghastly, and made me sick to my stomach. Yet this was not in the physical sense, as I had already seen much worse.

The rapidly expanding knot in my gut was purely emotional, because what was left of the sick man at the hospital now lay in a smashed, jumbled up heap of human flesh and bone, in the middle of the eastbound lanes for Interstate 10.

After making certain the truckdriver was uninjured, I cancelled the ambulance and asked for the justice of the peace, as well as the funeral home. Then I opened the trunk of my patrol unit and retrieved my issued raincoat, using the bright yellow slicker to cover the man's body. No one needed to see him like that unless they had no other choice.

I said the truckdriver was uninjured, but he certainly wasn't all right. The man was lapsing into a state of shock so I had him sit on the running board of his truck, away from the traffic. Other emergency units began to arrive and a volunteer fire unit, along with Texas DOT, began detouring traffic around the site. Bear Borrego came out to assist where he could, and Fire Marshal Steve Kenley lent his expertise in taking photographs of the scene.

While Shane kept an eye out and helped with taking statements, I made my way back over to the badly shaken driver after summoning the duty wrecker. The impact had ruptured the radiator on his late model Freightliner, and the truck tractor would have to be towed in.

I asked very few questions as he related what happened. When someone wants to talk you let them do so, especially in this sort of circumstance. What he had experienced would never be forgotten, no matter how long he lived or whatever else he saw.

The driver stated he was traveling in the outside lane at about 55-60 MPH, when he observed a hitchhiker standing on the improved shoulder. The truckdriver moved to the inside lane to give more room for safety's sake, but when he did the hitchhiker began waving and running toward his rig. The operator of the truck locked up his tires and continued to the inside lane to avoid impact, but the hitcher kept coming and then deliberately jumped into the grille of the Freightliner.

Still in shock, the driver mumbled that the deceased was smiling and waving as he did so. After talking himself out, I had the driver write down his statement while I examined the scene more closely.

The physical evidence matched exactly what the truckdriver described, there was over a hundred and fifty feet of straight skid marks angling to the inside lane. The impact area on the truck was squarely in the grille, no damage to the headlamps nor to the front bumper. The deceased had knowingly and with deliberation jumped squarely into the path of the truck.

The impact itself was severe enough to knock both shoes off the dead man, and send his body airborne for over sixty feet before hitting pavement again. As the deceased bounced and rolled along, the right-side truck and trailer wheels ran over his body.

After the truck was towed away and some semblance of quiet came to the scene of the suicide, I marked the area for a future scale diagram and the road was reopened for traffic. The sun dipped below the horizon, the last rays of light across the sky faded away. Then I was left alone to consider many thoughts that both puzzled as well as disturbed.

But one word would sum these various thoughts up best:

Why?

There could be no real forethought or prior planning on the dead man's part. Walking from the bus stop, he had to cross all four lanes of traffic to get to the eastbound improved shoulder. This told me he had fully intended to hitchhike to Houston at that time.

But why leave the bus stop in the first place? He already had a passenger ticket to Houston, a ride in relative safety and comfort to where he wanted to go.

And why the sudden change in thought process from hitching a ride to committing suicide, and why this particular truck?

Was it a sudden overwhelming emotional impulse bred from a feeling of absolute futility and despair, which lasted just long enough to make him literally throw his own life away?

What of the truckdriver and the inescapable guilt and regret placed upon him for the rest of his life? Did the dead man give a scant second's thought to how this would affect his unknowing executioner's own soul and spirit, for all his remaining years?

That night after my shift I laid in bed staring at a dark ceiling, my mind in another dark place while searching for even darker answers. There were none forthcoming, and before drifting off into a troubled sleep I decided it was probably just as well.

From next shift forward my total focus was on the investigation. This was a suicide, not a traffic accident, but it still had to be proven on paper as to what really occurred. Like any other fatal I ever worked, I lived with it until the investigation was completed and the multitude of written reports filed away.

In the meantime, it was not a very nice place to be.

But the only way through was forward, so forward would be my course. In this was a necessary, even vital, piece of business needing attended to. I had to find a next of kin and have them notified.

I knew the victim's name but it was a very common one, and the address he gave to the clinic was at least three years old. Inside his wallet was a birth certificate and social security card, and the first three numbers on the card did not match the area for that last address. But someone out there knew this person; be they family member, friend, or a co-worker, and that somebody needed to know.

Also in the wallet were some business cards and pay stubs, strung throughout the West Coast for the past several years. This was before the internet and our now digitalized age, so I picked up the telephone and began calling.

On the other end of the line were answering machines that malfunctioned or often times no one answered at all, and when they did there was suspicion and outright ugliness upon identifying myself. Evidently my case involved someone who possessed quite a checkered past, far more than even his criminal history stipulated.

But one or two did listen, and said they might know someone who 'knew someone who knew someone' that could help me.

Three days later, this jammed up ice pack of missing information began to break. Shane Fenton called and said a male claiming to be a brother had phoned the hospital. The nurse on duty gave him our office numbers and she notified Shane as soon as the caller hung up. Not too long afterward, my phone rang and it was the brother.

Or I should say one of three half-brothers. This family was not a normal one, and there seemed to be even more suspicion and animosity for each other than toward me as a peace officer. But after some long distance diplomacy and appeals to conscience I finally obtained a physical address for the mother of the deceased, in the state of Washington.

With this break I made contact with the local police department. It was a small town and the person who answered the phone knew the mother as well as the deceased, and said he had handled him before. When I detailed the circumstance for my calling, he said he would phone the mother and tell her.

Our conversation changed tone with that last comment. No, he wasn't going to just pick up a telephone and glibly tell some poor woman that her son was dead. He was going to send an officer along with a preacher or a priest, or a close friend of hers, or preferably both and inform her in person.

"Oh," was the somewhat startled reply. "I'll have to talk to the sergeant about that."

"Please do so" I said. About an hour later, I was notified the mother had received a death notification concerning her son and it was done in proper, respectful fashion.

Later I was to learn the deceased man was an intravenous drug user as well as an alcoholic, and that he had been kicked out of several recovery programs. He also exhibited prior suicidal tendencies, and recently was diagnosed as having AIDS. The mother felt this would happen sooner or later, and her greatest fear was he would end up as just another John Doe.

The combined efforts of the people of the community of Ozona kept this from happening. If there was any real good which came from this dismally sad episode, I suppose that would be it.

And perhaps that one or two minds were changed about who peace officers really are, what they really do, and why.

SOOTHSAYING AND BUZZARD CONTROL DEPARTMENT

During my career I was blessed to work with a lot of good people, some of whom wore the cinco peso badge of a Texas Ranger. Unlike times past, rangers these days usually start out in the highway patrol and work themselves into the Ranger Service through promotions to Narcotics, Motor Vehicle Theft, Criminal Intelligence or the like.

You must have at least eight years in the DPS as a commissioned officer before any consideration as ranger material, which is considerably longer than all other billets found elsewhere in the organization. The selection process is exacting, as it should be for an elite group who can trace their roots all the way back to 1823. This was when they were first created by a man who became known as the Father of Texas, Stephen F. Austin.

The Ozona DPS office had a ranger position assigned since its opening in 1973, and likely a half dozen came through during my time as a highway patrolman. It was a privilege to work with such men, and be around them on a day to day basis.

But even out of such a group of highly vetted, highly qualified men there are those who stand out as being special. To me, one of these was Texas Ranger Danny Rhea.

Danny took the position of ranger in Ozona around 1988, if memory serves me correctly. I had only been on the force less than two years, so when he spoke I tended to listen.

Ranger Rhea had been a cryptographer in the United States Navy, a highway patrolman, a license and weight troop and was a member of our Criminal Intelligence division before pinning on the ranger badge. He was nobody's fool and "knew some things because he had seen some things." Anybody who gave Danny Rhea short rift, in any way, was making a bad mistake in doing so.

As the years went by he became a friend, as did his family. To this day I am honored to be considered by them as remaining so.

A few years before either Danny or I arrived in Ozona, out-of-state authorities arrested a suspect involved in a local killing. When he confessed to the crime, he didn't stop there but went through a litany of others much like Henry Lee Lucas or Samuel Little, both widely known serial killers who committed several of their heinous acts in West Texas.

During this string of shocking confessions, the suspect claimed to have murdered an entire family along old US Highway 290 close to Fort Lancaster, and disposing of their bodies in a nearby canyon.

BLACK AND WHITE

Now anyone who knows anything about the lower Pecos River country will tell you there are dozens of large canyons running every which direction, so the suspect's admission led to many more questions. Added to this puzzle was the fact that very few answers were forthcoming as the confessor could not, or would not, be more specific.

For the next few years those canyons nearby were swept repeatedly by deputies, constables, highway patrolmen, rangers, border patrolmen and game wardens, along with area ranchers, oilfield pumpers and deer hunters, all looking for some evidence as to where this might have occurred. They did so not only on foot but also by horseback, four-by-four, helicopter and fixed wing aircraft.

In the end, not a single trace of this reported mass murder was ever found.

But this did not stop the morbid fascination with such a bloodcurdling revelation, or the continuing line of people who claimed to know something about those killings. Some sought notoriety, others genuinely wanted to help. All were interviewed exhaustively and each and every lead, no matter how strange or improbable, was followed through upon.

And no one was more involved in doing so than the Ranger Service, along with other agency divisions such as DPS Criminal Intelligence.

I want to say it was in 1992 when a self-described psychic in the Houston area approached authorities, and began speaking of dreams and visions she had concerning this case. She went on to say that she was sure this family had been murdered, and was certain she could walk right to the spot where their remains would be found.

Though such a fantastic claim might be ridiculed out of hand by many, I do not know of a single experienced road troop who will not give some sort of nod to a 'sixth sense,' though they may do so only in private. Each of us can remember a certain sensation or feel about a past situation, where we went with gut intuition spawned beyond the boundaries of the five normal senses.

In police work, you personally experience so many strange occurrences as to have a sort of familiarity with those flirting knowledge from the other side of the veil. Any man who believes he has seen it all most likely hasn't, and is usually making that declaration from a very limited perspective.

Besides, nothing else had borne fruit so far. There are missing persons reported by the hundreds of thousands each year across our nation, in 1990 alone the figure was nearly 664,000. Furthermore, an average of 90,000 a year are never accounted for. If there was any chance of removing some names from such depressingly long list, the high improbability was still more than worth the effort.

So, arrangements were made for the DPS Aircraft Section to fly the psychic to Ozona, where Danny Rhea picked her up that morning and drove her to the immediate area some thirty miles west of town.

This locale was both rugged as well as remote, even when US 290 was still the main corridor from California to Florida. But after Interstate 10 was completed through Crockett County and bypassed the spot by several miles to the north, it became much more so.

From here the nearest food and gas was the tiny burg of Sheffield, better than ten miles to the west. The surrounding rough terrain is peaked by outsized boulders and infested with cedar and mesquite scrub, offering little to no shade from the vicious midday summer sun. For those seeking man-made shelter nearby, there are only some picnic tables at the seldom-visited roadside park on Lancaster Hill.

Rangers to a man are fastidious dressers, as they are expected to be as professional in appearance as any officer alive, and looking ready to meet the governor or appear in district court at any given moment. In that they dress in the manner of their forebears which means a western hat, boots, tie, long sleeve shirt, and crisply pressed trousers. A dress coat, usually of western cut was either worn or kept handy, depending on the weather and assignment.

As always, Danny made for an imposing impression in his neatly groomed six foot and something frame, dressed the traditional ranger way. But nobody told him about having to climb up and down every canyon found within a five mile radius, and to do so in the middle of a hundred degree day.

You see, that psychic assured everyone in Houston she could walk right to the exact location in question, and it was just off the roadway. Soothsayer she may have been, but she was lying like a rug on both counts.

For that entire long summer day she wandered into one canyon and out the other, saying that she just 'knew' they would walk up on the spot at any moment. Dutifully, Danny knocked out her tracks every step of the way, remaining as courteous and professional as any man ever could in the same circumstance. In his heart he clung to that one, tiny hint of hope that something might come of this effort, even with such a flighty, unpromising start.

The hours went by and it grew hotter still as the uncompromising sun continued to beat down. Danny, a seasoned hand with years of experience, had water and victuals stored in his unmarked Caprice. Yet there was nothing that could be done about the furnace-like heat and once in those canyons, there was not much of a breeze either.

Finally, as the sun hung close to the western horizon, Danny had to call a halt to her little wayfaring expedition. They were way behind schedule in getting the psychic back to the Ozona airport, and on to her home town the same night.

Once back to his parked unit, Danny turned the a/c on full blast and headed east for Ozona at a fast clip, allowing no grass to grow underneath that car. He hoped to shave off some time in the return trip to make the situation better for the DPS pilot, who still had to fly all the way back to Houston. However, this was not to be.

A couple of miles down the road with that small block Chevy at full song, an unwary turkey buzzard took wing from the tall grass along the shoulder. There was no time to react other than to hang on to the steering wheel as the large scavenger awkwardly fluttered up, and then went right through the car's windshield.

For those who do not know, a West Texas turkey buzzard is one of the vilest, filthiest, most odious creatures on God's Green Earth, and those unhappy characteristics are not improved upon when dying in the back seat of a four door Chevrolet. And of course, the carrion eater had to throw up all contents of its trade before expiring to wherever dead turkey buzzards go.

Providentially neither Danny nor the psychic were injured in the accident, though the Caprice was ultimately totaled. This was partly due to damage done and partly because they could never neutralize that horrific lingering odor.

Danny had a sheriff's unit come and arranged for the woman to be taken to the airport, then went about his business in securing the needed towing and filling out the necessary paperwork. Suffice to say, it was way into the wee hours before he finally managed to get home.

And even after all this he never, ever lost his gentlemanly composure and sense of professionalism. That was the kind of officer Danny Rhea was, and one of the many reasons why he was chosen to be a Texas Ranger.

That is, until the next day.

I was in the office the next morning, and noticed the gaping hole in the windshield of his Chevrolet parked at the rear of the building. I circled the mortally wounded Caprice to better see what had happened, though not too closely as the car stunk to high heaven.

Randy Hall was manning the radio, so I went on inside to get the straight skinny. He was waiting for me behind clouds of cigarette smoke and grinning with glee at the chance to tell a funny story.

First order of business: No one was hurt other than one turkey buzzard terminated with extreme prejudice. Then he told me Danny's tale of woe in its totality reference his outing with the Houston psychic.

After hearing what occurred and having a little levity put into my day, I marveled again at Danny and the peace officer and gentleman he was. That was when the germ of an idea came into my head.

Walking into the highway patrol office I fished out some typing paper and a black marker. Working quickly, I brought my idea to reality and showed it to Randy. He began grinning again in somewhat wicked fashion.

Then I took some scotch tape and right below the sign that read 'SERGEANT DANNY RHEA TEXAS RANGERS' on the door of his office, I placed the following addendum:

'SOOTHSAYING AND BUZZARD CONTROL DEPARTMENT'

When Danny came in I was still there, and somehow he knew immediately who this particular culprit was.

"Ben English!" he roared and I hit the back exit at a run.

That was a lot of years ago and Danny and I remained friends until he passed away a few years back. I still miss him and his counsel, they don't hardly make that kind of man anymore.

And I know that he really liked me in return, otherwise he would have killed me that morning and told God I died.

NO ONE SHOULD HAVE SURVIVED

When I started through the photographs in the sealed manila folder the thought came to me again, no one should have survived this wreck. I was always pretty good at identifying vehicles, especially during those years, but on that night I distinctly recall looking at an off-red passenger vehicle so badly damaged I had no idea as to what make or model it was.

There was a dead man lying near the crumpled, crushed mound of metal, rubber and glass, yet there should have been four. The following is their story and why I decided to include this tragic event in this book, because other than by God's Grace what happened should have been a whole lot worse.

It was already past midnight on a humid August evening, I was finishing up a minor accident investigation at the DPS Office in Ozona. I heard the phone ring in the communications shack and Bob Falkner answered, speaking in low tones. But somehow, I sensed the subject of the conversation, and my body began to tense up with a surge of adrenalin as well as anticipation.

He appeared in the doorway and his face told it all.

"Ben," he said quietly, "I think you got a bad one at Howard Draw Bridge."

I was out the door and had my Dodge rolling in less time than it would take to tell how, pointing the Pentastar hood ornament toward the interstate as I engaged the lights and siren. Howard Draw was fifteen miles west of Ozona, and our ambulance crew was all volunteer and likely asleep at home when they received the call. Seconds count when someone may be dying, and I needed to be there right now.

My unit was not the only one out that night, I heard Shane Fenton come on the air and say he was right behind me. Checking my rear-view mirror, I could see his rollers in the darkness merging with interstate traffic. I willed the Diplomat to go even faster, and somehow that black and white knew what needed done. According to the log, I checked on scene some seven minutes from the time Bob notified me. Shane was not too far behind.

Then I was on the binders hard, coming to a slewing, skidding stop in the median as a citizen frantically waved a dim flashlight and pointed under the east side of Howard Draw Bridge. Other civilian vehicles were parked about, their prior occupants trying to lend help as best they could.

I bailed out of the Dodge and ran to the edge of the drop off, where I observed an incredibly damaged red colored vehicle below, and a body about thirty-five feet away. Simultaneously several people began to talk all at once, saying the person was dead.

It was pitch black underneath that bridge, and those $1.99 flashlights people were using to try to light up the area weren't helping much. I ran back to my unit and began repositioning it at the edge of the drop off, to make use of the high beams as well as the twin spotlights. Meanwhile Shane had arrived and barreled past me on foot, going off the edge with his issued Streamlight. There was a steep concrete embankment leading to the bottom, and he took it in record time.

While moving my Dodge, I updated DPS Communications on what we had and put out the call for assistance, as it was obvious the mystery car had overturned numerous times before coming to rest. If there had been anyone else inside the smashed vehicle, there was no telling where they might have ended up.

Numerous people were still trying to talk to me, leading to a real Tower of Babel scenario. Their words and perspectives were varied and confused, even contradictory and no two could agree on the same. Finally, I asked those present to please be quiet and did a quick verbal interview on each citizen there.

Some of the pieces of the jumbled puzzle began to come to the fore, important ones. Putting those pieces together, I learned a young woman and two infants had also been involved in the crash. An alert truck driver was driving past and narrowly avoided striking them as they stood in the roadway, the woman with a child under each arm.

His sudden braking and coming to a stop attracted the attention of other motorists, as did his CB transmission saying he was taking them to medical attention in Ozona. All three had serious injuries. That was when people began to stop and try to help.

This information produced a new dimension and purpose to the primary mission at hand, the location and recovery of survivors. One always hopes that anyone who stops has the best of intentions, but you don't hang someone else's life on just that one hope.

I took down a quick description of the truck and notified DPS Communications, asking Bob Falkner to call the clinic and to pass along the truck description to L. D. Whitton and Norbert Ortiz. They were working a two man unit that night around Sonora, and after hearing what was going on were riding hell bent for election in my direction.

At the same time Shane Fenton had organized several of the civilians present, and repositioned his Crown Victoria to the drop off opposite to better light up the creek bottom. Now he was having them walk line abreast to sweep the area. I say "line abreast" somewhat loosely as the line was about as ragged as it could be, but everyone was doing their best and getting it done.

Shortly afterwards I learned the truckdriver had brought the three survivors to the clinic; a twenty-year-old woman, a year and a half old infant and a six-month-old baby. There were several broken bones involved and they were badly banged up, but everybody would be okay. It was also confirmed the other three accounted for everyone inside the car at the time of the wreck.

At that very moment I could have kissed that truck driver, whoever he might be or however ugly. Instead, I said a quick, silent prayer of thanks and kept checking things off my personal 'what's important now' list.

L. D. and Norbert arrived a few minutes later and started handling things topside so I could take a closer look at what lay below. My descent on the steeply angled concrete embankment was a careful one, as a couple of men had already lost their footing on it.

Once at the bottom I stood not twenty feet away while looking at the vehicle, with no clue as to what this wadded-up piece of compacted junk might have been. I moved on to the dead man. Though there was little blood present, he had suffered massive head injuries. There was no identification and no wallet on the body.

Surrounding the vehicle in every direction were personal items, diapers and pieces of luggage and debris, scattered about as if an F3 tornado had gone through the draw. I began a written inventory before noting that Jim Hearne, justice of the peace, had arrived to pronounce the victim. We took care of that as L. D. began taking photos of what was left of the disemboweled machine.

Jim Hearne was a retired Border Patrolman, and it didn't take him long to figure out we had more than we could say grace over at that particular moment. So once finished with his official duties, he joined Shane and I in walking out the route of the horrendous crash. A woman's purse was found and I inventoried it in the presence of the judge. Inside we found the identification for not only the dead man, but also the three survivors.

With that identification and the California license plate still attached to the vehicle's rear bumper, I climbed the embankment again and radioed Ozona Communications for checks on both. The plate came back to a 1988 Chevrolet Camaro IROC-Z, verified by the last six digits found on the car's VIN tag.

The return on the California ID card was a bit more involved. The deceased subject had a criminal charge for Grand Theft, and a slew of traffic violations including two different license suspensions and a couple of Failure To Appears. Ironically enough, every one of the numerous moving violations involved this IROC-Z.

We finished walking out the Camaro's path of destruction, marking pertinent pieces of evidence with spray paint while Norbert did the same on the bridge approach above us. He reported numerous wooden guard rail supports splintered into oblivion, as well as a long section of crumpled metal guard rail. Around our location, scads of small wood splinters littered the western side of the creek.

Young cedar saplings nearly ten feet tall were randomly plowed asunder or left untouched, paired with deep scrapes and gouges where the Camaro flipped, cartwheeled and somersaulted its way across. Some blood sign was found where the car first impacted the ground, along with some baby articles, denoting that one of the infants had laid there for some time.

Later investigation revealed the young family was moving from California to San Antonio, and had been traveling almost non-stop since first starting out.

Earlier that evening they came through a series of bad thunderstorms between Van Horn and Fort Stockton, which slowed down their progress considerably.

Once clear of these storms the wife and two children gradually drifted off to sleep. The older infant was in the back and wearing a safety belt, but the six-month-old was acting cranky in the cramped confines of the small car. The mother took her from the child safety seat and put the baby in her lap to console her. The deceased driver, now the only occupant still awake, decided to make up for lost time. He was not wearing a safety belt, either.

Nearing Howard Draw Bridge the dead man apparently drifted off to sleep too, and the red Camaro IROC-Z slammed into the inside guardrail at better than 100 miles per hour. Along with the safety rail itself, the impact sheared a total of sixteen support posts and damaged the seventeenth. The Camaro continued on east straddling the bridge railing itself, riding atop the rail for a distance before plummeting into the creek bed some twenty-nine feet below. At this point, the speed of the Camaro was calculated at slightly over 74 MPH.

When the right front corner of the car impacted the creek bed, it hit with such force that the entire body partially collapsed upon itself. The six-month-old went into the front passenger floorboard, breaking both legs.

The driver's body was propelled across the interior of the Camaro, breaking his wife's jaw and knocking her out cold, beyond just being asleep. Near simultaneously he struck the inside of the passenger door itself, so hard as to bow the middle of it about five inches to the outside.

As the Camaro bounced back up and began a vicious cartwheel, the momentum threw the baby out the now glassless passenger window and sprung the driver's door open.

The car finished the first cartwheel and then went through a series of flips, skids and half somersaults. Somewhere early in the ensuing carnage the driver's door was stripped off and the driver's body ejected, before the IROC-Z finally came to rest on all four wheels some 220 feet from that first impact into the creek bed.

Then, silence and darkness save for the sound of an occasional vehicle going by overhead, and the reflected light from their headlamps.

Time estimations can be a chancy thing in such a circumstance, but it is my belief the woman remained unconscious and still strapped in by her safety belt for around a quarter hour. She had a shattered jaw and numerous welts and contusions, and when she came to that same silence and darkness was all around her. Badly hurt, in deep shock and beyond confused, the first sounds she could hear were those of her children crying for help.

The one-year-old was still in his safety belt, and she reached around and managed to find the release button to free him. Pulling the infant boy out of what remained of the Camaro, she began calling for her husband. There was no answer, and it was so dark she could not see his body when mere feet away.

She told me later she crawled out of the crushed car and began searching for the six-month-old, who sounded as if she was far away. Stumbling across the eroded ground and from one sapling to another, she kept walking half-blindly toward the cries until she found the baby and gathered her up.

Making her way back to the near obliterated IROC she kept calling for her husband to help her, to tell her where he was. When there was no response, she made up her mind that she needed to help herself now, along with the two children. The mother tucked one under each arm and started up the concrete embankment, where she could hear the sparse traffic passing above.

This was the same embankment where I would see at least two men slip and fall, grown men with flashlights and able to see what was before them. This young mother was about five-foot-four and weighed around 120 pounds, and was seriously injured enough to be transferred to a regional hospital some four hours later.

But at that particular moment she marched her way to the top of that steep incline carrying two small children, as if she was out for a Sunday afternoon stroll in a city park. That was when the truck driver saw her with her kids, standing in the roadway.

She was still asking for her husband as he bundled the three of them into the cab of his truck, and then all the way to Ozona.

That was thirty years ago, yet there is hardly a time I have crossed over that bridge and not thought of her and those two small children. She'd be fifty years old now, the same age as when I retired. Those two children were almost the same age as my two sons, so they most likely have their own families these days.

But who knows what life holds for another, as none of us can really calculate what will happen in our own over the next five seconds. I just hope that none of them ever have another night like the one under Howard Draw Bridge.

WHOM THE HELLHOUNDS MOCK

The year 1992 was a bad one when it came to seeing human lives devastated, the kind of tragic waste and strange circumstance that stick in your mind and pull at your heart when pondering the thin threads of life. Within nine months I had worked the two mentioned prior and the third came three days after Christmas.

There were many other memorable events that occurred in this one year, but these were the three that I remember most vividly and wonder the most about. It is perhaps not a good thing to keep timeline tabs on your life by what seared your soul most, but that is the way of life for most peace officers no matter where they work, or what their exact job title might be.

It was nearing 10:00 pm on a cloudy Monday night, I was patrolling Interstate 10 about seven miles west of Ozona. The shift had been quiet, there was not much traffic as those traveling for their Christmas holidays were mostly already back home, and those preparing for the New Year would not begin traveling for another day or so.

Then the shortwave radio in my Dodge came to life, and all that quiet evaporated in little more than a scant second or two. DPS Communications was reporting a major accident with injuries nearly twenty more miles to the west on Interstate 10.

Acknowledging the call, my mind refocused on getting there as quickly as possible. Since the nose of the Diplomat was already pointed in the right direction, I hung my spurs in the dash and held on with both hands, willing as much speed as possible out of the squared-off four door.

As I neared Bachelor Hill, the cloud cover was low enough to obfuscate the roadway and I backed off accordingly. About a mile more, the glow of headlamps and the dull pulse of emergency flashers became visible through the intermittent clumps of fog.

At this particular location the east and west bound lanes for the interstate separate, and a creek bed runs between the two sections making the chance of crossing there impossible. So I barreled to the top of the hill as fast as I dared, crossed the median and swept down again to where those stationary vehicles were scattered about.

My first priority was in trying to keep other traffic from blundering into this spot and causing another collision. I turned on every light I had on that Dodge, including both spot lamps to help illuminate the scene. Hopefully these lights, along with the red and blue emergency lamps, would reflect and diffuse into the fog, and warn motorists to slow down to what lay ahead.

BLACK AND WHITE

I notified DPS Ozona of my arrival and bailed out of the Dodge with Streamlight in hand, and at a dead run into some sort of nightmarish accumulation of sights and sounds best reserved for some level of Dante's Inferno. I could see a small, crumpled up four door sedan off to the right, beyond the paved portion of the roadway, with much of the passenger side sheared away.

Some distance past was a black and blue conventional cab truck-tractor, laying on the driver side and further on an overturned semi-trailer. Excited voices were all around running the gamut of confusion, frustration, despair, comforting, full of anger and near unnatural screams that made one think of a tortured animal driven to insanity, rather than a human being.

All the while my red and blues pulsated surreally, the afterglow reaching up and out in mute warning before being swallowed up by the multiple blankets of fog. Overpowering everything else attention-wise was the occasional bark of radio traffic on the outside speaker of my unit, acknowledging my arrival and the responses of other units coming to assist.

The very first person I came to was David McWilliams, a local teacher and coach who was doing the best he could in trying to slow the traffic. David was someone whom I came to know well over the following decades, both as a citizen as well as a man. He filled both roles in ways that made one feel somehow blessed to be in his presence, and this was one of those times.

Known affectionately to one and all as 'Coach Mac,' David told me I had one injured and trapped inside the small car, and one injured lying beside the truck tractor. Then he added that his wife at the time, Peggy, was tending to the truck driver.

That was the second ace I had been dealt in this ugly hand, as Peggy was an RN at our local clinic and as solid as they came in this sort of situation. Telling David to be careful of the oncoming traffic, I bolted from him to the heavily damaged red car where the screaming and shrieking was coming from.

There was a young woman standing there, doing all she could to try to calm a hysterical woman still seated behind the wheel. Glass and debris lay scattered about, and the forward part of the roof was peeled back as if a giant can opener had been taken to it.

The young woman calmly remarked in between the near constant wailing, "Pay no attention to what's in the passenger seat, it's only a doll."

I looked down through what remained of the flattened windshield and into the front passenger area. There was a child seat secured by a safety belt, and sitting in the seat was the body of an infant. Everything from the bridge of the baby's nose and above was gone, and I was looking down inside at what was left. You could see the dead child's tongue and top of the throat.

Then the young woman said it again, as if in a trance. "Pay no attention to what's in the passenger seat, it's only a doll."

That was when I realized she was repeating the same words over and again. A forlorn chant to keep her sanity, and to keep her focus on trying to help the screaming driver.

The young woman probably wanted to scream too, and I would not have blamed her.

Running back to my patrol car, I grabbed the mike and advised Ozona DPS that I needed two ambulances, the jaws of life, traffic control, a justice of the peace and the local funeral home. DPS acknowledged and started the wheels rolling on their end. Others were already enroute.

Grabbing a small tarp, I ran to the demolished car and covered the grisly remains in an attempt to aid the good Samaritan, who was still trying to keep herself from going into shock from what she had been forced to see. The trapped driver continued screaming in an incoherent, almost raging fashion, yelling wildly about being pursued by 'them' and that 'they' were trying to kill her and her daughter. She was also screaming that she had to get out of the car.

I turned to my next problem at hand, traffic control. Two or three vehicles had already sped through the scene, oblivious to Coach Mac and his small, weak flashlight. Gathering up some other civilians who had some kind of light in their hands, I organized them in an attempt to move the passing traffic into the inside lane. The corner of the overturned semi-trailer protruded some three feet into the outside one, and it would be only a matter of minutes before someone plowed into it.

At sometime around then I realized I was no longer the only officer on the scene, a deputy sheriff had also arrived. But he was not helping with traffic control nor with the injured; the deputy was just standing there with a pale, blank look on his face. He had lifted the corner of that tarp and gazed within, and for all intents and purposes had checked out mentally from everything else from that moment forward.

I called out his name but at first he did not respond. I did so again, more forcefully and insistent. His eyes shifted to where I stood mere feet away, followed by his head and then his body in a slow, dreamlike manner. The look in his eyes told me the lights were on, but nobody was home.

Moving in closer where no one else could hear us, I began talking to him in measured tones, telling him to come back to me because I really needed him right now. This was a good man, a brave man, a man I had confidence in and whom I called friend in this world. But he was also a new father with his own baby at home, just like that dead baby lying in the front seat of that partially dismembered passenger car.

As others read these lines, I am fairly certain there will be at least a few who will question my friend's behavior. They might admire themselves enough to think they are mentally tougher than that, and would have responded differently. Maybe they would have, but more than likely they have never been in that very same exact position, at that very same exact moment.

You see, it is my belief every human being capable of empathy for others is hard wired with an emotional circuit breaker. When it is all coming at you from every direction, all at once and with just the right, or more accurately wrong inputs, sometimes that circuit breaker trips. My friend's emotional circuit breaker had done so, and it needed resetting. And anyone who claims he doesn't have one really does not know, or is a liar or a sociopath. You have to figure out which for yourself.

I continued talking to him, watching his facial expressions as his thought process recycled and began running again. Within a minute he was back with me from wherever his mind had taken him, and once again to the man I knew.

"Are you with me now?" I asked.

"Yeah, I'm okay."

"Good" and I called him by his first name again. "I need you to take your unit to the top of the hill. We need to start slowing down this traffic before someone else gets killed."

"I'm on it," and my friend was in his Chevrolet patrol car, and back in the ball game again.

My next pressing need was to check on Peggy McWilliams and the injured truck driver. While gathering information from her as to what she knew or suspected, I learned the truck driver had crawled out of the cab before collapsing. He had a bad head wound with a good deal of bleeding, along with possible spine and internal injuries.

She also said she had quickly examined the hysterical woman trapped in the passenger car, and could find no real physical injuries other than a deep cut to her right arm. Peggy had applied pressure to stop the bleeding, then had a bystander take over while she took care of the truck driver.

Peggy added, "She's been going on like that for an hour now. There's something not right about that woman."

I had already made a mental note of the same thing concerning the shrieking woman, but the length of time came as a complete surprise to me.

"An hour?" I exclaimed.

"Yeah, David had to go to the Childress Ranch and call the sheriff's office. People just kept driving by, we would have but saw the glass and debris in the road. There was a woman, too, waving a flashlight and yelling for help."

Peggy went on to describe the injuries of both subjects, and I relayed the information to our responding ambulances. The McWilliams family did their fellow man tremendous service that night, and I will always be proud to know them.

Within ten more minutes or so both ambulances were on the scene, along with the volunteer fire department and the badly needed jaws of life. Not too much longer Norbert Ortiz arrived from Sutton County to assist, as well as my new sergeant Paul Davis.

With the extra hands available, I made my way to the red passenger car and helped free the hysterical woman from her trapped position. I also wanted more input as to how this accident occurred. From the first moment of my arrival, the physical evidence was not adding up to being any 'normal' collision, however one might define that particular word. Something was very awry here.

But trying to get any information, no matter how simple the question, was much like trying to converse with a crazed, raving lunatic. She was screaming as loud as her voice would allow, ranting repetitively about bodies in the trunk, that somebody was trying to kill her as well as her daughter, and that God was telling her this.

All the while I was puzzling over the evidence present and trying to put it together; the position of the vehicles, the direction and type of damage, the debris and tire marks on the pavement. At impact the red Nissan Sentra four door must had been in the middle of the roadway, almost on top of the center stripe and facing the wrong direction.

Before leaving one of the ambulance crew came to me, stating the trucker was confirming what my own two eyes had already decided. The Nissan had been sitting in the middle of the road, facing the wrong way. Also, the truck driver claimed there were no visible lights on the Sentra. Upon hearing this Norbert started for the mangled vehicle, me right behind him.

It did not take us long to ascertain the headlamp switch was turned to the off position. Paul Davis and Judge Hearne saw it too. Also inside the vehicle, wedged in the front passenger floorboard and mottled with the infant's blood, was a black and white woman's purse. I removed the purse and placed it in the trunk of my patrol car.

The baby's body was pronounced by Judge Hearne and removed as reverently as possible, before being placed in a hearse. Then the wrecker removed what was left of the Nissan and cleared the scene, while the highway department put up warning signs and barricades. It was decided to leave the truck in place until daylight, which would allow the wrecker company to procure the specialized equipment needed.

Paul Davis went back to town to assure blood was drawn from the Nissan's driver. Others drifted away, probably to a warm bed and time to think about what they had seen and heard. The passing traffic died away, and the night took on the same quiet, serene quality it possessed before that first radio call.

Once the quiet settled in again, I walked out the accident scene from start to final resting points. There was a goodly amount of physical evidence present, enough for most anyone with some common sense to figure the deadly chain of events.

There was no question the Nissan had been sitting near the middle of the roadway, facing west. With all the lights on the car extinguished in the patchy fog, the driver of the Freightliner never saw the red Sentra until it was too late.

At the very last moment, the truckdriver locked up his brakes and veered to the left but was unable to avoid colliding. The right front of the truck tractor slammed into the right front area of the Nissan, and the momentum of the commercial vehicle took it partly over the top of the parked four door.

This was what did such tremendous damage to the front passenger area of the car. The undercarriage of the eighteen-wheeler first crushed and then partially sheared the roof away, causing the dreadful head injury on the small child. The driver, seated on the other side of the Sentra, survived without so much as an engaged safety belt.

The positioning of the car acted as a one-sided ramp and upset the balance of the truck-tractor rig, sending the commercial vehicle into a wobbling yaw and off the right side of the highway before the semi-trailer detached and both overturned. The impact propelled the car backwards from the collision point, and out of the roadway. If either of those vehicles had come to rest in the two traffic lanes, others would have crashed into them causing far greater damage, injuries and death.

A call came in from Jim Wilson, who was sheriff of Crockett County during those years. Jim was making absolutely certain blood would be drawn from the woman driver. Over the radio, he sounded unusually adamant about doing so. I informed the sheriff that Sergeant Davis was enroute and would be there shortly.

Later I learned the driver of the Nissan screamed, cursed, ranted and fought the ambulance crew all the way to the clinic. While trying to get an IV into her, she began talking about the drugs "they" had given her and that she had white powder residue under her dentures.

Upon arrival at our little hospital, she was wheeled into the emergency room and Doctor Sims began examining her. At about this juncture in time, her paranoid state switched gears again and she started wailing wildly about being shot, and that "they" had put the dead bodies of the others in the trunk of her car.

Though Marcus Sims could find no sign of a bullet wound, he had Sheriff Wilson come to the ER to validate this and attempt to question the out-of-control patient. At times she would struggle with the staff in an attempt to get away and Jim was unable to ask anything because of her behavior, but both the doctor as well as the sheriff agreed she was in some sort of drug-induced state of mind.

This was the reason why Jim radioed to verify blood would be drawn for laboratory analysis.

Once done marking the tell-tale evidence at the scene with spray paint, I met Norbert at the Ozona office and together we inventoried the black and white purse. Inside was some money and identification for the driver as well as the dead infant, along with the other usual accruements found in a woman's handbag.

However, there was something else inside. Contained in a small plastic bag was an amount of an unknown powdery substance, along with a shortened soda straw.

For all the years I worked with Norbert, he was our go to man when it came to anything involving controlled substances. Ultimately Trooper Norbert Ortiz was awarded a Director's Citation for his high level of knowledge in drug interdiction work. Furthermore, he was loaned out repeatedly to train others in the significant skills he had perfected.

Looking at the plastic bag I surmised it was some sort of illicit drug, but Norbert narrowed it down for me immediately.

"Either cocaine or methamphetamines, Ben" he estimated. We bagged the evidence and tagged it, and made ready to ship the substance to our nearest DPS Laboratory for analysis.

The next afternoon I was headed for Shannon Hospital in San Angelo, to interview the truck driver involved in the crash. He was in iffy shape and had been placed in their ICU ward. Explaining my situation to the floor nurse she allowed me in, but only for a few minutes.

Standing in his room I introduced myself and asked if he could answer a few questions. It was obvious he was in a bad way, yet he said that he was glad I had come to talk with him. We visited quietly in the semi-darkness and I found myself liking the man.

His answers as to what happened dovetailed nigh perfectly with what we had already determined at the accident scene. But once finished, he said he had a question for me.

I waited.

"Mister English," his voice rasped in the confines of the darkened room, "was anybody hurt in that little car?"

I swallowed hard, looking for the right words as my mind spun with the weight of honesty versus the possible ramifications of what my answer might mean for his recovery. But he had been truthful with me, and I couldn't do anything but do the same for him.

"Sir, I am really sorry to have to tell you this. But a two-year-old child died."

In the shadows I saw his face set and then sag, as if the age of another fifty years was placed on his shoulders, as well as his soul. Tears started forming in his eyes as he vainly tried to blink them away, and began rolling down his cheeks.

BLACK AND WHITE

He didn't say a word, he didn't have to.

I hastened to tell him what I had learned about the driver, and where the investigation was going. I also tried to console him by saying that no one, including myself, could have shut his rig down in the amount of distance needed to avoid colliding with the car.

That was the truth, too.

I stayed with him as long as I could and we talked some more, until the head nurse eased in and gave me the hit the road signal. After telling the driver I would pray for him, I said goodbye and headed for where the floor nurse waited.

Stopping in the doorway, I looked back one last time. He was watching me, and raised his hand a bit to give the weakest of waves. Then he looked straight ahead again, all alone as the darkness surrounded him much like that fog had the night before.

But this wasn't just a physical darkness, it was one of thought and of spirit.

There were a few times in my career when I absolutely hated my job, and what it did to others as well as myself. This was one of those times.

I turned and walked out the door.

A few hours later I was on the phone with one of the driver's relatives from California. She was a nice enough lady and I answered her questions about the wreck as best I could. She also seemed to warm to me a bit, and near the end of our conversation began confiding in some background information concerning the family.

What I heard made me want to look and see if Rod Serling might be seated somewhere in the empty office, smoking one of Randy Hall's cigarettes as he narrated an episode to The Twilight Zone. We had thought upon the dead infant as the driver's daughter. The child wasn't, she was her granddaughter.

The relative's strange story continued. At the grandmother's insistence, the granddaughter had been named for the woman's older daughter, who had been killed in a car wreck several years ago. Due to this tragedy, the grandmother had a nervous breakdown that took some time to recover from.

Once the grandchild was christened with her dead aunt's name, the situation became even more bizarre. Unemployed and residing in the same domicile as her surviving daughter, the grandmother had done everything possible to mold the child into the daughter she lost. In the relative's own words, it was "spooky."

With an upcoming family reunion occurring in south Texas, the grandmother was absolutely relentless about having the granddaughter accompany her. Other members of the family were actively against this, more so because the grandmother was so unyielding about driving all the way from California, rather than taking a commercial flight.

One has to wonder why both the grandmother, as well as the conflicted family members, were so powerfully entrenched in their opposite perspectives. Was it past experience, future prescience or simply an odd sensitivity for the present? Such overwhelming emotions on both sides, all coming to fruition along a lonely, foggy stretch of Interstate 10.

And the traffic accident from years back that took her other daughter's life? The person behind the wheel of that particular death car was the very same who was screaming and wailing so insanely just the night before, with the body of the near decapitated grandchild sitting lifelessly beside her.

Before my shift ended, the deputy who had helped me at the scene stopped by. We visited for a while, and I told him everything that had happened in the investigation so far, including the grimly eerie telephone conversation.

After giving him the rundown, he nodded and said he wanted to apologize for his behavior the night before.

I shook my head slowly from side to side, heading him off. This man of outsized heart had proven himself to me many times before, and was a credit to the badge on his chest. I told him that, and there was no need whatsoever to apologize to me for anything.

"It could be that you were seeing something, sensing something beyond what the rest of us were last night," I remarked. "Perhaps because you had your own baby at home, or maybe because something reached out from another time or place, and touched you."

"Who knows?" I added, in as much as asking myself the same question. "But I do know this, we all have that emotional circuit breaker. In a way you're lucky, because you know now what triggers yours and can be ready next time."

He nodded again and got up to go on patrol. He stood there several seconds, studying me. Then he asked, "What makes you so tough?"

The question caught me off guard, and I responded only half-facetiously with a nervous laugh. "Me? I've been wanting to bawl like a baby since this deal started, and there will come a time and a place. But we have to hold it together when around anybody else, because we're the good guys with the guns and badges."

I paused before adding: "And if we lose it, everybody loses it."

Ultimately this young man would go off to another agency in another place. I heard he became a DARE officer for a rather large department, and a very special one. His future success did not surprise me in the least.

I was unable to get written statements from David and Peggy McWilliams until the next evening, so I called their residence and arranged to come by when both were home. After doing so, we sat in their living room to discuss what happened and how they felt now, and for me to answer any questions they might have.

It was the least I could do, because both had been there and stood tall when it really counted. When I got up to leave, David walked me to the door. He had some parting words.

"I don't know how much they pay you to do your job, but it isn't enough."

His statement stuck with me the rest of the evening, and I thought about it many times more in the years to come.

Truth is, there's not enough money in the world to make most folks be a patrol officer, nor enough training or education. It is a calling, something inside that just will not rest until you do something about it.

And sometimes, on rare occasions, that calling can be better called a curse.

A CUSTODIAL SUICIDE

When someone claims they, or someone else, has the ability to "read people," those words are usually only meant in a general sense. At least, by those who really understand just how deceiving, unpredictable and often irrational human behavior can be when influenced by other factors. Though the vast majority of the species are creatures of habit when in familiar places and circumstances, those same habits can go to the four winds in other scenarios.

These conditions often have to do with physical, mental or emotional duress, or most often a combination of the three. Then they can exhibit the polar opposite of their normal behavior and also be at their most dangerous, either to themselves or somebody else.

You don't know what they will do next because they don't either, which was one of the reasons I decided to include this story.

It was late morning on a Saturday, springtime had come and with it a brand new patrol unit to replace my aging Dodge Diplomat. The new kid on the block was a 1993 Chevrolet Caprice slick top, just the way I liked 'em for interstate work.

These were the Caprices that many highway patrolmen affectionately nicknamed 'Shamus,' after the black and white killer whale so popular at Sea World. They would become my all-time favorite style of patrol unit, and what happened on this day alone proved one of the many reasons why.

I had just completed a traffic stop about two miles west of Ozona when I received a sheriff's office alert, advising of a theft of gas from the Shot's Number Two convenience store. This quick stop was situated on the west edge of Ozona and the theft had occurred within the past few minutes. The suspect vehicle, described as a dark colored Chevrolet pickup, was last seen traveling west on the access road straight toward me.

The trouble was my current position was inside a roadway cut, some distance before an access onramp to the interstate. Also, there was intervening high ground between the two locations, which basically meant I likely did not see them nor did they see me when passing by. I fired up the Chevy and pointed that bow tie hood ornament west, gas pedal matted to the floor.

All of those Shamus were good runners, but this one in slick top configuration was especially so. Within five more minutes I was booming along at over 140 MPH, coming up fast behind a black over silver full-sized GMC pickup displaying Louisiana tags.

Once I was close enough to run the registration through DPS Communications, I dropped back. Way back, as I had a strong feeling that whoever was driving would rabbit as soon as I turned on the grille lamps. I also knew that Shane Fenton and Sheriff Wilson were not too far behind.

I gave them the GMC's description, speed and location, and rolled along as the pickup truck made several minor traffic violations. The person behind the wheel was driving via rear view mirror, meaning they were spending more time watching me than where they were going.

Less than ten minutes later Shane and Jim came rocketing up behind in separate units. I had already advised both that I felt the driver would run the moment my lights flipped on, and I had observed a plentitude of moving violations as other resons for the stop. This was important, given the discrepancy in descriptions from what the store clerk reported.

Jim positioned his unmarked unit to his satisfaction, and Shane did the same. The sheriff advised they were ready and for me to try to make a traffic stop. When my grille lamps came on, the GMC surged ahead.

The chase was on.

I notified Bob Falkner, the duty communications operator, that we had a pursuit in progress. The GMC ran up to about 100 MPH and flattened out, likely because this was all the speed the old truck could muster. When I first closed the gap for the attempted traffic stop, I noted four people sitting in the cab. A white male driver, a black male on the far passenger side, and two young girls sandwiched in the middle.

This changed the situation and the available options considerably, and I knew that Shane and Sheriff Wilson were thinking the same thing.

The sheriff advised Shane to get in front of the GMC to try for a rolling road block, with the sheriff on the inside lane and my unit close behind the truck. Shane's big Ford muscled ahead of the rest of us, and positioned itself in front of the GMC.

At first our tactic seemed to work. In concert all three of our units began to drop speed, boxing in the truck and causing it to do the same. But as the speed fell off, the driver of the GMC became more aggressive behind the wheel. He began swerving at Sheriff Wilson, who was forced across the inside fog line and had to abandon his position.

Then the driver of the GMC started working over Shane. In both cases he came within a scant few inches of colliding with the sheriff's units, as our speeds climbed back up and hovered again at the century mark. He managed to get beside Shane's Crown Vic and began squeezing him across the lanes, and toward the loose stuff in the median.

Seeing an opening to the outside and wanting to give the GMC's occupants something to worry about, I kicked that L05 350 V8 in the rump and my Caprice shot forward. I rolled up beside the GMC and began pacing them, looking into the eyes of the black male while he watched me do so.

Suddenly the GMC made a big swipe at Shane and the deputy was forced to brake hard to avoid collision as the fleeing driver nearly lost control. When the suspect steered for the middle of the roadway, I knew there was too much side momentum going to keep the truck out of my lane. He would run smooth over me before he could straighten that GMC out.

This was when I really planted that Chevrolet's gas pedal, and was rewarded with a downshift and enough acceleration to propel myself forward and out of harm's way. In my driver's side mirror, I watched as the GMC's chrome front bumper swished within inches of my left rear corner, occupying the space where I had been just a split second before.

Our situation was getting out of hand, and any miscalculation on anyone's part was going to get at least one of us killed at this speed. I made a snap decision, rolled down my driver's window and began slowing down.

The GMC came up again on the inside, now trying to get past my Caprice and keep running. To where I am certain the driver had not a clue, but I was also certain his destination would involve an enormous wreck not too far down the road.

I took a long look to my left for a final estimation as to the state of affairs. The black male was looking at me again, a sneering grin on his face. But he stopped grinning real quick when he found himself staring down the muzzle of a Smith & Wesson .357 Magnum.

Now I wasn't about to shoot into the cab with those two young girls inside, or shoot the suddenly contrite black passenger. Nor was I going to take a tire off, as that would likely lead to the GMC going out of control and flipping over. But I did want to give those occupants the distinct impression their present circumstance had ventured beyond serious, and they had no surety that I would not shoot.

My improvised psychological ploy began to bear fruit. The black guy's eyes went saucer wide and he pivoted quickly in his seat, reaching across and grabbing the driver's shoulder while pointing with his other hand in my direction. He was screaming at the driver to pull over, I could hear him over the roar of the engines and the sound of tires on pavement.

And for some reason, the GMC began to slow. I say 'some reason,' as I could tell it was beginning to run rough and lose power. Later I would make a quick examination of the truck's engine and find it two quarts low on oil. If you are going to run any powerplant wide open for any length of time, not enough oil in the pan is a sure shortcut to blowing it up.

The GMC finally rolled to a halt and we arrested the two male occupants without further incident. The two girls were even younger than I first thought, one was thirteen years old and the other only twelve. Both were runaways out of Baton Rouge.

The two male occupants were in their early twenties, and the driver had a criminal record for Felony Theft. At the arrest scene, the driver was overheard saying he had stolen the truck from his parents. For whatever reason, the parents never reported it as such. All four were put in the sheriff's office units for transport, while I remained to inventory the ailing pickup and sign it over to the responding wrecker service.

As Jim was placing the last one in his unit, he turned to me and grinned, exclaiming "Well, you sure called it right when you said they'd run!"

I grinned back, I think all three of us were relieved we had pulled this off without somebody getting hurt. In fact, one or two from inside that truck might have shared the same opinion.

I just wish I had been a little more prescient in what was to follow.

Once the truck was signed over to the wrecker driver I headed for Ozona, stopping by the DPS Office to pick up the teletype returns from queries that Bob Falkner sent to Louisiana. He was kind of relieved too, as in his long experience he had seen many such incidents go wrong. Terribly wrong.

When I arrived at the sheriff's office things were in full swing. Sheriff Wilson was trying to contact Baton Rouge for further information and Shane was working on the needed reports, as well as what to do with the female juveniles. Our new jailor, Kent Pullig, was processing the two arrested adult males. Kent was a brother to Kirk Pullig, who would later become sheriff of neighboring Reagan County.

For once I wasn't the guy having to do all the paperwork, so I stood by as moral support while Kent booked in the two males. Everything was going fairly smoothly until Pullig asked the driver about having any serious medical conditions.

"Yeah," the suspect responded. "I'm HIV positive."

Well, that sort of brought the house down. The black passenger exploded with indignation, and looked like he was going to swing on the white guy before I got between them.

"You sonovab----! Why didn't you tell me?!!!" roared the black arrestee, furious at the possible ramifications. It didn't take a genius to figure these two pillars of virtue had been swapping out the two underaged girls. At the thought of that, I kind of wanted to swing on somebody myself.

Those poor kids.

After the bedlam subsided and the two were separated, Shane asked me to check on a car load of welfare cases parked by the sally port. This was a fairly common instance in these small, rural communities astradle Interstate 10, vehicular-borne people who were usually looking for free food or gas. In Ozona the local churches had a ministerial alliance, and kept a slush fund for the truly needy. The sheriff's office handled the fund, which afforded us the opportunity to cull out some really bad actors.

And this was one of those times. After gathering their identification, I went inside the jail to run them through DPS Ozona. One of the occupants came back as wanted with multiple felony warrants. Jim heard what was going on and came to help me with the suspect, muttering something about it being one of those days.

Truth was, we were only getting started.

We arrested the suspect without incident, handcuffed and searched him, and turned him over to the already beyond busy Pullig, who was still processing those two males from the pursuit. I hopped in my Caprice and drove to the DPS office to gather up the newest teletypes pertaining to this arrest.

Bob was at the top of his game, as usual, and checking on the criminal background for the last subject. By the time I arrived he had received further responses concerning our latest prize having a lengthy felony arrest record, as well as a very violent one. I called Jim on the phone and let him know, so the appropriate precautions could be taken immediately.

Upon my return everything seemed to be going well at the jail. Kent had everyone in their respective cells, and kept the two male occupants from the GMC separated when doing so. I was sitting in the facility's small kitchen thinking about my missed lunch and the chance of scrounging something up, when a voice shouted out loudly in alarm.

My first thought was a jail break and I sprinted for the control room. Observing no one there, I quickly checked to make certain the electronic door locks were secured. The two juvenile runaways were in an adjoining area and I began asking them questions as to where the jailor had gone.

That was when I heard movement down the hallway that led to C Cell. Running for the passageway, I turned the corner just in time to see Shane Fenton laying a body on the concrete floor.

It was the driver of the GMC.

Shane pulled away the knotted linen from the young male's neck and started CPR. I ran for the nearest telephone to call an ambulance while Kent, who had originally found the subject hanging in his cell, went to locate the sheriff.

Later I found out that Shane heard something while walking past the passageway, and heard Kent cry out. The deputy went into his star running back mode and charged the cell at the end of the corridor. He was almost to the open door when Kent managed to release the linen noose from an overhead pipe, and Shane caught the body as it started to fall.

From that very second forward the situation was a total blur. Everyone did what they could, but the clinic called sometime later to let us know the driver had been pronounced dead.

A custodial death in a county jail is a very serious matter, and a near nightmare in real time for any sheriff as well as his staff. In the state of Texas, the rangers are called in to conduct a comprehensive investigation as to what occurred and why.

Kent was by far the most shook up of us all, not only because he had just started out but also due to him feeling most responsible. After all, he was the duty jailer and had been the one who placed the recently deceased in his cell. Furthermore, he didn't have the opportunity to do a standard welfare check owing to having been so busy.

We sat in the office as he held his head in both hands, about ready to cry. Like any man of real conscience and sense of duty, he was being harder on himself than anyone else could ever be. His was a thankless job where one's successes often were taken for granted, or never known at all. But any possible mistake glared out without delay or hesitation, and this loss of human life was something he would live with for the rest of his days.

As Kent played through what had happened in his mind, he became more disconsolate, questioning himself and his actions over and over. In my eyes, he simply had too much to do and all of it at the same time. To me, not only Kent but every one of us had done everything we could, in the best way we knew how.

I told Kent this. I also said what happened could just as easily occurred to any of us. Once someone takes it in their head to do themselves harm, it is nigh impossible to keep them from eventually committing such an unnatural act. More so, the more violently inclined often turn their suicidal instincts into the murderous sort, and end up hurting or killing someone else.

My own thoughts went back to those moments and miles as Jim, Shane and I maneuvered our units at near triple digit speeds, conducting an evolving death dance in two ton vehicles with someone who only a bit later would take their own life.

I thought about Jim Wilson being nearly run off the road and then Shane actually having it happen. I thought about the GMC swerving toward me, and my spurring that new Caprice forward as the chrome bumper of the truck occupied the space where I had been only a second before. If I had been driving my Diplomat, we would have collided.

One slight slip, one swerve, one single wrong move or split-second late reaction, and somebody would have died out there. That GMC would have surely rolled, and neither of the underaged runaways had any sort of a seat belt on. As bad as the day had been, it could have been so much worse so easily.

Then came the chilling realization that our now deceased driver was probably working himself into the exact mindset which would end up killing him, while at the same time we were doing all we could to keep anyone from being hurt.

Ultimately the rangers finished their custodial death investigation. No one person was held responsible in any manner, save for the one who committed the awful crime of killing themselves. The jail, like the sheriff's office itself, needed more personnel on duty at all times. But more personnel meant more tax dollars expended, and most every sheriff knows how that plays with most commissioner courts.

Kent Pullig resigned his jailer position some time later and moved to Reagan County, raising his family there and becoming a pillar of the community, as well as a willing volunteer in many worthwhile capacities. He made the sort of citizen that small towns must have to exist. I would not have expected anything other from him.

I never heard anything else about those two runaway girls, though I prayed for them for many days afterwards. What happened in their lives was not only wrong, but could have been a death sentence for each later on.

One also has to wonder what would possess two girls so young to run so far away from home. Were things so despairingly bad where they came from? Was this the only option they could come up with as a way out?

Or was it a lighthearted dare, a carefree lark or did someone of influence talk them into doing so for selfish purpose?

Did one person die as a result of that fatal journey, or did four?

So many questions, so many unanswered what ifs.

As I said, ours was a profession habitually filled with ignorance to any of our successes, and yet constantly made aware of any possible oversight or mistake.

JUST BAD LUCK IN WEST TEXAS

I used to say that Interstate 10 was the greatest show on earth, and behind the wheel of a black and white provided for the best seat in the house. There was ample reason to make that claim too, as about when you thought you'd seen it all, something new would start your direction.

Of course, that was not only because of the interstate itself. A network of county, state and federal highways, a well as other connecting roads ran through Crockett County like some sort of complicated web spun by a drunken spider. In turn, these were emplaced in a jurisdiction with a southern boundary in spots not thirty-five air miles from Mexico.

Crockett County was said to be the fifth largest in Texas, with over 3,000 square miles of wide-open country mixed with rock strewn canyons, craggy hills and desolate mesas. Ozona, while being the county seat, possessed that title by default because it was the only town within the county, and in population might have stretched some folks' opinions of what a town should be. The community was not even incorporated.

This meant no police department, a small sheriff's office, a constable, a game warden and both a volunteer ambulance service as well as fire department. Locally stationed highway patrolmen assisted on many calls for these agencies, and they did the same for us. Sometimes there was only one other officer on duty and he might be fifty miles away, so you often enough handled those calls alone.

There was always plenty to be done. An officer could end up involved in everything from a jaywalker to a murderer, and all within the same shift. Billy Mills, long time sheriff of Crockett County, used to say that when he was a young officer and you had a railroad running through your town, you always tried to be there when the train arrived. This allowed you to see who got on, and who got off.

Then he would pause for effect, and surmise that with Interstate 10 running through the middle of Ozona the train was running 24 hours a day, seven days a week and 365 days a year.

Or as I have heard more than a few veteran officers mutter sarcastically under their breaths, "Ain't nothing like being gainfully employed."

This constant coming and going brought a certain red 1965 Mustang convertible into Ozona one evening, I just happened to be at the 'train station' and watching when it took the off ramp into town. The 'Stang was a real beauty, the top was down and it was the loaded-out V8 version, and immaculately cared for.

Then I noticed the driver and sole occupant, a white male and my internal cop meter bounced off the red line.

That guy behind the wheel did not fit this car, not one wee little bit.

As the Ford cruised by the shirtless driver stared straight ahead, and I could see jailhouse tattoos on his arms and shoulders. Tattoos were fairly rare in those days, and I keyed on the prison-style etchings that marked him like a multitude of trail brands on an outlaw steer.

Not only did this guy not match that Mustang ragtop, those tattoos detailed nothing but bad news about his manner of making a living.

I ran the displayed Florida license plate as I eased along some distance behind. The red Mustang pulled into a self-serve gas station and I drifted by, waiting for a registration return.

The plate came back to a 1983 Pontiac four door.

Responding to the return, I advised PCO Frank Galvan of my situation as well as location. Frank had not been on that long but was plenty capable. His first day behind the console was when Willie Dale was killed, and he did a stellar job even then.

After making sure I was out of sight, I hung a hard right and again approached the convertible from a different direction. Parking along a side street and watching through some heavy undergrowth, I waited for the Mustang to start rolling again. Though I was not sure about the true status of the license plate or the driver, I found it prudent to not make an approach until both were completely away from anyone else.

Once he was back on to the interstate, I notified Deputy Dan Griffith of my suspicions and requested he start rolling my direction. While leaving town I had spotted his unit on Texas Highway 163, so I knew he wasn't far away.

After picking my ground for a traffic stop, I flipped on the grille lamps of my Caprice and the Mustang pulled over. As I was getting out of the patrol unit, the driver began making furtive movements with his hands and was ordered to put both of them on the steering wheel.

He complied.

He also complied easily enough when instructed to step out, and to keep his movements real slow when doing so. Once outside the car, he was advised to move behind the Mustang and over to the side of the road, facing away. I visually examined the convertible's interior, it was as clean and well-kept as the rest of the vehicle.

This was unusual for a stolen car, but everything inside me still said it was stolen and this guy was wanted for something, someplace.

I asked for his driver license and he said his wallet had been stolen by a hitchhiker outside of Houston. When asked for the Mustang's registration and insurance papers, the suspect said that both were inside the wallet.

Naturally.

When Dan arrived he obtained the subject's name and date of birth, while I took a closer look at the VINs displayed on the convertible. Those years of Fords had two, one near the left front fender and the other on the trailing edge of the driver's door. Both were the same and ran through DPS Ozona for identification.

I also gave the driver's full name and date of birth, which turned out to be an alias. Shortly thereafter, a broadcast from Frank notified me of the suspect's real name and attending cautionary advisories for both the driver as well as the car. The Mustang was stolen and the driver was an escapee from a penitentiary in South Carolina, and on the state's ten most wanted list.

The prison escapee was placed under arrest without incident and transported to the county jail by Dan Griffith. Meanwhile, Sergeant Paul Davis and another trooper arrived to assist.

While searching the car some interesting things were found, including a sizeable coin collection along with an equally sizeable amount of jewelry. This was quickly turning into something more than a normal stolen car case.

But for now I needed the convertible where I could take my time looking through it, and not have my attention divided on the passing traffic to avoid being run over. Glen Burns and his wife Sue came out with their duty wrecker, and towed it to the office while I followed behind.

Those two were the salt of the earth in every way, always there and ready to help when most needed. Some years later Sue would be killed by a drunken illegal immigrant in a head-on collision north of Ozona. That wreck took away Glen's main reason for living, and his absolute despair inspired by this tragic loss would ultimately take Glen from us, too.

They were the kind of people who make the world continue to go around, broken as it may be.

Meanwhile at the jail, the suspect was adamant in regards to the coins, jewelry and clothing found in the Mustang, saying the items all belonged to him. Deputy Griffith later advised me the suspect went into this at length, as well as with some passion. Dan didn't believe him and neither did I.

Once at the DPS Office I conducted an exhaustive inventory of the red convertible. All the coins and pieces of jewelry were logged individually and secured in our evidence locker. Frank Galvan looked in and quipped it looked like someone had knocked over a San Antonio pawn shop, owing to the numerous coin wrappers and city amusement tokens.

And that was exactly where we started in our search for the rightful owners. Frank helped draft a teletype to law enforcement agencies in that area, querying about any recent jewelry or coin collection thefts.

At this point the investigation became a waiting game. But we had the patience required, and it was not as if the suspect was going to be released any time soon. We already had enough to keep him locked away for a long time to come.

Before going off shift that same night, a phone call came in from the Mustang's owner. He was concerned about the condition and was near overjoyed upon learning the car was in remarkably good shape. The owner lived in Columbia, South Carolina, and had given up all hope of ever seeing his convertible again.

During the conversation I mentioned the jewelry and the coin collection. The owner said he knew nothing about those, the only items he was aware of had been some golf clubs in the trunk. I made a note of that for future investigation, as no sign of any golf clubs were found anywhere in the car.

There was also the question from a prior observation, regarding the car keys found in the red Ford. They were evidently the original ones with factory markings and script, quite worn and were in the ignition when the suspect was stopped. When asked about this, the owner stated that was not possible as the keys were in his pant's pocket even as he spoke.

I found his statement interesting for more than one reason, and held off saying anything else about the subject.

The next day I was contacted by South Carolina authorities reference their escaped prisoner. During our conversation I asked if they knew anything about stolen coins or jewelry in connection to the suspect. They did not.

Meanwhile, our prior teletyped queries had received zero response so I decided to redefine our possible contact area. A teletype was sent out to all stations along Interstate 10, starting at Jacksonville, Florida. Descriptions were given of both the suspect as well as the Mustang, along with some more particulars on the jewelry and coins.

And the wait began anew.

After supper I drove over to the jail and gathered up Bob Hartman, the on-duty deputy was a thoroughly experienced peace officer. Bob had been on the job for a long while, working in different departments and holding different positions throughout the state of Texas. I asked if he would mind sitting in on an interview of the suspect.

Bob said he would be happy to.

After being read his rights again we began questioning the escapee, who seemed willing enough to talk. In his statement he claimed to have stolen the Mustang after breaking out of prison. The suspect had initially hot wired the car via the starter solenoid, an auto theft trick that worked well on older Ford products. Found inside the vehicle were the golf clubs and jewelry.

He had gone about forty miles when he happened to look in the ash tray and found the matching car keys. Adding this bit of legitimacy by inserting them into the ignition switch, he swung by a spot where he had hidden the coins during a car theft and burglary five years before. Ironically enough, these were the same crimes that ultimately landed him in prison.

From there he headed south and into Florida, pulling some Florida tags off a parked Pontiac in Daytona. After this the escapee began traveling west and ultimately linked up with Interstate 10, stealing gas along the way with a siphon hose. Other incidentals were taken care of by pawning some of the coins off, as well as the golf clubs.

After learning the location of the burglary from five years ago, I made contact with the authorities in Aiken, South Carolina and it all started coming together. A detective who worked the case told me not only a coin collection had been stolen in that burglary, but also a sizeable amount of jewelry.

Bingo.

The rest of the investigation was mostly anticlimactic, the jewelry collection and what were left of the coins were returned to the rightful owners, who like the owner of the Mustang believed they would never see their property again. This was followed by several written 'atta-boys' from the burglary victims, the Mustang owner, the South Carolina prison system and the authorities in Aiken.

In sum, I felt pretty good about the whole deal. That sort of job satisfaction cannot be bought at any price.

But there was one more bit of icing for the cake, one of those stranger-than-fiction elements that seemed to crop up along that shining superhighway known as Interstate 10. When I visited with the detective in Aiken, he thanked us for "catching this old boy again."

Again? I asked what he meant by that?

He laughed and went on to explain the rest of the story, as Paul Harvey used to say. When the suspect committed that burglary, he also stole some guns and a vehicle parked at the residence, a like-new red Mazda RX-7 sports car.

Just like this time, he had headed west along Interstate 10, siphoning gas and pawning those guns to keep him flush in spending money. That is until he was nabbed by none other than Trooper L.D. Whitton, my fellow academy classmate who was working out of Sonora during those years. L. D. put the 'habeas grabus' on this star-crossed lad not six miles from where I would get him five years later.

See what I mean about the greatest show on earth, and why this story is entitled Just Bad Luck In West Texas? I wonder if that fellow ever drove a red car again west on Interstate 10, and if he did so what he must have been thinking.

And speaking of thinking:

L. D., what were you doing poaching in my county like that anyways?

TROY HOGUE

Jess Malone should be the one telling this story, as he knew Troy far better than I. After all, they shared the same little Mustang patrol unit for a couple of years while working out of Iraan together. I hope that one day Jess sees his way clear to do so. But until then, this will have to do.

It was in the later part of 1988 when I first met Troy, if memory serves me correctly. Jess called me on the radio to meet him somewhere near the river for introductions. Troy was Jess's new rookie, but that particular word really did not do Troy any justice.

Though he had only recently graduated from DPS Academy, Troy Hogue came to us from Big Spring where he had been a lieutenant for the local police department. It seems the Big Spring area brought us many a good man over those years; men like Chris and Curtis Becker, Erwin Ballarta and Nick Hanna come to mind immediately. Troy was right in the same league.

We hit it off from the start and as the months went by and the three of us were embroiled in one brouhaha after another, I became acutely aware of just how really special Troy was.

He had all the attributes of a superlative peace officer. Troy Hogue was intelligent, personable, easy going, non-judgmental, a shrewd student of human nature, and in uniform looked like he just stepped off a DPS recruiting poster. He cared about his profession, his family, his co-workers and the people he came into contact with on a daily basis.

He was a man with a big heart who was slow to anger, but you had better think twice before trying him on for size. Troy was as tough as boot leather, and not anyone to trifle with. Still waters run deep, they say, and they can also give you a shellacking to remember.

It was obvious that Troy was special in Malone's eyes, too. This was of real significance to me, as Jess could be exacting about his choices in whom he let closest to him. Those two proved to be quite the team.

Time passed on and a few years later there was an opening back home and Troy transferred to Big Spring. We all understood why, family came first and Troy was a family man to the core. But he was missed all the same by many, including myself.

Though now out of the area I would still see or hear of Troy on occasion, the last time we visited was at DPS Academy. I had been detailed as a firearms instructor for a recruit school and Troy was in Austin for a promotion board. We bunked together, and talked about all manner of things both past and present.

BLACK AND WHITE

When Troy showed up in our room that evening, he was a little despondent. The promotion board passed on him, I think it was for Highway Patrol Sergeant. I still remember wondering who in their right mind would pass on this guy as a leader of men, for I would have been proud to work for him.

I didn't hear anything from or about Troy for another six months, and that was on the night of December 30, 1994.

I was working evening shift when called into the office by the duty PCO. Though I cannot remember who it was, the teletype message I was handed seared itself into my memory for all time.

Troy Hogue was dead.

The news shocked everyone who had ever been around him, and reverberated across the state of Texas. He was not the kind of man easily overlooked or forgotten, and many places where he hadn't been still knew him by kinship and reputation.

Curtis Becker was our Texas Ranger in Ozona at the time, and someone who I came to know fairly well. Curtis had also started out as a rookie in Big Spring and Troy took him under his wing, as he had so many others. Now he was part of the investigative team in Troy's line-of-duty death. I never realized how hard this was on Curtis until later.

It was through him I learned what happened, and the circumstances leading to Troy's murder.

That evening Troy and his rookie partner were called to a minor vehicle accident on Interstate 20, at an exit ramp into the small community of Coahoma. A deputy sheriff initially responded to the call, and once at the scene requested a highway patrol unit to work the wreck.

The driver was an intoxicated juvenile, known areawide as someone out to make a name for himself in all the wrong ways. Though only seventeen, he had already been a perpetrator in prior criminal acts and came from a family much the same. Fifteen days prior, this budding boil on humanity was placed on juvenile probation for aggravated robbery and felony escape.

And tonight he was armed with a loaded .455 Webley, a break open British military revolver from the World War One era.

Troy and his rookie arrived at the wreck scene and began questioning the juvenile. Though it was obvious the seventeen-year-old was intoxicated, Troy patiently asked what had happened and the driver began talking about swerving to miss a cat.

When he pointed in the direction of where the imaginary cat supposedly crossed the roadway, all eyes went to the spot. In that fatal moment and for no apparent reason, the drunken young fool pulled the Webley and began firing.

His target was Troy Hogue at point blank range.

Two rounds were expended, and one of them struck Troy just above the left eye. My friend was already dead before his body fell to the ground.

A struggle over the gun ensued between the deputy and the assailant, and the rookie troop joined in. They were only able to get the Webley out of the killer's hand when the deputy slammed an elbow into the shooter's temple.

At that point the seventeen-year-old gave no further resistance, stating then he had no idea as to why he shot Troy.

Curtis speculated in the last fraction of a second, Troy somehow saw the gun and tried to duck out of the way. This conjecture came from the angle and path of the fatal bullet.

Within the next few hours, the news of Troy's murder was printing out on teletype systems across the state.

The funeral in Big Spring was on a miserably cold, windy day this part of West Texas is infamous for. I was on the regional honor guard at that time, and trying hard to do whatever was expected of me. The memory of Troy Hogue deserved at least that much.

I watched men I knew personally; incredibly strong, tough men step up to that casket and nearly go weak at the knees in grief. Others would stand there in respectful silence, while tears flowed freely down each cheek as if they would never stop. It was as if we were all burying a small part of ourselves alongside Troy, and saying goodbye to not only him but also this same portion of our better selves.

At graveside it was so bitterly cold that when it came time for the rifle volleys, some of our Mini-14s malfunctioned. We had no blank firing attachments for our muzzles, so each round had to be hand chambered. If the rifles had been left inside a warm patrol car, the drastic change in air temperature caused condensation and the rifle receiver and bolt assembly froze together.

But the highway patrolmen on the rifle detail grimly carried on, doing their duty even while they silently cursed the weather, their rifles and the heartbreaking circumstances that had placed them there.

After the service, I picked up one of the .223 blanks we had fired and placed it in my pocket.

The drive home from Ozona was a quiet one, I was by myself and in no mood to listen to the radio or much else. The wind died down some and the cloud cover started to lower, and the smell of moisture came sweeping in from the north. As night closed in, large falling flakes of snow reflected in my Caprice's headlamps all the way from Sterling City to Ozona.

Of all the days I have lived before or since, that early January day in Big Spring was one of the saddest.

The following weeks went by and things began to turn back to normal, or as normal as it gets while prowling about in a black and white. Yet there are degrees of normalcy for each of us, and sometimes the grieving goes on in the most personal, unexpected manners for those still dealing with unrelenting pain and sense of loss.

One late evening I was at my desk after working a wreck and heard sobbing coming from the ranger's office. Following this unmistakable sound of human misery, I looked through the open doorway and saw Curtis sitting there crying. The top of his desk was covered with photographs and statements concerning Troy's still ongoing murder investigation. The photos were graphic, as likely were the words and paragraphs in those reports.

With the slightest bit of sound I telegraphed my presence to Curtis. He looked up and into my eyes and slowly shook his head from side to side, and waved me off with a hand.

I quietly closed the door behind me.

More weeks and then months passed by. A trial was convened and the shooter was convicted of capital murder. Rather than be given the death penalty, he was sentenced to life imprisonment. One of the jurors could not be convinced that he deserved to die, saying he looked like somebody's child.

I wondered if that juror would have the same opinion if he had seen that 'child' take another human being's life in such a despicably cold-blooded fashion, and without any rhyme or reason involved for such an absolute act of sociopathic-like immorality.

But this juror will have to live with that decision, same as each of us have to live with each of ours.

In 1997, a memorial dedicated to all slain DPS troopers was completed in front of the Homer S. Garrison Building, which houses the DPS Academy. Part of the memorial was a bronze bust of Trooper Troy Hogue, on a stand beside this silent wall of honor.

It took me a couple of more years before I could look at that bust.

In 2012 a new law enforcement center was dedicated in Troy's name, in downtown Big Spring. A DPS patrol boat, also named in his memory, was on display in front of the building during the dedication ceremony. Present also was a copy of the bronze bust that stands in front of the DPS Academy.

Each holiday season from Thanksgiving to New Year's is traditionally a dangerous time for officers on the road. We all knew that, and kept that fact in mind when we went about our patrol activities. But I believe in my heart that Troy never saw that punk kid as any sort of threat, he just saw him as a troubled seventeen year old boy in need of help.

Like so many of those who came along before, and in turn Troy tried to reach out in his special way.

That reaching out with a bit of human kindness and fatherly feeling is what led to the murder of Troy Hogue, and the fact still pains me greatly. However if he had not been reaching out, then he would not have been the man I knew and admired so much.

And that spent blank casing that I picked up at the cemetery, all those years ago? It sits in my study to this day, marked with the date fired and four words:

'A good man gone.'

Trooper Troy Merle Hogue, Texas Highway Patrol
End of Watch December 30th, 1994

MISSED IT BY THAT MUCH

A few years after I graduated the academy, a great hue and cry was echoing throughout police circles about officers nationwide being 'outgunned' with their traditional six shot revolver.

Much of this was sparked by the so-called FBI Miami Shootout, which occurred in April of 1986. Basically put, eight agents jumped out a pair of bank robbers inside a stolen vehicle. In response the bad guys, both Army MP veterans and hard core in tactical mindset, gave the Federal Bureau of Investigation a sure enough gunfight for the books. The end result was two dead felons, but at the cost of two dead and five wounded of the agents.

Now if the FBI is known for one thing among law enforcement, it is in not being able to admit to their mistakes. For those with an interest in such matters, examples abound over the past thirty years or so. When completing their internal investigation of this avoidable fiasco, in sum they laid the blame on the agents being outgunned.

A moment to think about that. You had eight agents with a total of two shotguns, seven revolvers and three high capacity 9mm pistols. The bad guys had a Mini-14 rife, a shotgun and two revolvers.

The vast majority of rounds fired were at near point-blank range, and measured in mere feet. Those agents had the advantage in the number of guns, the number of cars and the number of men involved. They should also have had the element of surprise, and that failing is often fairly enough disputed.

The crucial difference was actually in having the proper mindset, and with well-rehearsed tactics for such a violent, high intensity encounter. The bad guys were primed and ready, those agents weren't and they paid a high price for their neglecting in being so.

Stick with me on this. There are some very important lessons to be learned here in how most bureaucracies work, and police bureaucracies are no exception.

Though many agencies at the time did not have the institutional memory to recall, the same sort of situation occurred some sixteen years before in Southern California. Then known as the Newhall Incident, it also involved two hardened violent criminals facing off against eight California Highway Patrolmen, as well as an unarmed Good Samaritan who jumped into the action to help the fallen officers.

This time four of the officers were killed while both gunmen escaped with only minor injuries. Ironically enough, most of the blood drawn by any of the good guys was by the Good Samaritan, who managed to slightly wound one of the perpetrators with a service revolver obtained from a dead officer.

However, the ensuing shooting investigation by the CHP proved to be more honest in their self-appraisal. Training and tactics, rather than the excuse of being outgunned, constituted the real factors needing improvement within their organization. These changes led to the betterment of not only the California Highway Patrol, but law enforcement agencies across the nation.

Furthermore, CHP officers continued carrying their six shot Smith & Wesson revolvers into the 1990s. But no more incidents such as the Newhall tragedy ever occurred again within that time span.

Meanwhile, the Federal Bureau of Investigation went through a series of handgun changes that proved slightly confusing, if anything else. After officially announcing their findings as loudly and publicly as possible, they ventured forth in search of the mythical magic handgun and bullet.

The publicity campaign centered around the mantra of 'the police are outgunned' began in earnest.

Immediately the FBI decided that revolvers were passe and so was the high-capacity 9mm pistol. After all, three of their agents carried high capacity nine millimeters during the Miami shootout, so they certainly couldn't recommend that.

No, they were the Federal Bureau of Investigation and needed something special, something much more powerful. Enter the 10mm, chambered in a Smith and Wesson Model 1076.

About the same size and weight as a Colt Combat Commander, these stainless steel nine shot pistols with double action first round capability were good guns, and certainly powerful enough. The original 10mm cartridge developed more than double the muzzle energy compared to the hottest .38 Special or 9mm.

However there is always a tradeoff and the more powerful the pistol, the more need for muscle strength and skill to control the weapon. As with anything else involving proficiency, this boils down to proper aptitude and training.

The complaints started pouring in, some field agents simply could not manage the pistol and weren't about to spend the necessary time and effort in learning how. In truth, neither was the FBI hierarchy itself.

So they developed their own load for the gun, a reduced charge with considerably less recoil and roar.

Then more complaints, as now it was starting to malfunction. Consider this new development for a moment, a self-loading pistol has to work within a certain range of givens to function correctly. One of the most important givens is the load used in the gun. Change the power of that cartridge by much, and you have drifted out of the parameters required for duty gun reliability.

Cause and effect. Imagine that.

BLACK AND WHITE

Plus there was near continual griping about the gun being too heavy, too hard to conceal and the grip size being too large for some agents.

The much praised then cursed Smith & Wesson 10mm lasted about three years before being replaced by the Sig P226 and P228. This meant a step back to the 9mm chambering with the same ballistics, or worse, as those Smith & Wesson 459s that supposedly failed so miserably in Miami.

But hold on, yet another magic handgun and caliber were waiting in the wings. In 1997, less than ten years after the Miami shootout, the FBI chose the Glock 22 and 23 chambered in the .40 Smith and Wesson cartridge.

The .40 S&W was really nothing more than a shortened 10mm casing with a reduced powder charge. It quickly earned the undignified moniker of ".40 Short & Weak" among many with an interest in ballistics.

But the cartridge modification did allow the .40 S&W to be packaged in a 9mm sized pistol frame. That afforded many of their agents with smaller hands better control of the weapon in comparison to the older Smith & Wesson 1076. While not necessarily meaning better accuracy and higher qualification scores, this did mean they were less likely to drop the thing or have it malfunction.

Recently the FBI has moved on to what is called the Glock 17M. Not the standard issue Glock 17 like everyone else uses, but rather another special variant for the Federal Bureau of Investigation. And in 9mm again, and again with about the same ballistics as in 1986.

This latest and greatest sweet deal, gladly contracted by GLOCK Inc., added up to the princely sum of $85 million dollars.

Your federal taxes at work, folks.

Meanwhile in the law enforcement world at large, those FBI findings were making the rounds near incessantly. Mass media types who wouldn't know a Browning Hi Power from a Japanese slingshot conducted special reports on this evolving conundrum, aided and abetted by police bureaucracies and cash hungry gun companies.

And then the fever hit the Texas Department of Public Safety.

Standing against this growing whirlwind of trendy playthings and wonder pistols was a man by the name of Reeves Jungkind. Reeves was a meat and potatoes sort of individual with no nonsense about him. A master gunsmith and decidedly deadly with any kind of firearm, he was also the chief firearms instructor for the DPS.

Reeves believed in training, not placebos. In his experienced opinion duty sidearms for uniformed officers should be reliable, robust, accurate, powerful and simple to maintain as well as operate.

In his mind there was a place for autoloading pistols, and such pistols had been carried by Texas Rangers since the creation of the Department. But an officer needed to show proficiency with this type of sidearm before carrying it, due to the added complexity. As the old saying goes: the more complicated the plumbing, the easier it is to stop up the toilet.

The story goes that when Reeves told the DPS bureaucracy the proven .357 revolver was still what their uniformed services really needed, the powers-that-be responded by basically ordering him to test a variety of autoloading pistols for department-wide use in the near future.

Reeves, not the outdone, did conduct a comprehensive evaluation program. His first choice was the Sig Sauer P series. Rumor had it he chose the Sig in part because it was by far the most expensive of the guns tested, and he was certain the powers-that-be would balk at the price tag.

However, those same powers figured this had to be the reason why he selected the Sig. So to spite him, they scraped together the necessary funds to purchase these weapons for duty use.

And that is reportedly how the Texas Department of Public Safety ended up with the finest out of the box combat handgun of this era. Shortly thereafter, Reeves Jungkind retired.

Yet that choice of sidearm, for whatever reasons an excellent one, came with its own difficulties. The training given to troops in the field for the conversion was not as comprehensive as what they had received while going through the academy. Qualification scores suffered and rounds expended per shooting incident increased precipitously.

There were also a marked increase in malfunctions, and the number of negligent discharges literally went through the roof. Or in one memorable case, into the ground. For one young rookie in our area, that particular chicken marked 'fate' came home to roost.

It was about two weeks before Christmas and we had been so busy, as well as shorthanded, that our scheduled weapons qualification was pushed back nearly to the deadline. However, we managed to assemble together on the day in question to get the required qualification done.

That meant a lot of good natured ribbing and comments of every kind, but hardly ever complimentary. If one's feelings were easily injured, at that time the Texas Highway Patrol was not the place to be. But once on the firing line, things got relatively serious for a bunch of would be career comedians.

Standing at the three yard point, I fired my series and was reholstering when I heard a round go off to my left. During this stage the shooters usually finished at close to the same time, so a round going off so late aroused the curiosity.

'Dang,' I thought. *'Someone fired a long time after that whistle blew.'*

By habit I glanced that direction, wondering if I might catch the guilty party with gun still in hand. When I did, it was easy enough to pick the culprit out. It was my rookie, his hand still on the grip of his holstered Sig P226. He had a shocked, puzzled look on his face and a growing plume of telltale West Texas dust rising from his left boot.

In a mental flash I knew what happened. The rookie forgot to decock his pistol, the hammer stayed back and in reholstering he still had his finger in the trigger guard. When his index finger contacted the trigger as he shoved the pistol's muzzle into his holster...

BLAM!!!

Several of us immediately rushed to his side as the young troop stammered out he was "all right." Still in shock, he could not see his uniform trousers ripped along the thigh as well as the calf area, and his left boot had an odd look to it.

Once we talked him into taking the undignified position of having to drop his trousers on a public range, we could see a bullet burn on his buttock, about four inches in length and slowly starting to ooze blood.

On closer examination we determined the 9mm slug exited the bottom of the holster, creased his left buttock, traveled the length of his leg before entering the top of his boot, and then blew out part of the heel before burying itself in the dirt.

If it had been a .45 ACP bullet from our likewise issued P220, it could have opened up most of his left leg on the way down. I had seen this happen before while in the Marines, and the result was not a pretty sight.

Yet the rookie was still game, and finished the course of fire before being taken to the clinic by Tommy Scales. Sgt. Mayfield had me write a memorandum to explain what happened and after making its merry way to Austin, a manual change was instituted.

But all the memos in the world cannot make up for inadequate training, nor can the latest gee whiz Duck Dodgers equipment. Under Murphy's Laws there is one that reads: "The important things are always simple, and the simple things are always hard."

It is far easier to throw money at a situation rather than addressing the root cause and fixing it, especially in a bureaucracy funded by taxpayer dollar bills. Training is hard, it has to be hard to be effective. It is repetitive, time consuming and usually intensely disliked by some of those present.

Those in the upper levels of command are often recalcitrant about training, too. It eats at their budget and takes away available manpower, and usually there is not enough manpower to begin with. Nevertheless, the skill of any craftsman is measured by the mastery of his tools. When he, or she, is employed by an organization, the proper use of those tools reflects upon the organization itself.

In a very real way, that negligent discharge was as much the fault of the bureaucracy as it was the rookie's. He would have been far better off starting with a revolver, and only issued an auto pistol after showing advanced proficiency with what he already had.

Some decades later, a new trend started among many departments concerning the use of tasers. The idea was the availability of a non-lethal device that would disable a violent subject, rather than having to go hands on or in the worst circumstance, being forced to utilize a firearm.

Early on these devices came in two configurations. One looked like an oversized flashlight while the other was shaped akin to a handgun. The latter type proved to be the overwhelming favorite for law enforcement departments nationwide.

The reason often given for this choice? Because it was shaped like a handgun and thus less time consuming to train officers with.

Now think about this one for a minute. You are going to place a pistol shaped non-lethal device in a holster fastened to the duty belt, often positioned for as quick a draw as the sidearm itself. But to assuage the disbelieving skeptic, you have the Taser gun molded in yellow to help differentiate between the two.

Then you bring your officers in for a few hours of training, usually more if starting at a recruit level. Days, months, even years pass and the Taser remains inside the holster. A sometimes exception is when the individual department requires proficiency shown, which does not happen often.

With this in mind, do you actually think a different color makes one whit of difference to the user, especially when having to respond to a personal threat near instantaneously?

Sometime in the future, during a domestic or a traffic stop gone bad or someone needs to go to jail and doesn't want to, an officer is forced to deploy their Taser. That decision is often made in the compressed twinkling of an eye, accompanied by a virtual flood of adrenaline due to the clear and present danger of someone being seriously injured, or even killed.

And in that split second, when acting upon survival instinct more than anything else, the officer mistakenly palms a pistol rather than a Taser and pulls the trigger. Bad things happen from that instant forward, really bad things.

As I write these words, dozens of such incidents have occurred nationwide. In Minnesota, a twenty-six year veteran police officer was found guilty of manslaughter for mistakenly shooting a wanted subject with her sidearm, rather than a Taser. All the while, she was yelling "Taser, Taser, Taser!!!"

In that disastrous moment of miscalculation, her training failed her. Though there is likely plenty of blame to go around, the fact remains that an avoidable tragedy ensued, followed by a miscarriage of justice. I doubt if many of her higher ups lost much sleep over this incident, but I know the officer did. What happened is something she will have to live with for the rest of her life.

These are the tragedies that occur to police officers near daily, even when trying their best to do the right thing. Second guessing their actions is usually the sport of those who have never faced the possibility of not going home at shift's end.

At least, alive.

AN EVIL AMONG US

It has been said a society's worth is measured in how that society protects its most helpless members, the very old and the very young. Going by that scale our society has been slipping since my earliest memories, for we do less and less to shield either in our present culture.

What was considered heinous only a generation or so ago is now made excuses for, sold as 'entertainment,' or openly defended by fringe groups who can be best charitably described as totally clueless fools.

When people consider the absolutely most appalling, brutish act committed upon a fellow human being, a range of different levels of hellish depravities come to mind. When considering the memories of a highway patrolman who spent twenty-two years working rural interstate, one would think the most awful of all had something to do with this major thoroughfare.

Well publicized books, periodicals, television series, documentaries and movies often tell of these gruesome crimes, and of the soulless killers and mass murderers that ply their trade along the interstate systems. And yes, I had something to do with the investigation of a few during my time as an officer.

But the most despicable and vilest of all was the kidnapping, sexual assault and horrific murder of a nine year old girl in Ozona, committed by the monster who her family considered a friend and who lived only a few houses away.

This monster was a local also, someone whom I dealt with on an official level multiple times before this happened. Someone I detained and/or arrested more than once, all misdemeanors and on occasion involving alcohol of some sort. Not much came out of those arrests. As I said the monster was a local, and locals were not prosecuted much by the court system in Ozona at that time.

The monster set off all sorts of warning bells when I was around him. Something was severely amiss in a twisted, decaying soul that made one think of a dark, rotting place where only those of poisonous bent were allowed to enter.

Yet the monster tried every way he could to befriend me, even after my open disdain and intense personal dislike became blatantly obvious. He was treated no different than anyone else under the law, but I always had the urge to scrub my hands vigorously after putting them upon him.

And yes, to examine my own soul too. He was that malignant.

He was prosecuted in other jurisdictions where he was not a local for the same type of misdemeanor offenses, notably in Reagan County which adjoined ours to the northwest. He had family there.

Then he was arrested in Crockett County on a felony charge, for the molestation of a twelve year old girl within his immediate kin. Two things of note occurred at this juncture; that arrest proved every one of those bad feelings I possessed for this fiend, and there was something really wrong with our criminal justice system.

The monster never served a single day in prison, he was given deferred adjudication and sent to an area rehabilitation center. Successful completion meant the monster would have no criminal record for such a stomach-turning act.

And predictably enough, he successfully completed this rehabilitation and came right back to Ozona.

Not long after his return, citizens started coming to me about him. Volunteer firemen, EMTs, school teachers, oilfield hands, other officers. All had a very bad feeling about the monster, and all wanted to see something done with him beyond a rehabilitation program.

One does not rehabilitate true evil, one does not even try. You either do away with the diseased or put them where they can do no more harm. Child molestation is one of those rare crimes having the rehabilitation rate of a rabid dog, there is no psychological cure for either.

Each of these concerned citizens were saying this particular carrier was up to his same repulsive tricks again, riding around after dark with pre-teenaged girls in the car with him.

I managed to get a traffic stop soon enough, he was drag racing a seventeen year old kid in front of the local high school. That was before drag racing was a Class B Misdemeanor.

But I still took both down to the county jail for a little heart to heart. I released the teenager loose almost immediately and turned my attention to the monster. We had words about driving around with those little girls, and about doing so after dark. This evening there was no one in the vehicle with him, which narrowed my available options considerably.

Yet he readily admitted to doing so, saying he was doing nothing more than taking them out for some ice cream. At that very moment and while looking him in the eye, we both knew he was lying through his teeth and presently I could not do anything about it.

Then he went on to say he treated those little girls as if they were his own family. His somewhat ironic remark underlined what a sizable portion of our little community had already figured out, and this was the essential part of the problem.

I reminded him of those facts, and that many in our community were watching him. More so, I was watching him as well as my brother officers. Someday one of us would catch him again for what he had been arrested before, and this time there would be no so-called 'rehabilitation program.' Furthermore, he might do well to move someplace else as he was becoming so well known here, and for all the wrong reasons.

Sitting at the break table in that little jail, I pushed about as far as I could and still stay within the boundaries of the law and that badge on my chest. I chose my words and analogies carefully, all aimed at the futility of him staying in Ozona while in possession of his putrid malignancy.

Once finished I kicked him loose with one final warning: Sooner or later you are going to screw up and I'll be looking you in the eye again, while they put you away for good.

Then he was out the steel door and the duty jailor was asking me, "Do you think you did any good?"

"I hope so," I replied. "I really hope so."

Not more than about three months later, my hope was dashed away forever. The monster struck again in the vein of his fiendish type who not only refuse to stop, but carry their foul deeds down to even lower levels.

This time he murdered.

Jennifer Lee Gravell was a blonde-haired, blue eyed child brimming with life, as so many nine year olds are wont to be. That fateful evening in early August, her parents decided to have a neighborhood barbeque, and of course invited all their neighbors and friends.

And on that list, both as a neighbor as well as a family friend, was the name of this forty-seven-year-old lurking monster. He attended the party, had a few drinks and went home around 11:00 pm.

Jennifer went to play at a friend's home some houses over. When her friend's mother told her it was time to go home, Jennifer started in that direction. Somewhere along the route to her residence, the nine year old disappeared at about the same time as the monster went home.

And her path went right past the monster's house.

Jennifer's mother, Beth Gravell, began looking for Jennifer a bit after 11:00pm. She first tried the residence of her daughter's friend and was told Jennifer was not there. Beth noticed that the truck the monster drove was not at his residence. She continued searching the neighborhood for Jennifer.

Witnesses later reported seeing the truck, driven by its owner with a young blonde girl in the passenger seat. This was around midnight, and the monster returned home alone sometime after 1:00 am.

Still searching, Beth now saw his pickup truck in front of the house and stopped by to ask if he had seen Jennifer. He insisted that he hadn't. Beth, fearing for her daughter's safety, notified the sheriff's office. A search for the missing girl began immediately.

While this was occurring I was on my scheduled days off. During this late evening, myself and others had been helping my brother Lyndon and his family move into their new home. Lyndon was a deputy sheriff at the time, and those family members included his brother-in-law Bruce James, who was one of my fellow troopers.

BLACK AND WHITE

Some years later Lyndon's wife, Laurie English, would become district attorney for our area. Laurie made for a stellar DA, and still serves with distinction in that capacity. I sometimes wonder if such events, as those unfolding around us that night, made her so habitually vigilant in her prosecutorial endeavors.

Yet during those awful hours, none of us had an inkling as to what was happening not a half mile away. So close that a single cry for help could have carried to our ears in the night air.

But none was heard.

My first knowledge of the ongoing search came with a phone call the next morning, telling me what happened. My first question involved where the monster was, calling him by name. The caller said he had been out with the other searchers earlier, and was currently at the sheriff's office.

When the caller told me that, a wave of emotional nausea and helplessness swept through my very being, settling down where I keep my darkest of thoughts closest to me.

Cathy was already at work, preparing for a new school year. Since it was my day off I was caring for our two sons at home, six and nine years old. The three of us climbed in the cab of my old Dodge truck and began our own search.

Shortly after the noon hour, we were north of town checking behind some metal buildings along the highway when Trooper Tommy Scales and Joe Fincher, Chief Deputy for neighboring Sutton County, went flying past in separate units.

I had my portable radio, and it was obvious from the communications traffic that they were on to something. Levi and Ethan were still in the truck, so I jumped in and gave chase.

The two units turned on to Highway 137 as if going to Big Lake, but they braked suddenly and stopped in front of a tank battery only a couple of hundred yards from the intersection. Both men left their vehicles and began searching to the rear of the area. It did not take them long to find Jennifer.

Or rather, what was left of her.

Other officers began arriving, including Deputy Steve Kenley who asked me to go with him to the sheriff's office. He needed help in gathering the necessary equipment for the processing of the crime scene.

Upon our return, Shane Fenton requested my assistance in filming the location with a video camera. My friend and comrade in arms was now the sheriff of Crockett County, he looked tired and sick at heart. My mind went back to that cold, dark night along Taylor Box Road when we lost Christine Haire.

But even as bad as that was, what we saw this afternoon was incomparably worse.

My job was to video the gathering of evidence, and follow the crime scene team as they went about their grisly business. I will not relate as to what I personally saw through that view finder, but what was there will haunt me all the rest of my days.

I spent nearly two hours doing this, attempting to keep ahold of my professionalism as the camera lens captured the unspeakable horror before us. When finished, I turned the tape over to Shane and went home. Cathy would be there soon, and my two young sons had experienced a day they would not forget.

The next day or so, I learned from the lead investigators how we all ended up behind that tank battery. If there could be any sort of a blessing in such a horrible circumstance, it was the two men who spearheaded the questioning of the monster. I consider both personal friends then and to this day, and both were two of the finest criminal investigators I ever had the opportunity to work with.

Alton Davis was chief deputy for Crockett County then, a selection by prior sheriff Jim Wilson that allowed our small sheriff's department to punch way above its weight when it came to such matters. Jerry Byrne was our Texas Ranger, and one of the most capable and persistent men I knew in his line of work. Never was there a moment when Jerry brought anything but honor to the *cinco peso*.

Working together these two initiated a marathon effort in interviewing the monster, and in finally getting him to crack under their notably skilled probing. Once the monster started talking; his rotting, poisonous nature spewed forth for those present to see.

The night before, when Jennifer walked by his residence, he finally saw his chance. Under false pretenses, he lured her into his pickup truck and drove her to a nearby park.

There he attempted to sexually assault her, but when she resisted he bound her hands with electrical tape and gagged the child with a sock. In the middle of the assault another vehicle pulled in behind his truck, forcing him to leave.

He took her to a deserted area north of Ozona and completed his heinous acts of perversion in various ways. Following his doing so, he drug that little nine-year-old girl out of the truck, behind the tank battery, and mercilessly beat her to death with a tire iron. Using repeated, frenzied swings, the monster crushed her skull.

Then he left her violated, broken, dead body in the blackness to whatever else happened to come along.

In the process of research for this book, Alton Davis recalled:

"I guess that being able to maintain composure and holding everything inside during this horrendous case was the hardest part. During all the time I

spent with him, he never expressed or showed any remorse, only feeling sorry for himself.

Of the homicide cases that I investigated during my career, he had to be the epitome of Evil."

Nearly two years later, the monster stood before a court of law for what he had done. The physical evidence was overwhelming, shoe prints at the crime scene matched those found in the monster's home. The blood discovered on the shoes matched Jennifer's DNA.

So did the blood found in his pickup.

The child's underwear and sandals were discovered in a trash container at the residence, along with a wadded-up ball of electrical tape with numerous blonde hairs stuck to it.

The monster was found guilty of capital murder. In the penalty phase four days later, he was sentenced deservingly to death. During this part of the trial, the jury was made aware of what had been living in their midst, and how the criminal justice system failed to contain him time and again.

Due to being given deferred adjudication for his prior sexual assault of a minor, the monster possessed no felony criminal record. However, the jury was informed of the elements of this older case, including how he offered to pay this family member $50 a week to perform for him on demand.

Furthermore they were told how he allowed parties for teenagers at his house, supplying the alcohol. During one of these incidents, he grabbed the breast of a teenaged girl.

In this same encapsulation, prosecutors related the monster's long involvement in depravity and violent behavior, having molested a preschool relative when he was around eleven years old. He beat his wife in repeated instances, and had a misdemeanor criminal record for making a false report to a peace officer, driving while intoxicated and public intoxication.

All this, all this shame and terror and habitual cruelty. Yet the monster remained free to move among those whom he preyed most upon. It was only after the indescribably awful murder of Jennifer that he was finally brought to bay.

Again, Alton Davis recollects:

"While transporting from Ft. Stockton he turned to me and said, 'Alton the worst thing about all of this is I can't stand needles!'

I had a good come back to that but had to maintain my composure again. Even though the trial was over, what I said might be brought up at one of his appeals."

When they brought the monster to our jail after sentencing, I was waiting in front of the book-in area. Reminding him of our prior conversations, I asked the unexpected favor of being present for his execution. When he conceded to doing so, I pointed out it would likely be years, even decades before justice was served.

"Do not forget me," I said. "They allow you to have witnesses. I want to be there."

He nodded and moved on, finally in the shackles of confinement that he was so deserving of.

After he was gone, Chief Jailor Emilio Tambunga looked up and remarked, "Well, that was a Kodak moment."

"I reckon," was my reply.

"Think he'll remember?"

"Don't know," I said. "But if he doesn't, I'll figure out another way. That's one I personally want to see put down."

Emilio nodded and returned to his work, and I went out the door to return to mine.

Soon afterward, a tree was dedicated in Jennifer's memory in front of the elementary school she once attended.

Then the years began to pass by.

As with all such sentences pronounced in the state of Texas, it was brought before the Texas Court of Criminal Appeals which upheld both the conviction as well as the sentence.

The monster appealed for writ of habeas corpus both in state as well as federal courts. Each of these motions in turn were denied.

In May of 2003, Jennifer's father placed a gun to his head and pulled the trigger. Charlie Gravell's suicide was directly attributed by many to Jennifer's murder. He carried the guilt of not being able to protect his daughter from such a horrendous fate.

More years passed.

In October of 2005 with his scheduled execution date nearing, the monster's appeal to the sitting justices of the United States Supreme Court was denied.

That was the month when I received the necessary documents to witness his upcoming execution. Though the monster had forgotten my request from that decade before, someone else remembered.

Beth Gravell, now a widow and without one of her children, asked me to represent her family in what needed doing.

Yet the legal efforts to save the monster's life seemed unending. Finally, the Texas Board of Pardons and Paroles voted unanimously in a recommendation against any stay or commutation to life imprisonment. Governor Rick Perry followed their stand.

Early on the third of November in the year of 2005, I pulled my old '66 Thunderbird out of the garage and headed east for Huntsville. It was a quiet drive, giving me hours to reminisce on all that had happened since Jennifer's murder.

Her third-grade classmates would be graduating soon, and stepping out into the world as well as into their own lives. My two sons were now teenagers, and Benjamin Levi was already laying the groundwork that would ultimately lead him to the Naval Academy at Annapolis.

Ethan L'Amour was not far behind.

I wondered what path Jennifer's life might have taken had it not been for the monster. It was not the first time for my pondering of this hopelessly unanswerable thought, nor would it be the last.

Once at the prison, we were escorted into a room and briefed on what was about to occur. Packets were handed out with information pertaining to the execution process, a list of offenders still on death row, a witness roster of those attending and a copy of a letter from a local Baptist church, signed by parishioners saying they would be praying for us this evening.

We were also made aware we could make ourselves available to the press afterwards. That was something I had no intention of staying around for.

But I did have a question. Upon being brought into the viewing room adjacent to the execution chamber, I asked a prison official where one would stand to make certain the condemned would see them.

Nonplussed, he brought me close to the plate glass window and advised me to stand in a particular spot.

"He'll see you standing here," the man advised. "He has no choice."

I placed the exact spot in my mind for immediate reference.

We milled around awhile and visited. Jerry Byrne had come and so did my sister-in-law Laurie English. She was our district attorney by now. Melissa Perner, our local newspaper editor was also present. That was somewhat of a relief for me, as I knew at least one member of the press would actually get the story right.

At precisely 6:00 pm, they brought the monster in from the holding cell and began strapping him to the gurney. He looked over and seemed somewhat startled to see me standing there.

Somehow, I knew he was recollecting what I had told him those years ago: *"I'll be looking you in the eye again, while they put you away for good."*

That time had come.

He tried to turn his head and look away as the solution began to take effect. Soon enough he was in a deep sleep as the sodium thiopental coursed through his veins.

I kept my eyes locked on him.

He began snoring, then stopped. A few minutes later the monster was officially pronounced dead. It was a far more humane ending than having your hands tied behind your back, and beat to death with a tire iron.

We left the observation room and I said my goodbyes. Soon enough that Thunderbird and I were pointed west, toward the final afterglows of another day done.

Mile after mile the big Ford ate up pavement, the silence near absolute save for the sound of tires on asphalt, the unstressed moan of a big block V8 and the faint whisper of wind around the vent windows. It was thinking time again, something that none of us do enough.

Stopping at a convenience store along US 290 outside of Austin, I topped off with a tank of high test and wolfed down a sandwich. Then the crank of the engine starter and we were on the road once more, the surrounding blackness only pierced temporarily by the pale luminescence of headlights.

About halfway to Junction, I came to the conclusion the world was a very ugly place, and that I had somehow managed to wrangle one of the best seats in the house to prove that out.

But there was presently one less monster to prey upon the most vulnerable, and that made this ugly world just a bit safer for them.

Many times, I have heard academians claim that capital punishment had no deterrence value. Well, I could think of somebody who was definitely deterred from ever doing so again, and in an irreversibly permanent way.

The monster's next appeal for clemency would be before God All Mighty Himself and the result of that process, somewhere off in the unknown expanses of eternity, was way beyond my personal pay grade.

And that Thunderbird moaned on into the night.

In Junction I stopped off again, in need of a cup of hot, black coffee to keep me awake to Ozona. Inside were two Kimble County deputies I knew. We exchanged pleasantries and they asked half-jokingly what I was doing out that time of night.

When I explained in a few words, they wanted the entire story. After telling it, both shook their heads and one cursed softly under his breath.

Pulling in front of our home in the wee hours separating night from morning, I thought about how many times I had done so after an evening shift. All of the fights, the drunks, the bad wrecks, the blood on the ground and the senseless taking of life.

There is no good way to die, just bad and worse.

Jennifer Gravell was murdered in likely the worst of all, and justice for this most evil of all deeds was a long time coming.

But it did come.

Once inside the house, I crawled quietly into bed and was soon asleep, taking whatever satisfaction that could be had in that last thought.

TERRY MILLER

During most of my career in the Texas Highway Patrol, I was often temporarily assigned to the DPS Academy in Austin as an instructor. The subjects were varied but included Firearms, Defensive Tactics, Driving Skills, Officer Survival, Patrol Procedures and the like.

In that capacity I became familiar with a large number of recruits, including those of the A-97 class. It was a good group all in all, with many who would go on to make fine officers of all ranks and services. During these classes the instructors were issued rosters, and the recruits with special potential received a checkmark on my personal copy. Terry Miller had one beside his name.

Terry had been a police officer as well as a deputy sheriff in San Patricio County, north of Corpus Christi, before joining the DPS. After graduation he was sent to Freer and later transferred to Pleasanton in Atascosa County. My family helped pioneer that county a hundred and seventy years ago, and there is where this story focuses in detail.

Shortly after dark on Tuesday, October 12, 1999, a 9-1-1 call was phoned in to the Atascosa Sheriff's Office. Unbeknown to anyone at this time save for the perpetrators, this was nothing more than a bogus appeal for assistance to lure responding officers into a deadly trap set outside of Pleasanton. The incident became known as the Atascosa County Ambush.

Two deputies, Thomas Monse, Jr. and Mark Stephenson, arrived on the scene about a minute and a half apart. The murderer, armed with a Norinco SKS 7.62X39 semi-automatic rifle, opened fire from a ditch across the road from his mobile home. The shooter cold-bloodedly first killed Deputy Monse and then Deputy Stephenson upon their respective arrivals. Both were shot down without warning or challenge.

The soulless killer, a life-long loser who had for months been threatening suicide, left the ditch just long enough to make certain both officers were dead and to retrieve Monse's .40 caliber Glock sidearm. He shot each officer again multiple times in the face, at close range. In total Deputy Monse was shot eighteen times with rifle, shotgun and pistol, and Stephenson eleven.

Then this rotting, cancerous sore on all mankind went back to his hiding place and waited to see who else showed.

At approximately 8:50 pm Terry Miller arrived, dispatched by the sheriff's office as they could not raise their deputies on the radio. Evidently Terry saw one of the deputies, as he managed to radio an 'officer down' while trying to back his patrol car out of the kill zone.

He never made it, a barrage of rounds from the murderer's Norinco SKS impacted Terry's Ford, striking Terry twice and killing him instantly.

Terry Miller never even had the chance to unbuckle his safety belt.

About five minutes later two other officers arrived, responding to Terry's last words of 'officer down.' They were immediately engaged with heavy fire from the SKS and both were wounded in the fusillade. One of the officers had his arm nearly severed by a rifle bullet when it struck bone.

But more officers kept coming, undeterred by the gunfire because of personal conscience and a sworn oath to serve and protect. In front of them were the three bodies of their fellow peace officers, and those responding could not be certain if they were still alive or not.

Neither could they be sure of where the shooter really was. The officers were on unfamiliar ground, ground which in turn consisted of the perpetrator's home surroundings.

What little light available was concentrated, mostly headlight beams from the stricken patrol units parked haphazardly in the driveway. If you looked in their direction, you were in turn effectively blinded while trying to pick out any assailant in the surrounding blackness.

But then a San Antonio PD helicopter arrived and was able to pinpoint the shooter's position. Flushed out and now facing odds not in his favor, he committed his final act that illustrated so well the character of this suicidal degenerate. He took the pistol that belonged to Deputy Monse and shot himself.

A note was found on his person reading in part, "I have written this for one reason so that all will know why I have done what I've done, because of life's unfairness and uncertainties."

If it was not for all the blood shed and lives lost that night, those remarks would be better served as being part and parcel to some sort of sick joke. The shooter had been arrested the day before on a domestic violence charge, as he also had the habit of beating his wife near senseless on several occasions.

The arresting officer was Deputy Sheriff Thomas Monse.

The resulting beastly actions all boiled down to an attempt to get even with the deputy, who had the audacity to arrest him for repeatedly abusing the woman he supposedly loved.

This was how skewed the fiend's thinking was in his personal, completely corrupted concept of 'justice.' Over one hundred spent shell casings were found, all fired by someone with an absolutely obscene definition of this near sacred word.

Once the scene was secured the investigation began into what happened, and what led to this shocking crime. Within a day, it was determined the demented killer had outside help.

This second suspect posted the shooter's bail following the domestic violence arrest, and just hours later was helping the soon-to-be mass murderer move over $200 worth of ammunition purchased at a local gun store.

The two were living together in the mobile home that became the location for the shootings. They also had their respective families with them, including three small children.

Witness statements were taken that implicated this second suspect in still far deeper fashion, including the planning as well as first portion of the actual ambush involving the two deceased deputies. Furthermore, the second suspect made numerous conflicting statements inconsistent in logic, as well as in time and location.

Ultimately this suspect pled guilty to three counts of capital murder and was sentenced to death. That conviction was ultimately overturned by an appeals court and the person was sentenced to thirty years under a plea agreement. Since sentenced he has been denied parole twice, once in 2015 and again in 2020.

The senseless murder of Terry Miller is one of those lingering events where you find your own time line repeatedly crossing over the memory of someone else's. Shortly after his death, I was on evening patrol and making my motel and convenience store checks in the Ozona area.

While running license plates at a motel on the east side of town, I was flagged down by an attractive young lady standing in the parking lot. Bringing my patrol unit to a halt, I opened my door and stepped out as she approached. Introducing myself, I asked if I could be of assistance.

She flashed a big smile full of sparkle and said that I sure could.

The young lady explained she had been in Utah for a while but had gone to school with a boy she thought a lot of. The last time she had seen him, he told her that he was joining the DPS. She asked if I might know him, and how he was getting along.

His name was Terry Miller.

In the agony of heart and at that precise moment, the last thing in the world that I wanted to be was a Texas Highway Patrolman.

What do you say and how do you say it?

No matter what or how, the grieving begins anew for someone else. I don't remember the poor girl's name, but I do remember that smile turning into a grief-stricken sob in a matter of seconds.

I watched helplessly as that precious sparkle was utterly extinguished within her.

And time moved on.

Some months later I was in Austin again as an instructor. Before heading home, I stopped by a wrecking yard on East US Highway 71 to scrounge some parts for my old Dodge Charger. This place was where many of our wrecked units ended up, and the people who worked there were friendly to state troopers.

I had been to this yard several times and some of the hands knew me. While I was visiting with them about cars and such, the foreman approached me and said another one of our units had been brought to them. He went on to say there were some items found in the car they needed some help with.

Using a battered yard truck, we drove to a secluded spot near the back fence line for the property. As we made our way through the rows and piles of wrecked or abandoned vehicles, a badly shot up black and white Ford Crown Vic came into view.

It was Terry's patrol unit.

I climbed out of the truck and made my way around the Ford. There were numerous bullet holes through and through, and it was evident the shooter had been fairly close and fired with cold, calculating intent. The interior still contained the result of that rifle fire, in stark evidence I would rather not go into.

Once those rounds started coming in, Terry Miller never had a chance.

The boss man and two of the hands who were with us moved over to the rear of the unit, and stood quietly until I was finished. Then he motioned me over and unlocked the trunk.

I looked inside and saw a DPS issued gray straw hat, soiled by copious amounts of the same evidence seen in the unit's interior. My gut tied up in a complex knot of anger, sadness and despair.

"We don't know what to do with this," the man said movingly. These guys were hurting, too.

The foreman explained that when Terry's car was brought in, the hat was half hidden in the floorboard. He had it locked away in the trunk where it remained until now. There were tears in his eyes and his hands were shaking as he handed the hat to me.

We climbed back in that truck and drove away. I looked behind me, Terry's black and white was sitting there like an opened grave.

At the main building they retrieved a plastic bag for me. I put the hat in the bag and placed both in the trunk of my Caprice. You could see the look of relief in their eyes when I shut that lid.

It was a long, quiet drive all the way home to Ozona. I was in a quandary of what to do about that hat, and thought my options through repeatedly. In such condition you would not want to give it to a family member, or donated for some sort of display. Nor could it ever be cleaned enough to make a difference in the decision.

When I arrived home that evening, Cathy and I sat down and I told her what happened. I also told her of my plan formulated along the way. After hearing me out, she agreed.

BLACK AND WHITE

The next day, Cathy and our two small sons joined me in the back yard. I placed the hat on the ground and covered it with gasoline. Saying a small prayer, I struck a match to it. The four of us watched silently as the flames consumed this gruesome testimony to the high price paid when pure wickedness has its way.

When the fire was done, all that was left was the metal wire hoop that forms the brim. I took the wire, dug a hole, and buried it with as much reverence as I could muster. As far as I know, that spot has never been disturbed since.

In this job there are many things you do not want to forget. Then there are a few others you can't forget even if you tried.

And to this day, I still wonder if I did the right thing with that hat.

Rest in peace, Terry Miller.

Trooper Terry Wayne Miller, Texas Highway Patrol
End of Watch 12th October 1999

MY FASTEST PURSUIT

Many otherwise sane, level headed people have an inexplicable fascination with speed. Mind you I am not throwing any rocks from the proverbial glass house, as I have suffered from the same affliction for as far back as can be remembered.

Perhaps it was my dad's fault, as his idea for a family car with four kids was a 1967 Ford Mustang GTA 390, much like the one driven by Steve McQueen in the movie *Bullitt.*

Need I say anything more about my raising?

Nevertheless, the die was cast and I ended up having owned a total of seven vehicles by the time I graduated high school. The last one was a 1972 Fury four door, powered by a high performance 400 V8 along with the complete Plymouth 'Police Pursuit' package. Of course, I could not leave well enough alone so it received a hotter cam and headers, too.

I managed to get into a substantial amount of trouble with that car, and the die was cast yet again. To this day there are those who claim the only reason I became a highway patrolman was so that I could drive wide open legally.

To that allegation, I shall neither confirm nor deny.

But that old Mopar had a lasting effect on me, both in my choice of personal vehicles as well as a profession. When I called my dad to tell him thatI had been accepted to the DPS Academy, there was a long pause on the phone.

Then in a slow, measured tone he commented "Well, I guess it takes one to catch one."

And with no bag limit as to how many I could throw a loop over in the state of Texas, I caught a bunch of 'em.

But the one topping the list as far as sheer speed was a 1992 Kawasaki Ninja ZX-7 motorcycle, known colloquially among my Red Patch brethren as a "crotch rocket." In this case, you can underline the word 'rocket.'

During those years Tuesdays was when we usually had our area meetings, and often enough when we also had our special area traffic enforcement programs. Basically, a certain stretch of Interstate 10 was selected and units emplaced every five to ten miles or so. Nothing overly complicated or organized, you just went out and worked while trying to stay out of everybody else's way.

On this date I was assigned the mile markers on either side of Ozona. While patrolling just west of town, I noted a green and white sport bike merging from an entrance ramp and coming my direction.

BLACK AND WHITE

It was obvious the bike was accelerating rapidly, and I checked it on radar at 77 MPH in a 70 MPH zone. Good enough for a warning, so I engaged my red and blue grille lamps and crossed the median to turn west.

But that motorcycle wasn't slowing down, it was speeding up. Rapidly.

Since the rider showed no sign of having noticed my unit, and me knowing you never want to get into a drag race with a crotch rocket, I killed the emergency lights and mashed the gas pedal.

I was driving my all-time favorite patrol car, Ol' Rocket Sled. A slicktop 1994 Chevrolet Caprice LT1, these cars were some of the finest all-around pursuit units we ever had. And Ol' Rocket Sled, a parting gift from Corporal Larry Hill upon his retirement, was the best of the best.

Thank you, Larry.

The Kawasaki continued to accelerate, but that big Chevy was doing a little booming and zooming itself by now. We were holding our own, but about the time we reached 110 miles an hour a couple of things happened all at once.

Unknown to me, Steve Torres was headed into Ozona as it was getting around lunch time. All three of us met on a near collision course at the top of the hill for the Pandale Overpass. Steve saw he had a real mover, engaged the overheads on his Crown Vic, and turned hard left across the median to give chase.

And in doing so, he was right in the middle of both westbound lanes when I bounded over the hill.

I had the radio mike in my hand to advise any units ahead of my developing situation, and ended up screaming exactly five words into it.

"Steve!!! Get outta the way!!!"

Steve heard me and headed for the shoulder as I shot past, right foot still in the fuel injection system. The cyclist had seen Steve's overheads and was putting the spurs to his Ninja.

We had a real pavement scorcher going now.

Changing frequencies I advised Ozona that I had a pursuit in progress, gave my location and speed and asked about any other units to the west.

Les Hale was working the console, and advised Steve Torres was in front of me.

"Not anymore he ain't," I replied laconically.

By habit, I checked my rear view mirror. Steve's Ford was nowhere in sight. Then another bit of gleeful news, Les reported there were no other units in front of me for at least another forty miles.

Meanwhile, four more miles had gone by in somewhat less than two minutes. The Kawasaki still hadn't seen my unit and since neither of us could see Steve, the rider slacked off. This gave me the opportunity to reel in the distance and I settled in about an eighth of a mile behind, traveling around 130 MPH.

At this speed I figured he could still accelerate away from Ol' Rocket Sled a bit, but on the big end our respective numbers would be about the same. Plus I knew near every road in the 3,000 odd square miles making up Crockett County, and he didn't. No matter where he went, I'd still be with him.

And maybe, just maybe, when he realized a unit was already traveling at high speed behind him, he might give it up.

It was decision time. My right index finger rested on the rocker switch controlling the red and blues in my grille, the finger tapping lightly as I weighed the possible ramifications. My mind made up, I pushed down and the rider's head snapped to his rear view mirror.

With no hesitation whatsoever his right hand rotated to full throttle. The race was on.

I matched his speed until he flattened out around 150 MPH. Most people, even officers who drove the Caprice LT1, never realized there was a speed limiter on those cars set at 147 MPH, owing to the speed rating for the tires.

From prior experiences I did happen to know that, and I also knew if you feathered the gas pedal just right, you could get 148-149 MPH out of those cars.

I started feathering that pedal.

Another couple of miles in less time than it took to tell it, the cyclist made the deciding error. He took the Live Oak Overpass exit with half a mind to try evading on the secondary roads, and had to brake hard to do so. Going though the curve, he was traveling so fast his left knee was nearly touching asphalt.

I hit that ramp at 110 miles an hour right behind him, and felt all four Goodyears start to drift.

'Better hold on to this thing, cowboy,' I remember thinking. *'Or they'll end up naming this exit ramp after you.'*

Ol' Rocket Sled steadied herself and now we were all over that motorcycle. Seeing us rapidly overtaking his Ninja, the driver elected to jump back on the interstate.

But this time we were on him.

As the Ninja regained the main lanes for I-10, I crawled up on the steering wheel with a single thought in my head:

'All right, rabbit. Run!'

And run he did, but not with the same speed as before. Something was going wrong with his engine and when I realized this, I started grinning.

He made it back to 140 MPH before I noted the slimmest sign of smoke coming out of his tailpipe. The trail of smoke quickly became larger and so did that grin on my face. I knew then his Kawasaki wasn't long for this world.

Another mile or so the bike was slowing down to around 110. I unholstered my Sig pistol, eased up beside him in the other lane, rolled down the power passenger window and let him see my intentions were serious.

Then he made his second deciding error and it was nearly a fatal one. The cyclist let go of the handle bars and put both hands up in the air.

Again, at one hundred and ten miles an hour.

The bike immediately started into a wobble, and I yelled at him for being such an idiot. He might have heard me, because his hands went back to those handlebars in record time, and the motorcycle straightened out again. Seconds later he was on the brake and pulling over.

That little dance of near death took away the last of whatever resolve he might have still possessed about running.

More so, that ailing crotch rocket was seconding the motion.

Not knowing what I had other than someone who really did not want to pull over, I went into full felony takedown mode as the bike rolled to a stop. In short order he was belly down facing away from me, legs spread out and arms wide with palms up.

About that time, I heard the faintest sound of a siren echoing up the canyon. It was Steve Torres announcing his arrival, and there lies the crucial difference between a near-decade old Chevrolet Caprice LT1 and a near-new Ford Crown Victoria in those days.

Steve helped me with the handcuffing and pat down for our catch of the day, who was evidently waking up to the sad fact of how much trouble he had gotten himself into.

Over and over the young male kept saying "I didn't know they made a patrol car that would run that fast."

A check through DPS Communications revealed the subject had a suspended driver license, which he readily admitted to. He stated this was the reason he ran, and he knew he could outrun Steve's Crown Vic. Furthermore, he never saw my Caprice until I was behind him and turned my grille lamps on.

Then he said it once more for good measure: "I didn't know they made a patrol car that would run that fast."

I loaded him up for the ride to the county jail while Steve waited for the duty wrecker to arrive. We visited on the way in, and I learned he was a college student at Texas A&M. Polite in both manner and speech, he kept looking around the Caprice's interior as if searching for something to help with his open disbelief.

Finally, he shrugged his shoulders and stared out through the windshield. Once again he said: "I didn't know they made a patrol car that would run that fast."

I couldn't help myself by this time.

"Believe it," I responded.

He glanced over to me sharply while I remained looking ahead, watching the traffic. A long moment or so later, he was doing the same.

Pulling into the sally port at the county jail, I helped him out of the Chevrolet and headed inside for booking and lock up. Pablo Talamantez was the duty jailor, and a man who has been my friend for many years. One of his sons, Jimmy, would ultimately join the Marine Corps and later become a highway patrolman in Del Rio.

Pablo would sometimes give me grief about that, saying I had been a bad influence.

When I brought the cyclist in, Pablo had the proverbial curiosity of a cat.

"Why'd you run from this man?" was nearly his first question.

Of course, the response had to include a "I didn't know they made a patrol car that would run that fast."

Pablo laughed, showing his teeth and grinning. "College boy, you're lucky he wasn't driving that old Dodge Charger of his!"

The kid looked back over to me, his own curiosity piqued.

"Yeah," Pablo continued, warming to the subject. "He's a bad influence on young people. If you are around him long enough, he'll make you want to do something really stupid like join the Marines or the Texas Highway Patrol."

Now it was my turn to grin, and shake my head.

Pablo finished the book in process and led the kid down the hallway to his cell. After he returned, we visited. Talamantez wanted to hear what happened, as all he knew was what he gathered from my radio transmissions.

He also confirmed what DPS Communications had already told me. My prisoner had no criminal record. In fact, no record at all save for some traffic violations and the suspended driver license.

The jailor sighed, a man who when younger had taken a ride or two on the wild side himself, and now the father of sons who were much the same.

"Maybe he'll learn something, Ben." Pablo commented.

"Don't we all?" I mused.

"Yeah, if we live long enough. Pulling both hands off a motorcycle at a hundred and ten and going into a death wobble? That boy don't know how lucky he was."

"Nobody hurt, nobody dead, other than a completely roasted Kawasaki."

Pablo laughed again and said "And that's no great loss."

"Yep, I agree." I reached over and put my hat on my head.

"Where you going?"

"Why, back to work!" I exclaimed. "I can't sit in a nice, comfy jail all day long. There's real crime fighting to be done out there, you know."

"Just remember Speed Cop," Pablo retorted. "You're never too old to do something stupid!"

And as usual, Pablo was right. No one is ever really too old to do something stupid.

Including joining the Marine Corps or the Texas Highway Patrol.

IN THE HIGHEST TRADITION...

There are some men who fit a certain uniform so well, both in appearance and character, they seem to be born to it. So it was with Cody Cory, though in his case twice over. You see, Cody had been a grunt in the Marine Corps before joining the Texas DPS and fit either cut equally well. Not only in the manner of being recruiting poster material, but also with a special determination and raw courage that burned inside.

A big, strapping young man built like an escapee from the front cover of a Louis L'Amour western, I first met Cody when he was going through recruit school. He made a lasting impression on me, an impression that only deepened and solidified with the passage of time. There are some men in this world who will do to ride the river with, while the vast majority are best left ashore and safely out of the way.

Cody Cory is the kind of man you want around to ride any river, cross any desert or climb any mountain. This story will help explain why.

The Saturday of May 4, 2002 was just a bad one all the way around for THP Area 4B07. I had been called out early to a wreck northwest of Ozona, then later dispatched to assist Robert Bybee on a fatality in the far corner of Schleicher County. After that, I went home upon finishing a full shift and then some.

But the day was not near over for some other troops in my sergeant area, and especially for Cody.

Early that afternoon he responded to a reported motor vehicle accident with injuries, about fourteen miles east of Sonora on Interstate 10. Even while still some miles out, he could see a solid plume of black smoke rising into the sky.

Arriving on scene, Cody observed a late model white Ford Explorer impacted hard against a rock wall cut for the highway right-of-way. The vehicle had sustained tremendous damage to the front and leading sides, and the engine compartment was aflame.

People were running frantically about, trying to put out the fire as well as assist the badly injured driver trapped inside. Traffic was reduced to one lane owing to the thick smoke, and an assortment of vehicles were parked haphazardly by those trying to help.

Meanwhile, other citizens were stopping commercial trucks to obtain more fire extinguishers. Amid the excited shouts, curses and pleas for assistance were empty canisters littering the ground around the demolished SUV, testimony to the multiple efforts already made to suppress the developing flames.

Due to the congestion, Cody had to park his patrol unit some distance away from the wreck. Grabbing his own fire extinguisher from the trunk, he headed into the spreading chaos and panic at a full run. The Texas Highway Patrol had arrived in the outsized presence and purpose of a single man.

The trooper first discharged his extinguisher into the engine compartment, but with nil effect. The gasoline-fed blaze continued to gorge itself greedily.

Cody moved quickly to the passenger side of the Ford, as the driver's door was wedged tightly against the rock wall. Inside alone and behind the wheel was a large male in his fifties, bordering on obesity. The man, terrified of the flames and in agony from his severe injuries, was screaming for someone to help him.

The trooper began trying to calm the driver, and to ascertain his condition. When Cody advised they needed to get him out, the injured man screamed his foot was trapped under the seat of the vehicle.

Peering inside the crushed Ford, Cody could not see past the dash and console shoved back and over the driver. The mass of the man's body was concealed by the destruction, and the doors on the passenger side remained jammed shut.

Sizing up the situation, the trooper realized the only way to bring the man out was through the driver's door, still solidly emplaced against the rock wall. He also surmised his window of opportunity to do this was shrinking rapidly, as the conflagration under the Explorer's hood continued to grow in strength.

Rushing back to his patrol car, he contacted Sutton County S.O. to determine status and location of the volunteer rescue team. Their response made a very bad situation far worse, no one from the volunteer unit had answered the call. Looking to the wrecked Ford he could see the fire still spreading, and hear the piteous pleas of the driver shrieking for help.

However, others were listening to Cody's radio traffic and of the ominous report that no other assistance was available. Kurt Knapp was on patrol in Crockett County and upon hearing the broadcast, pointed the nose of his black and white east and laid that hammer down as far as it would go.

Thinking back some twenty years later, Cody reminisced:

"To this day I can still see a clear line in men I meet. There are men who will quietly sit by the radio and listen to chaos ensue, unsure of what to do.

Then there are men like Kurt; who hear a slight change of inflection in your voice and drive from fifty miles away as fast as a car will go, loading guns and charging head first into the hell they had no part in creating, to try to save you.

The world is less without him around."

DPS Ozona Communications was also listening in. The PCO on duty immediately paged Norbert Ortiz, our Sutton County night unit. But Kurt was still fifty miles away and Norbert twenty, and whatever was going to be done to save that driver had to be done now.

Upon receiving Sutton County's response, Trooper Cory grabbed a big hammer and wrecking bar he kept in his patrol unit, and charged into the fray once more.

The vehicle fire was gaining ground against all efforts, but he specifically tasked a couple of citizens to flag over the passing trucks for more extinguishers. While Cody realized they could never get ahead of the blaze, more extinguishers might buy them another minute or two to do what needed done.

In the same continuum of requests, suggestions and commands, he turned to a pair of citizens who had been with him from the very beginning, and who happened to have a one ton dually truck parked nearby.

Upon being asked, they said they also had a chain of sufficient length.

Explaining his developing plan in the briefest of words, he had the truck chain up to the back bumper of the Explorer and drag the SUV away from the wall. But while successful in doing so, Cody was then confronted with a driver's door that was nigh melded to the rest of the Ford's body.

In the Marine Corps infantry, we have a saying that goes back for generations of grunts: '*Improvise, adapt and overcome.*' At this critical moment, I am certain Cody was thinking along those exact same lines. More so, he was acting upon them.

Taking the hammer and wrecking bar, he tried to first break the door latch but was unsuccessful. Seeing the fire working its way into the passenger side of the interior, he grabbed another extinguisher and ran over to cover that spot. The dry particles from the canister slowed the infiltration of the blaze, but in some ways the accompanying dust made his fast-devolving predicament even worse.

Running back to the driver's side, the highway patrolman began pulling at the top of the door frame with his bare hands. Cody Cory was, and is a powerful man, and with adrenaline boosted strength he managed to begin peeling the upper door frame away from the Explorer.

While the two citizens held the emerging gap open, Cody was able to wedge his body between the roof and upper door. Assuming a modified weightlifter's squat, muscle and sheer grit made sheet metal and steel give way, forcing the gap wide enough for him to crawl partially inside head first, and examine the driver's floorboard.

Once in that somewhat precarious position, the trooper could see how the driver's foot had been grossly dislocated in the crash, and was jammed up securely under the bottom of the seat.

As the flames ate their way into the interior of the Ford, Cody struggled and pulled with all his remaining strength to free the man's foot. Between the smoke, damage to the vehicle and extinguisher residue he was now using the sense of feel more than his eyes, and he could also feel the heat from the fire only a few scant inches from his back.

To Cody, it was obvious he would not be able to free the foot and get the man out. His vision was blurring, his strength was failing him and the heat was becoming intense. He had run out of time.

Remembering that awful moment all these years later, Cody recalled:

"I told him that if we're going to make it out we had to leave his foot here. The driver nodded to the affirmative."

Hanging upside down, half in and half out of the SUV, Cody somehow managed to grasp his boot knife and began cutting the stretched-out tissue covering the massive dislocation. The driver began screaming again from the pain, and the aluminum grip of his knife became slippery with human blood.

But the trooper wiped what he could away, and continued on with the gruesome task. Grimly he worked the blade into flesh, sinew and bone until he could see where the end of the tibia was, and how only the instep of the man's foot was connected to the rest of the leg. Grabbing the tibia, he used the large bone for leverage and pulled the rest of the foot from under the seat.

The heat inside the vehicle had become unbearable. In the irony of disparate elements that have one common denominator in a fight for survival, the instant the driver was free he began pulling Cody down, much as a drowning person does a would-be rescuer.

The highway patrolman found himself pinned to the floorboard as the injured man climbed up and over him, attempting desperately to pull himself out of the soon-to-be inferno. Now underneath, near on fire with eyes stinging and coughing uncontrollably, Cody found himself fighting for his own life.

With a different kind of fire blazing from within, Trooper Cory was able to shift his position from underneath, take control of the larger, panicked driver and extract both men from certain death.

Just outside of the advancing furnace, the waiting hands of the two civilians awaited them. The badly injured driver was safely carried away and down to ground, where a nurse rendered aid and stopped the bleeding.

I would like to say to the reader that the driver survived, to make this a story with some sort of happy ending. Unfortunately, the harsh realities of an officer's daily life while on patrol triumphed instead. Sometime during the frantic, heroic efforts to save his life, the driver passed away. Massive internal injuries were later determined as the cause of death.

Meanwhile, assistance began to arrive in the presence of those who risked their own lives to come help. Troopers Kurt Knapp and Norbert Ortiz began bringing order to the chaos, taking the necessary actions to keep everyone safe at the scene, and to preclude any further public endangerment. Sutton County

Fire and EMS eventually did arrive, though by this time the Ford Explorer had burned all the way to the tail lights.

While Norbert began the fatality investigation for Cody, Kurt drove Cody home to clean up and change uniforms. Trooper Knapp had to use his rain coat to protect the passenger seat of his unit, as Trooper Cory was near completely covered in blood.

At the Cory residence Kurt waited while Jody, Cody's wife, scrubbed the blood off her husband. Then she helped him into a fresh uniform to send him back out to the scene. Once there, he reassumed his responsibilities as lead investigator of the accident.

Some months later Trooper Cody Cory, THP Sonora, was awarded a Texas Department of Public Safety Director's Citation. This was in recognition for actions taken in a horrendous situation that no one could ever imagine, save for those who have been there themselves. His truly admirable display of determination, fidelity and selfless heroism were not only in the highest traditions of the Texas Highway Patrol, but also the United States Marine Corps.

When we visit, Cody will occasionally refer to me as 'Brother Ben.' Those are words of a bestowment of honor that I hold in the highest esteem.

Trooper Cody Cory, THP

KURT KNAPP

This book has been hard to write at times, and no more so than with the beginning of this story. It is the first of three, interconnecting three men who meant a great deal to me. They were also friends to each other and were in assorted escapades together, including those when I was not around to take notes.

They lived their lives much like the rest of us with the same concerns, difficulties and day-to-day challenges. Each was different from the other in various ways; of different backgrounds, ages, temperament and goals. Yet they were the same in what really mattered in a man, and I think this bound them together from the first time they laid eyes on the others.

Kurt Knapp was the youngest; a tall, gangly baby-faced young man who made you think of someone's kid brother. He seemed to always have an easy going, confident smile that lit up his features and acted as a picture window into the heart inside.

Kurt was only twenty-three when he graduated as part of the B-98 class, at the DPS Academy. It was there he met the second individual in this trilogy, a truly unforgettable man by the name of Carl Mayfield. Carl was my sergeant in Ozona, and had been selected as a recruit counselor for Kurt's class. Carl knew the makings of a good hand when he saw one, and recruited Kurt into our area to fill an empty slot.

And boy, did he ever do so.

I was Carl's corporal then, and had a hand in getting Kurt snapped in during his probationary period. There was never a dull moment when Kurt was around, and I think every other veteran troop in the area would agree with that summation. He was always into something, always had an opinion, always with a joke and always with that same mischievous smile on his face.

It was about this same time I became acquainted with the third member of this forming trio. His name was Pat Sirois, a command sergeant major in the United States Army. Pat was nearing retirement and was thinking of becoming a peace officer. He would occasionally spend a couple of days in our home, riding with me while I was on patrol and gleefully playing the part of the proverbial evil uncle to my two sons.

Of course I introduced him to Carl and Kurt, who in turn immediately struck up a friendship with Pat. Peas in a pod, you might say. In my mind, I can still picture Kurt and Pat walking side by side. Kurt ambling along while Pat, who was even shorter than myself, was taking three steps to Kurt's one and both of them swapping stories at a mile a minute pace, and both grinning hugely while listening to the other.

One day Carl decided he needed to do a supervisor's check ride on Kurt. Pat was riding with me, so they went east on the interstate and we headed west. About an hour later, DPS Communications radioed for me to get back to the office and report to the sergeant.

Upon arrival we learned that Kurt's Ford had given up the ghost for some unknown reason, and Carl needed my unit to complete the needed check ride. I started to hand him my keys, resolving myself to the task of inglorious paperwork on a simply glorious weekend afternoon. He stopped me from doing so, saying that Pat and I could ride along in the back seat.

So, all four of us clambered into Ol' Rocket Sled and away we went. Kurt not only had his sergeant watching his every move, but also two back seat drivers named Sirois and English, razzing him about anything and everything he did. What a deal for a rookie to find himself in, while trying to impress his boss.

That afternoon was one of the best times I ever had in my entire career, or in my life. I laughed until nearly giggling myself silly at Pat's remarks, Carl's observations and Kurt's retorts. Any conversation about any subject was loaded up with jokes, wisecracks and one liners among three masters of the art, and no sacred cow was left ungored.

Part of the fun was when a traffic stop occurred. THP slick top patrol units were becoming somewhat rare by this time, especially a slick top Caprice with no spot lamps and an odd arrangement of takedown lights mounted in front of the grille. This in itself sometimes caught the offending motorist flat-footed.

But the real surprise was when they pulled over and stopped and not one, nor two, nor even three men stepped out of that patrol unit. There were four, three in uniform and one in civvies who walked around and observed what was happening with an air of good-natured authority.

Some thought he was from the AG office, some thought he was a congressional aide, and one believed he was a fleet representative from General Motors letting us test some sort of new police interceptor.

And who were we to argue with them?

Then we were all back in the Caprice and rolling again while 'debriefing' Kurt. Carl was enjoying himself hugely, still doing his job as a sergeant in working with a rookie, but only taking minor jabs at Kurt for one small thing or the other. Pat, though, was a different story entirely. He noted every movement, every pause, every question or statement and every single word Kurt uttered and made something of it.

Of course, all Kurt could do in return was grin and just shake his head. Lasting friendships were nurtured that autumn day, friendships as well as a special brotherhood that grew only stronger with the passage of time.

The months passed and soon enough Kurt was off probation and working the road on his own. One Tuesday afternoon Carl was off someplace and I was left to check the weekly area reports. Coincidentally, Rocket Sled needed an oil change and service. Kurt was working the same shift as I was, so I dropped off the unit at a local shop and bummed a ride with him over to my residence.

Since it would be a while before the Caprice was ready, I felt the nagging need for some sort of wheels even while assigned office duty. So I tossed my issued rifle and shotgun in the back floorboard of my '71 Charger R/T, and nonchalantly deputized that overbuilt, misshapen god of speed into official duty.

Kurt absolutely loved that old Dodge and thought it was so cool that I would actually use the car for patrol work, even when only going to the office. I told him to be safe and not stir the beans too much, and he drove off with a final remark about the red Charger, grinning all the way.

An hour or so later I was at my desk, suffering the slow death of a thousand paper cuts and wanting to be on the road where I really belonged. Suddenly Frank Galvan, the duty communications operator, started shouting from his console. Kurt had a full carload of *muy malos* pulled over and was calling for backup.

I grabbed my hat and ran for the front door where the Dodge was parked, fumbling for my keys as Frank shouted out more information. There were five males in that one car, and four had prior arrests for some kind of killing. The fifth one had an outstanding felony warrant and also a violent criminal history.

When that punched out 440 Magnum fired I didn't pull out of the parking lot, I launched that Charger. Frank later said it looked like a fighter plane catapulting off a carrier deck. I shot under the overpass for I-10 and hung a hard left into a near perfect four-wheel drift, feeding her just enough gas to keep that Mopar big block out of its natural tendency to understeer.

As I blew past Maness Texaco with tires squalling for mercy, the hand on duty hollered encouragement and gave a big thumbs up. It sure felt a lot better for the soul than checking weeklies, even given the circumstances.

Then down a short straightaway before braking for the narrow entrance ramp onto the interstate. I picked off both apexes in textbook fashion and when that Charger's nose cleared the last curve I was hard on the gas and working that Slap Stick.

The rear end wiggled a bit when I punched the pedal to the floor, but I stayed with it and let the car settle into a straight line again. The tach revved up to 6200 and we upshifted, looking into the horizon and seeing Kurt's red and blues twinkling a good mile and a half away.

The tach climbed up to the redline again, and I hit the shifter once more as the speedometer swung past 120 MPH, then accelerated beyond as that big block dropped into its main power band. The red R/T laid its ears back and was running for the roses, and my peripheral vision narrowed while the speed continued to build.

Another mile further and hard on the brakes again; pumping smoothly to keep them from getting too hot while trying to whoa down all that Mopar momentum. I can see Kurt covering the five with his issued Sig P226, and his body movement is saying he's not messing around. The five males have their hands up, but their body language is saying they ain't quite convinced yet.

The Dodge comes to a smoking, shuddering halt on the caliche shoulder, in a controlled slide the last few feet as I cocked the front wheels full left. Those wheels could give me a little more cover if things happen to go really bad.

Kurt never even looks around; he's watching them like a wired-up mongoose studies a den full of hissing cobras. In one fluid motion my boots hit the ground and up comes the Remington twelve-gauge, chambering a round of triple ought. Kurt barks out a repeated command and I level down with that shotgun.

Whatever recalcitrance they were showing before goes away like empty candy wrappers in a West Texas wind. A twelve-gauge pump tends to have that sort of effect on people, no matter how bad they may think themselves to be.

Once the show was over and the wanted suspect secured, I slapped Kurt on the back for scoring one for the good guys. That was the moment when Kurt christened the Charger R/T.

"I heard The Beast coming when you started out of town" he explained with one of those grins, "And I knew the cavalry was on the way."

And the name stuck, picked up by other area officers and townspeople alike.

From that day forward, that Charger meant something extra to Kurt. He was always asking me about what I had done to it, or passing along compliments about the car he heard from others.

Once I made the mistake of telling him I might sell it one day, same as all those other hot rods that had come along before. Kurt was aghast at the thought, and made his opinion known he didn't think much of that idea.

Looking back now, I am so glad he did.

The months continued on, followed upon by the years. Kurt transferred to Fredericksburg, and he and Jennifer had started a family. One little girl and one little boy.

More time passed. Late one Friday evening I was in the office again, handling some more of that area paperwork that never seemed to cease. Sgt. Mayfield was in his office, doing the same.

The phone rang and I instinctively cleared my mind; thinking it might be a wreck, a motor assist or something along those lines. However when I heard Carl pick up in his office and start talking, I relaxed again.

BLACK AND WHITE

Yet something was wrong, really wrong. And the more I could hear Carl's voice, the more wrong it became. You work with a man long enough in all sorts of serious situations, and you can tell by the inflection in his voice even when you can't make out the words.

And Carl was trying far too hard to sound poised and all business.

As he hung up, he was already calling me into his office. I did not waste any time in doing so. There was an empty, gnawing feeling in my stomach, growing larger as every second passed.

It was a car accident, but not like anything I had been bracing myself for. This one was a lot closer to heart and hearth.

"Kurt's been in a bad wreck outside of Comfort" Carl said, mentally willing himself to keep his voice steady. "It don't look like he's going to make it."

We talked a bit and he gave me the details as he knew them. Kurt was working a STEP program on Interstate 10, and had evidently checked a speeder heading the other direction. It was pouring rain, so he had some speed up to get across the median in case he hit a soft spot.

At some point he lost control of his Crown Vic, and slid into the path of an oncoming vehicle.

After we talked through what we knew, I went back to my desk and tried to force myself to do some of that paperwork. But first I said a prayer for Kurt, and then for Carl as I knew his heart was breaking inside.

This was about all the mental focus I was capable of at that point, as Kurt kept creeping back into my thought processes. Some time later the phone rang again, and again it was for Sergeant Mayfield. The conversation was brief, restrained and numbing in nature. Carl hung up and looked at me for a long moment, steeling himself for what had to be said.

"He's gone, Ben."

That was all Carl could get out before using his right hand to shield his eyes. I let him be and made my way back to my desk.

Then I did the same.

The rest of that shift was spent notifying some of the local people about what happened. Kurt had been well known and well liked in Ozona, and Carl drew up a list of names for me to break the news to in person.

The state of Texas lost a fine young man that night, someone who had so much to offer in so many ways. His wife lost a good husband and their two children would never really get to know their dad. As for me, I lost a friend and the rest of us lost one of the good guys there never seems to be enough of.

Rest easy, Kurt. The Beast is still in my garage, safe and sound and standing ready for duty.

Those keys will never see another pocket as long as I'm still breathing.

*Trooper Kurt David Knapp, Texas Highway Patrol
End of Watch May 8th, 2004*

HURRICANE RITA

I was supposed to go to New Orleans and help with recovery efforts involving the aftermath from Katrina. After seeing all the excitement on FOX News reference the Big Easy as well as what was occurring throughout southern Louisiana, I promptly called Sergeant Mayfield and volunteered my professional services.

Well, actually that is not exactly true. To be more precise, I also volunteered my newest rookie partner, Ryan Dalton. There was a price to be paid when someone had me for a field training officer, and this was prima facie proof.

Three times the word came we were going. Three times we were then told to stand back down. Ryan and I became experts at packing and unpacking our Crown Victoria, using every square inch of available space.

Upon hearing of our possible shipping out for disaster relief duty, co-workers and citizens reached in their pockets and purchased supplies to take with us. Bottled water, food snacks, mosquito repellant, cans of Fix-A-Flat, Handi Wipes and all sorts of basic medicine cabinet items. People's hearts in Crockett County are as big as their native West Texas, and we soon had far more supplies than what we knew to do with.

Yet we still had not made it any further than the east county line, before somebody called us back.

I lived out of my old Marine Corps sea bag sitting by the front door of our home for over a week, until word was passed down that we were definitely not going. Even so I kept everything packed for another two Sundays, just in case. When the following Monday rolled around, I finally decided it was safe to put my gear away.

The next morning Ryan and I were at intoxilizer recertification in San Angelo. During a break I was told to call Sergeant Mayfield in Ozona. When he picked up the phone, he started the conversation with one of his characteristic chuckles fairly dripping with irony. Evidently there was another hurricane entering the Gulf of Mexico, called Rita. Our orders were to report to the DPS Academy in Austin on Friday, and we headed back for Ozona and started packing again.

That Friday morning, we drove to the office, making final preparations to arrive at the academy by mid-afternoon. Area troopers Steve Torres and Rito Renteria were also being sent, so we linked up with them and started east in two separate units.

The four of us stopped at an eating place in Johnson City, and that was where we had our first contact with some of the evacuees from the coast. They were tired, frustrated and apprehensive, but also very glad to see us.

Each had their own story to tell. Many spoke of the sadness of having to leave their homes and the fear of what they might find upon their return. Others talked of long lines of traffic, and of being only able to cover a mere eight miles in eight hours. Already there was a growing shortage of available gasoline and food along the evacuation routes.

Most had some place in mind to go, but others didn't. Complicating this situation was Rita appeared to possess a somewhat fickle nature, and could not make up her mind as to where exactly she wanted to make landfall. Because of this, not only were the Houston and Galveston areas being evacuated, but also many other heavily populated locales along our coast.

The logistics of moving so many people under such uncertain circumstances was a mind-boggling task, but we as a state were getting it done. Texans are a resolute lot by nature, we come by it honestly due to shared history and traditions.

The four of us arrived at the academy and made it to our first briefing, which really did not tell us a whole lot. Again, this was mainly because no one was quite sure as to where our unwanted guest would come ashore. Afterward I found our field commander, Captain John Madden, and delivered a satellite phone he needed. Madden was taking a strike force of fifty highway patrolmen to an advanced waiting area in Lufkin. They would ride out the storm there.

With a gathering combined force of over five hundred highway patrolmen and supervisors, the lodging capacity at DPS Academy was already filled. As part of the overflow, the four of us were sent to the nearby Texas Parks and Wildlife dormitory to get some rest. This was the last decent amount of sleep we would have for the next eight days.

My alarm went off at 0630 next morning, and we were back at our academy in time for breakfast and another briefing. We were told what we already knew from the latest weather updates, Rita had finally made up her mind and painted a bullseye on the mouth of the Sabine River.

Our Cajun neighbors were being hit yet again, adding to the misery Hurricane Katrina had brought less than a month before. Near ground zero and on our side of the Sabine was Port Arthur. Concern was already growing for this heavily populated as well as industrialized area, as real time reports had Rita raising tremendous havoc there.

We received our assignments breaking us down into groups of ten troops, each led by a highway patrol sergeant. Todd Jennings would lead ours. I had worked with Todd on several prior occasions and was confident in being a part of his detachment. The other two sergeants from our district were John Land and Don Graham, who had proven themselves on our Civil Disturbance Management Team many times.

If anything else, we were going to be working for some competent people.

BLACK AND WHITE

In this briefing we learned where we would go next: Houston. Bags packed, gassed up and ready to go, we formed into a six vehicle convoy, five black and white units led by Todd's unmarked Dodge Intrepid. Leaving the academy and pointing our noses east on U.S. Highway 290, we quickly began merging with other convoys of six, then twelve, then fifty DPS patrol vehicles heading in the same direction.

Almost immediately we hit the first snag of the operation, which subsequently earned the title of Problem Number One. Tens of thousands of evacuees, learning that Rita has spared the Houston area, now clogged the roadways trying to get home. Our convoy, still gaining in numbers, snaked though their midst with red and blues activated and sirens blaring.

We ran in the inner lane, then the outer, then on improved shoulders or by making our own roads in the barrow ditches. Time was of the essence, as the plan was to be moving into the affected area even as Rita was clearing. But we could not make any real speed as we couldn't get the civilian vehicles to give way. The tension rose and our radios crackled with terse instructions, lead vehicles were to force their way through if need be.

But such drastic measures were not needed as our intentions dawned on the civilian motorists and the lanes began to clear. Moving along we started picking up speed and within twenty more miles, all the responding DPS vehicles had formed a giant convoy of about 250 patrol cars.

This made for an impressive scene. Texas Highway Patrol units of that time were not low key in either paint scheme or appearance. Body panels were painted in large swaths of contrasting black and white with bold gold emblems on the front doors. For a final touch, both front fenders and the trunk were emblazoned with the words 'STATE TROOPER.'

Every marked unit involved was a late model Crown Victoria, and virtually identical to all the others with matching overheads. In each Ford were two troopers, in full uniform and with their game faces on. Even with nearly twenty years on the job, the sight left me with a lasting memory. A man can do far worse than wear the red patch of a Texas Highway Patrolman.

The crowded lanes began opening up and we were now flying past other traffic at 80, 90 and sometimes 100 miles an hour. Citizens began giving us the thumbs up, or taking our photos. THP units howled in one solid line through towns like Giddings, Brenham and Hempstead, with local police and sheriff's officers blocking major intersections so our progress would not be impeded. Small crowds lined the roadways, smiling and waving and holding makeshift signs on cardboard that read: 'LOOK OUT RITA,' 'DPS ROCKS' and 'GET 'ER DONE.'

Again, the memories that remind a man of what he stood for, and why.

On such a heady entrance we arrived at the regional headquarters in Houston, only to have Problem Number Two raise its ugly head. Availability of gasoline, or lack thereof, was critical. Much of the entire city was deserted and all the stations were closed. The regional headquarters had gas but there were exactly two pumps for over 250 cars, and that sort of math never looks promising.

The line crawled along. Patience in this sort of scenario is not in the vocabulary of most highway patrolmen, and our frustration meters began to peg. Todd Jennings, along with some other first line supervisors, received word about National Guard fuel trucks at the Astrodome. Todd scrambled back to us and said to get there any way we could, and fast.

He did not have to repeat himself.

We arrived at the Astrodome to find another waiting line, yet this one was going much faster. Or at least until we were about the eighth unit back and they ran out of gas.

So, we sat and waited, knowing that precious time and daylight were being wasted. None of us wanted to be a Johnny-Come-Lately and assigned some silly task to just keep us busy or worse yet, be turned back around. Doing some scouting about, we finally located another gas truck before being promptly interceded by a bunch of feds in rental vehicles.

I looked over to Todd Jennings and plainly saw the thought of murder in his eyes. But instead, he struck a deal with the unexpected interlopers and the two groups alternated vehicles to fill their tanks. In the interim, we learned of our location assignment. Port Arthur, that same ground zero for our side of the Sabine. As an aside, we never saw that bunch of feds again.

With full tanks our six units regained I-10 pavement and we put the pedals to the floor. Ahead we could see truly colossal thunderheads staggered at different levels of altitude, as the remnants of Rita drifted north.

Forty miles out we began encountering some of her recent handiwork. Our progress slowed to a near crawl in spots as we eased around collapsed billboards, wadded up road signs and downed light poles. Scattered throughout our route was debris of every description. Gently we tippy-toed through the shrapnel-infested obstacle course, trying to save our near precious tires.

This would become a constant, ongoing task for the next several days.

Our command post was set up in a Holiday Inn located on the northwestern edge of Port Arthur, an improvised CP shared with the Port Arthur Police Department. Other than neighboring local agencies, we were the first outside force to show up. Sizing up the situation, we shoved the ever-present debris out of our way and parked the patrol cars by the Waffle House across the street. More tellingly, we parked by what was left of this establishment.

The Holiday Inn was showing some wear, too. In fact, the entire scene was chaotically off kelter, even eerie. There was no power, the water and sewage systems were not functioning, and incoming reports were constant about blocked roadways and massive damage to the region's electrical grid.

BLACK AND WHITE

What was termed as a 'command post' was much the same. The local officers had no idea as to what happened to their homes and many did not know the exact status of their families. Yet they were still in the game and swinging hard with everything they had. The message was unspoken yet crystal clear, this was not going to be another Orleans Parish and they weren't the New Orleans Police Department.

Sitting in our patrol car on standby, I reverted back to some of my old habits as a grunt in the Marines. We were now where we were supposed to be, so I found something to eat and dug a paperback out, making myself as comfortable as possible. Hurry up and wait was something I had grown accustomed to in my various livelihoods.

A somewhat familiar voice interrupted my reading and I looked up to see Geraldo Rivera, who wanted to know where he could get some gasoline. I started to laugh out loud at this little inside joke, but instead motioned him toward one of the sergeants and got back to my Elmer Kelton novel.

A young trooper walked over and exclaimed in half awe "Ben, that was Geraldo Rivera!" I told him I knew that and continued reading. As a general rule I didn't have much use for most of the mass media, they were usually too busy genning up sensationalist stories to take the time in carefully reporting the facts.

But in Geraldo Rivera's case, I might concede to an exception. Later I would see him in places one does not expect to find a big-time journalist. From what I could observe, he took his responsibilities seriously and was not afraid to get a little dirty in the process. Or to put that mike aside to pitch in and help, if the need arose.

Shortly thereafter a detail of fellow troopers took off for Port Arthur proper. Their mission was to go in now, while the rest of us would relieve them at midnight. A few minutes later we start getting our unit assignments. All they could say about ours was to secure the mall at 39th Street and Jefferson City.

Being the map fiend that I am, I pulled out a previously liberated imprint of the area and quickly found 39th Street. But I could not locate anything referring to a 'Jefferson City.' That made for the unexpected arrival of Problem Number Three.

We were also instructed to relocate our units to a more secluded spot and try to get some rest. I hate it when they say that, as I would much rather proceed to our patrol area and do some reconnoitering while still having daylight. I barely dozed, but Ryan got in a few good winks as we crashed in our units.

With a mind full of possible other problems, options and remedies, I sat there staring out from under the lowered brim of my issued straw hat. It was still very warm and the humidity bordered on near suffocating.

Stepping out of the car, I pulled off my shirt and body armor to air everything out. As if right on cue, I heard an air wing's worth of oversized coastal mosquitoes peeling off to make their runs. It didn't take me long to get back in that Ford, and dig out those cans of insect repellant for future use.

The surrounding area reeked of a wet, moldy odor that seemed to cling to our clothes, as well as the upholstery of our patrol units. It permeated the air you breathed and every pore of your body until it became an open stench.

Thinking back to my Texas history classes, it was little wonder several of the Indian tribes of this region had been cannibals. Perhaps they just had to make somebody else's last remnants of life even more miserable than their own.

Another briefing was given around midnight. Troops were warned about random shots being fired at local PD units and to be doubly on guard during our shift. We were also informed there were no detention facilities available, and to not bring anyone in unless there was no other recourse. Everything was to be handled by our own best judgement.

Midnight found us moving in and attempting to find our assigned positions. Note the word 'attempting,' as many did not have any maps or only those of a basic main highway sort. My recently procured map was best in class, but Jefferson City still remained an unknown.

Of course, there were a lot of unknowns about now. The night was pitch black with no moon and no lights, other than those from other units groping about in the gloom while trying to figure out where they were. Many of the highway signs were missing, as were residential markers and business billboards. Ruptured gas mains hissed in the darkness like hidden nests of giant pit vipers. Downed poles and uprooted trees blocked access to some of the streets, and we had to detour around more than once.

And finally, to add sauce to the goose, were the power transmission lines. These were either snapped off, dangling free or lying across our intended path and were obstacles to be reckoned with all on their own. By now the electrical grid was completely defunct, so there was little chance of summary electrocution for the unwary or unlucky.

Yet they still managed to present a major hazard. The cables were often dark grayish in color, which blended in all too well with the surrounding concrete and asphalt. This proved especially true in the harsh artificial glare of our headlamps and takedown lights. Several local units were damaged or knocked out of service by these slender, camouflaged in open sight booby traps. Our units suffered no such fate, or at least no one admitted to it.

Ryan and I slowly continued up and down 39th Street, at least the parts we could navigate. Large pieces of roofing and siding from surrounding buildings littered our improvised path, slowing our progress even further.

Finally we met up with a local Port Arthur officer and compared notes with him. He quickly decided that someone had gotten their own wires crossed when detailing us out, and what they meant was the Jefferson City Mall located on 39th Street and Twin City Highway.

We asked him to point us in the right direction and he gestured into the blackness, to our immediate southeast. Turned out we had driven along the edge of this five-block long mall at least a half dozen times, during our seemingly fruitless search.

Again, it was that dark on the first night.

Making a quick box recon of the mall we located at least twenty businesses, including three banks and two pawnshops. Directly to the rear was a large apartment complex, and a check of that area revealed many of these folks did not heed the evacuation notice. We made certain the back doors facing the apartments were secure, and selected the best spot offering a broad field of view with a modicum of concealment.

The two of us sat with our windows partially cracked, fogging the interior of the Ford with mosquito repellent while listening for any movement. One thing nice about the endless amount of shattered glass and scattered debris present, it was very hard for anyone to move about undetected.

When the hurricane hit, the local mayor emplaced a curfew from 7:00 at night until 6:00 in the morning. This did not help our day shifts much, but it was a highly effective tool for us nighthawks. We saw four vehicles during our shift and four traffic stops followed. Three were legitimate, employees of refineries and public works trying to get their plants up and running again.

However, the fourth was iffy. We could not run computer checks on him or his vehicle, due to the damage done by Rita to our regional communications system. We shook him down and examined the car as much as legally feasible, but came up with little more than a bad gut feeling.

So, we kicked him loose after discussing a hypothetical scenario, and what could happen to him in that same imagined situation. I was never sure if my impromptu surmisings did any real good, but we didn't see him or that vehicle again.

During our shift, we met a pair of Port Arthur officers basically working the same beat as our assignment. They gave us a good deal more information about the mall and confirmed our earlier suspicions concerning the apartment complex. Our teaming up worked well, we were glad to be there and they were definitely happy to have us around.

At about 4 a.m. a clicking noise from the left front of our Ford announced the troublesome birth of Problem Number Four. I knew what it was even before climbing out to take a look. Sure enough, we had a large roofing nail in the tire.

The good news was it did not appear to be leaking. The bad news was the nail was buried in the sidewall, ruining an almost new Goodyear Eagle GT.

Shortly after 6 am we stood relieved by the day shift and limped our Crown Vic back to the Holiday Inn.

When we arrived, the building was still in an awful mess. The conference room for the hotel was now an ad hoc nerve center for our combined recovery operations. It had very little lighting, no air conditioning, no running water and plenty of damage left by the storm.

Everyone had been working without rest in trying to improve the situation, but little progress was being made. Those present were facing a host of monumental tasks with little more than the determination in getting the job done.

I scrounged some bottled water and a few snacks while Ryan gassed up the Ford, and we tried to find out where we could get the tire replaced. For now, there was no such luck. Scuttlebutt had it DPS Headquarters sent out a mobile repair crew for our units, but such a visionary thought was short on reality. The tire was still not leaking so we moved on.

The troops from our night shift were all dog tired and looking for a place to rest their heads. Unfortunately, 'there was no room at the inn,' to borrow a phrase. So, we made our way to a nearby parking lot, circled the wagons and crashed in our patrol cars.

Each unit was so loaded down with gear and supplies that we couldn't lay our seats back, so we pulled our shirts and body armor off and just tried to relax. The ambient temperature was already hovering around ninety degrees with about the same level of humidity, and we sat in those metal boxes with glass windows under an unrelenting sun, trying to get some shuteye.

Any sane person could see Problem Number Five evolving. We finally opened our hoods for better air flow, and left the engines and a/c systems running. Again, the cars were really cramped, even for a small guy like me. Crown Vic front seats are nowhere near best in class, and the headrests are at the wrong angle for anything other than neck pain. Also, there was no way to position your legs without your knees and ankles letting you know it wouldn't work.

I put my uniform hat over my face for a little shade and started to doze off, staring at the inside of a Resistol and wondering if forty-seven was getting too old for this kind of carrying on.

The insistent knocking on a passenger window about a half hour later brought me into a fatigue-induced fog. It was Todd Jennings, saying some rooms had been found but we needed to move fast to claim them. Ryan and I immediately bailed out of the black and white, trying to wake ourselves up as we followed along behind.

Our detail gathered together at what was normally the front desk. We stood there in anticipation, noting what the passage of time and temperature level was doing for the hotel's degrading scent. It reeked of something associated with wet gym towels that had been allowed to sit for too long; except this was far, far worse. Joining in on the odorous chorus, was the backed up sewage in the nearby men's room under constant use.

However, improvements were being made even as we waited for those rooms. Some of the mess was being cleaned up and generators wired into the hotel's electrical system. One of the conference rooms adjoining our makeshift CP had bottled water, soda pops, junk food snacks and sandwich makings. I managed to lay hands on a somewhat bruised banana and felt like a king.

While stuffing my face full of my new prize, Sergeant Land told me how those rooms suddenly became available. Originally the hotel floor in question had been appropriated by the media, to keep close to the action occurring inside the command post.

Turned out it was a little too close, our people in the CP couldn't pass gas without somebody's microphone picking it up. The local officers strung 'Police Only' yellow tape to cordon the section off, but to little real effect. So the entire mass media contingent was unceremoniously booted out to make room for us. I was not certain if it was this karma-like news flash or the recently consumed banana, but I was starting to feel all sorts of warm and fuzzy inside.

Minutes later Ryan and I received the room number, sharing our four walled treasure with Trooper Lopez from Abilene. Though the room itself was smelly, hot and dirty, it did have real beds and a decent couch for sleeping. Compared to the front seat of a black and white Crown Vic, our new digs were downright palatial.

First though, we had to do a little house cleaning. Judging by the number of empty beer cans and bottles of booze, the prior tenant had a real drinking problem or was in the middle of a little hurricane party. Reminding myself as to who the likely culprits were, I seized upon a theory as to why they never seemed to get a story straight. The three of us hit the sack at about 11 am and began making up for lost sleep.

That lasted until around three in the afternoon. Though the portable generators were working, it was barely enough to keep the room livable. The windows could not be opened and even if possible, the combined outside air temperature and humidity made for a heat index of 115 degrees.

The weather stayed like this for the next several days. Each of us kept waking up and wiping the sweat away before dozing off again. I finally gave in and got up, grabbing my washrag and shaving kit for a stroll downstairs. In the aforementioned men's room was a trickle of cold water suitable for a shave and rag bath. Then some black Kiwi polish on my boots and I was good to go again.

Ryan and I set out for the reported DPS repair truck, and found both truck and crew behind the hotel. They were having their own battles; the heat, the lack of sleep, the constant demands for service and the little to no spare anything. All they could do was pull the nail, stick in a plug and hope for the best.

I asked them what they needed most and some of their requests were simple stuff. We went back to the hotel and started scrounging, returning with our arms full. They were grateful and we made some acquaintances that would come handy. After all, these were the folks who made the wheels literally go around.

We stashed away some more snacks and bottled water in the Ford, and downed a makeshift meal in the CP area. By 6 pm we were back at Jefferson City Mall and relieving the day shift.

But some of the night units were not patrolling far, as they are sucking on fumes and gasoline was nowhere to be found. Those with less than a quarter tank were instructed to ease into their areas and remain stationary until more fuel arrived. Dalton had topped off our tank that morning so we were in fine shape. However, gasoline would continue as an ongoing concern for our operations.

This was the first opportunity we had to actually see the area by daylight. In my time I have navigated a lot of rough country at night, only to find my back trail looking even more so with the coming of day. This was one of those times. That mall and the surrounding locales had been totally plastered by the huge storm.

Many of the stores had windows knocked out, signage missing and siding blown away, while others were demolished. This go-round the two of us scouted the entire complex on foot, long guns at the ready. During our prowl, we discovered where a vehicle had been driven through the front doors of a grocery store.

By looking at the muddy tracks, I speculated this was done right after Rita passed through. One would hope they were after food, but the evidence pointed toward lottery tickets. We found no one around and moved on, making a mental note for future reference.

Since we had a little daylight to play with, we loaded back into the patrol car and began a mounted recon of the outer surroundings. About three blocks north of the mall we found a couple of new car dealerships. The Chevrolet house was much akin to some of those stores in the mall, and nothing remained of the building other than a partially collapsed shell. Their inventory had been moved elsewhere.

A bit farther on we came across a competing Ford dealership, complete with close to a dozen new Mustangs parked out front. This caught Dalton's eye, as he had a yearn in the worst way for a Mustang GT with a manual transmission. I stopped and he scrambled out to scout the premises and those new iron ponies. After checking around for any looters, we continued on.

BLACK AND WHITE

It was starting to get dark again, and the overall atmosphere was way over to the creepy-crawly side. There was no traffic, no lights and no moon. Nothing but varying degrees of destruction everywhere you looked. You also didn't see any people but you knew they were out there, watching. My mind went back to a post-apocalyptic film from the early 1970s entitled *The Omega Man*. All we needed was a bunch of night zombies wandering around to match the movie's story plot.

As the blackness enveloped us, we managed to link up with our local police compatriots from the night before. With us holding close to the mall and they in roving mode, our combined coverage was fairly effective. Radio communications were still mostly defunct, no traffic allowed unless declaring an emergency.

So, our response plan was simple, whoever got into something would hit their lights and siren and the other unit would zero in on those. The tactic was somewhat primitive and definitely not stealthy, but for now the only ball game in town.

The interesting stop of the evening came when I spotted a big, rusted out, ratty looking Delta 88 four door driving slowly along the Twin City Highway. There was a bit of time-honored cop math which figured 'one big, rusted out, ratty looking Oldsmobile usually equals to at least one felon,' so we pounced along with our neighboring PD unit.

Upon doing so we were confronted with the nastiest bunch of semi-pro dirtbags we had come across so far. Our sense of smell was absolutely overcome by a rancid combination of dirt, alcohol, urine and yes, human vomit. With bloodshot, bugged out eyes, long greasy hair standing on end, filthy clothes and missing a couple of front teeth each, the Oldsmobile's occupants made for a sorry sight indeed.

Now, what was I saying about that movie and night zombies?

Anyway, we checked their IDs, emptied their beers, patted them down and searched their car, and let the PD guys read them a memorable riot act with emphatic as well as colorful language. After doing so, we cut them loose.

We never saw this bunch again, either.

Later on the word was passed down that gasoline was in supply again. We really didn't need any, but had the PD unit cover for us so we could top off. This became a habit of necessity, due to unpredictability of gas being available. None of us wanted to be caught flat-footed in an emergency situation.

The rest of the night was exasperatingly quiet, and by the end of the shift our biggest enemy was boredom. Once relieved we drove back to the CP, fighting droopy eyelids all the way in.

I awoke the next afternoon feeling more refreshed than in the past few days. The air conditioning was staying on most of the time and we actually had tap water in our bathroom. More so, it was hot water.

After a badly needed shower and another shave, I made my way downstairs to the command center. One of the local officers present told me about hot chow being served at a place called Sanderson's. Against all odds this establishment had reopened and meals were being cooked by the local fire department, along with some civilian volunteers to help feed hungry first responders.

Dalton and I made a bee line and had our first real meal in three days. Everyone was super nice and could not do enough for us. In fact, they were so nice we barely made the evening briefing. Ours was a new assignment, a heretofore unnamed spot called Checkpoint Seventeen. In real world parlance, the location was a mile east of the Neches River Bridge on Texas Highways 73 and 87. This spot was the most remote point of our stationary operations.

We gassed up once more and reported for duty shortly before 6 pm. Checkpoint Seventeen was set up on a divided four lane highway with the westbound lanes blocked off due to high water, so they were running two way traffic through the east lanes.

Our orders were to let no one through other than those involved in recovery efforts. All other vehicles were to be turned around, per decrees from the area mayors. The driver of each vehicle was warned to stay to the right when using those eastbound lanes, we didn't need a head-on collision on top of everything else.

We took over and I was in a particularly good mood. I felt rested, had a hot shower, a shave and a hot meal. Even the weather wasn't too bad, a breeze coming off the water cooled us and gave promise of keeping the mosquitoes at bay later on. It was just too good to last and sure enough it didn't. Problem Number Six was less than twenty minutes away.

I noted the gray, late model Lincoln Town Car when it pulled up behind some other vehicles at the checkpoint. What caught my attention was the expression on the driver's face, he was already mad clear through. Ryan approached the Lincoln while I handled another vehicle whose occupants only spoke Spanish.

My attention refocused on that Lincoln as things obviously were not going well. Ryan walked over and asked if I could talk to the driver, who was not taking 'no' for an answer. It was a wise decision on Ryan's part, he was fresh out of the academy and still on probation. I could fade a good deal more heat if push came to shove.

I strolled over to the open driver's window, putting on my best West Texas grin in an attempt to preemptively defuse his anger. The driver was a big, older white male and my smile had absolutely no effect. His face looked like a large, ugly thunderhead, signaling everyone in advance that really bad weather was coming.

Politely introducing myself, I asked where he was going.

"Groves!" he barked in a curt, impatient reply.

I proceeded to ask if he was part of any emergency or relief service, or if he might be bringing in any supplies. I felt badly for these poor people and wanted to swing as wide a loop as I could, looking for even half an excuse to let them through.

All I received in return was an angry "No!' and an ill-boding stare.

Now faced with no other option, I began explaining the reason why he couldn't pass through.

The situation was deteriorating rapidly. The driver interrupted my explanation by basically exploding, demanding to know who gave those orders. He was half shouting, half screaming about knowing the mayor and other local officials, and he was not going to put up with this.

I let him rant on a bit before suggesting if he knew the mayor, then he should be able to make contact with hizzoner for permission to come in. Once granted we would be happy to allow him through. However, for now he needed to turn around.

The man began cursing us vehemently, threatening to come through and no one was going to stop him. Blustering with all that he had, he dared us to shoot him for driving through a road block.

I told Ryan to get the Stinger tire deflation system from inside the trunk of the Ford. Taking the contraption from him, I tossed the device across the front of the Lincoln and took about ten steps back.

The driver was warned once more to turn around, before he put himself into a really bad situation. In response he began shaking his head from side to side like a maddened Brahma bull, yelling he was coming through and we would have to shoot him.

Meanwhile Ryan, seeing it all headed due south, reached in the Crown Vic for our Remington 870 and went to port arms. When the driver of the Lincoln saw the shotgun, he went absolutely berserk.

Purple faced with gobs of spittle flying, he shrieked out a continual string of obscenities when he wasn't daring us to kill him. With all self-control gone, the enraged man suddenly announced he wasn't scared of our guns because he had one too.

His right hand came up in a fist, clenching a revolver.

At that precise moment everything went into slow motion, kind of like an action sequence from a Sam Peckinpah movie. I still don't remember palming my pistol, the Sig P226 just appeared in my left hand with the sights lined up on the driver's nose. Off to my left, I heard the doomsday echo of a load of triple ought slamming home as Ryan worked the shotgun.

All the while my mind was racing forward, far ahead of my physical reactions. As I gathered up the trigger to the Sig, those thoughts braked hard and seized on a bit of information that would save someone's life today.

The old man's revolver was a Colt New Police .32 from the late nineteenth century. On a good day with fresh ammunition, that gun had about as much chance of penetrating the Lincoln's sloped windshield as I did spitting through it. And this was the only way the seated driver could presently engage us.

Then I was the one screaming, shouting at Ryan not to shoot.

I have described Ryan Dalton several times as a rookie, a young man of twenty-five just five months out of our academy. Such was really not a fair description, as my youthful partner had a five-year hitch in the Marine Corps in hell holes like Afghanistan and Iraq. For some instinctive reason that God only knows, he did not let go with that fatal load of buckshot.

If you are looking for a hero on that day, look to Trooper Ryan Dalton. Too many others would have fired anyway be it out of frustration, fear or perceived self-preservation.

Yet what we were facing was far from over. As lead officer I was doing most of the talking, ordering the driver to put the gun down. The old man was still cursing and threatening us with every word he spat out, waving the Colt around wildly and shaking his head from side to side. The growing chant of "go ahead and kill me" was his one continuing refrain.

Among law enforcement circles this refrain has another name: 'suicide by cop.'

We backed away to the Crown Vic and I told Ryan to turn the video system on, radio for assistance and ditch that shotgun for our Mini-14. We were now close to sixty feet away, and at that range I had seen buckshot fail to penetrate car bodies. Meanwhile I kept my sights square on the driver's nose, repeatedly instructing him to put the gun down. In response was a never-ending outpouring of rage and defiance.

Our state of affairs was evolving into the proverbial Mexican stand-off. If he stepped out of the Lincoln with that gun, he was going to get shot. If he tried to maneuver the car so he could engage us through an open window, he was going to get shot. If he accelerated the car toward us, he was going to get shot. Other than that, we held our fire and let him continue venting.

The old man was slowly lowering the Colt below dash level, which I considered a hopeful sign. But he was still full of some sort of malignant fury that borders on temporary insanity. At one point he began to taunt me, yelling I did not have the guts to shoot someone.

I distinctly remember thinking at that juncture, *'I can't believe this guy.'*

I knew help was coming. One of the first commandments in my line of work was to slow the action down, time was almost always on our side. As if to vindicate that philosophy a local reserve officer was driving by, saw what was happening, and blocked the roadway further to our east. If enough units arrived for a combined show of force, we might resolve this without someone being killed.

But the driver had other ideas. Somewhere in his stressed-out mind he must have decided now was a good time to leave. He put the Town Car in reverse and started backing up, but I was anticipating that sort of move. No one was going to leave this checkpoint after pulling a gun on me.

I shifted my sights to his right front tire. A smooth, steady squeeze and the Sig pistol bucked, sending a .357 slug into the tread. I rode the recoil down, realigned on the left front and squeezed again. The second round took out that tire.

The Lincoln stopped briefly, and the driver looked around like he was trying to spot cross traffic. At the same time, I put my sights on the center mass of his head. I found myself marveling that I could actually hear those front tires losing air. Normally, those same two shots with no hearing protection would have had me partially deaf on a training range. Yet now I could hear air escaping at this distance.

Amazing.

The gray Town Car started backing again and I fired a third time, busting the left rear. Ryan, pulling a little flanking maneuver, put a pair of rifle rounds in the right rear. The Lincoln braked to a stop once more and the driver looked quizzically at me for a long moment, then demanded to know if I had shot off all his tires.

"Yes sir, sure did!" I hollered back, neglecting to add that he might be next if he did not knock this nonsense off.

However, there was no need to. When I answered in the affirmative, his demeanor changed completely. He went from a raging, dangerous lunatic to being just a confused, befuddled old man. All the fire and bluster was gone, quenched by a dawn of reason following a dark, storm filled night. The change was jarringly abrupt and, in a way, somewhat troubling.

The driver's shoulders slumped in resignation and he stepped slowly out of the gray car, leaving his revolver on the front seat. Advising Ryan to cover me I made my approach, holstering my pistol when coming within arm's reach. He was pinned against the Town Car and taken to the ground, cuffed and patted down.

It was over with.

Reaching in the open driver's door, I pulled out the old Colt. Opening the cylinder, I ejected the six round nosed lead cartridges and looked at the head stamps. 'Colt .32 Peters' they read. Good grief, how long had it been since this caliber was sold under the Peters trademark? The revolver and ammunition were secured and we waited for the cavalry to arrive.

And then my own quiet rage came, silently settling upon me like the pall of death itself. That old man had come within an eyeblink of forcing me to kill him.

Within a few more minutes we had two captains, a lieutenant, three sergeants, several troopers and at least a dozen local officers on the scene. It must have been a slow night every place else but here. Captain Paul Davis, once a rookie sergeant in Ozona, took me over to the side. After hearing my story, he asked incredulously why I did not shoot the driver. I replied it was not necessary to accomplish the mission.

For a long moment he studied the cuffed figure being interviewed by Sgt. Land, shook his head and walked away.

After that interview, John Land informed me the driver said the incident was all his fault. He was already mad and could not control his temper, and could not force himself to back down. Both he and the Lincoln were hauled away and Sergeant Frye, the Bridge City area sergeant, began the required shooting investigation. Meanwhile Sergeant Land advised Ryan and I to top off magazines and get back to work. We were shorthanded and could write our statements later.

Land started for his unmarked unit and then called my name. Looking around, I saw him grinning, giving me the thumbs up. I had known John Land for a long time and respected him, and that simple gesture of support felt better than any Director's Citation ever could.

A couple of troopers stayed with Dalton while I went into Bridge City with Brad Frye, to secure our evidence at the local PD. That night, Ryan and I took turns handwriting our statements by the glow of the Crown Vic's interior light, still manning Checkpoint Seventeen.

Later we learned the driver of the Lincoln was seventy-six years old, a Korean War veteran and had no record, not even a traffic violation. But during our near fatal encounter he was an armed, active threat to anyone he might have come into contact with. This fact reminded me of a life's lesson learned long ago. Basically good, decent people do desperate things when believing they were in a desperate situation.

And desperate people can make for very dangerous folks.

The rest of our shift was punctuated by other strange occurrences throughout the night. At around 2:30 am a small blue car flew past at flank speed, not touching the brakes until barreling through the 'Road Closed' barricades. The driver skidded to a stop, and Ryan jumped in our unit to investigate.

At the same time I was dealing with another old, ratty Oldsmobile (remember the cop math rule) crammed with seven males who were redlining my trooper meter. After sending them packing, another car pulled up and the two occupants identified themselves as TABC agents. They were shadowing the Olds for their own purposes, so I briefed them on what I saw and surmised.

Ryan came rolling up as the agents drove away, briefing me on the blue car. It was a refinery hand working some long hours while trying to repair damage caused by Rita. He was for all intents asleep when he blew through those barricades.

About thirty minutes later, the blue car was back again and traveling the opposite direction. The worker pulled up and with a sheepish grin, told us he had forgotten it was his night off. Now he was headed home for some much needed sleep. I said that sounded like a really good plan and the fellow tootled off toward Bridge City, waving a friendly adios.

After those particular incidents, as well as others, I had a new name for Checkpoint Seventeen. I began referring to it as 'Checkpoint Charlie,' which once existed between East and West Berlin. With all that had happened during our shift, I considered the unofficial rechristening an appropriate one.

This was the last night for our version of Checkpoint Seventeen, within hours it was moved farther away from the bridge. In addition, there would be at least three marked units present with high visibility warning signs and traffic cones. Our escapades during that one night alone proved the pressing need.

Back at the hotel, Ryan and I sacked out for some much-needed rest. Yet sleep did not come right away, I lay there thinking through the shooting incident and how really close we came. I realized that had we killed the old man, there was not a grand jury in the state of Texas who would have second-guessed us.

However, I also knew I would not have slept very well for a long time. That self-judgement lingered with me as I drifted off, and I slept well then.

The restful luxury of a clear conscience lasted about five hours before Ryan's cell phone sounded off. It was Sergeant Mayfield, asking to speak to me.

"Ben" the familiar voice drawled, "I sent you down there for recovery efforts, not to shoot up the place."

"Well Sarge, I can't lie to you." I deadpanned in return. "It was Ryan who started it."

Ryan went a little wild eyed as Carl chuckled over the line. We visited for a few minutes more, me covering what happened and my sergeant asking pertinent questions. Once he was satisfied, we were doing well, he hung up.

By then I was wide awake so I got up, grabbed a shave and read for awhile. After that, a short trip down to the CP where I ran into one of the local officers I had visited with before. Upon being asked how things were going he replied "Fine, if we can keep from killing each other."

His stark observation brought home what had occurred since Rita was a category five hurricane positioned off the coast. These officers had been working near continually for over five days straight. Many hadn't seen their families, and had not a clue as to the damage done to their homes.

It was a high stakes crapshoot in that respect, as word trickled in of only minor damage for many while an unlucky few lost almost everything. Yet they were still in there, still holding true to an oath to serve and protect. If this is not total dedication to one's profession, I do not know what is.

However, things were getting better. The broken windows had been boarded up, allowing the air conditioning system to put a dent in the building's oppressive heat. That cesspool of an adjoining men's room was finally cleaned out and odorized, and everyone now had a place to wash up and sleep, if and when the opportunity arose.

Food, real food and not just junk snacks and soda pops was made available. My eye caught a stack of Gatorades in a corner, and I liberated a couple bottles for Ryan and I. There was also one big, fat, juicy orange I quickly made good use of.

I also noted the trickling in of more federal people. Up to that date, most all you saw were National Guard. Within another twenty-four hours, FEMA and other associated agencies made their presence felt in large terms. Until now, it had been mostly a state and local first responder show.

These groups went into the devastated areas first, did the disaster equivalent of triage and told the feds what was needed. All in all the concept seemed to work rather well.

However, our first line of defense was formed by the individual citizen and associated volunteer groups. This was the major crucial difference between what was happening in Rita's aftermath when compared to New Orleans. It was the individual citizen who stepped forward with their own trucks, boats, chainsaws, generators, fuel, water and food. They were the ones who manned the kitchens, medical facilities, cleanup crews, search and rescue teams as well as a hundred other vital tasks.

They did not sit on their duffs and wait for someone to solve their problems, rather they went to work and met those problems head on. I have always been proud of being a Texan, but I was especially so during those days of hour-by-hour tribulation and triumph.

After a solid meal and pleasant conversation with some of these everyday heroes, Ryan and I received our new assignment. Tonight, we were on roaming patrol, and would remain so for the rest of our stay. Roaming is what a highway patrolman does best.

Our first destination was Sabine Pass, about twelve miles south of Port Arthur. Of all the locales in the area, this little fishing community was the most exposed to Rita. An evacuation occurred early on and that was a good thing, as an estimated ten-to-twelve-foot wall of water surged through during the storm. We drove past numerous refineries under repair and soon enough came to Sabine Pass.

Or at least, what was left of it.

Bits and pieces of homes and businesses were strewn about in every direction, downed power lines went on for miles and large fishing boats sat shipwrecked in the middle of the highway. Dead animals were everywhere, but we saw some live ones too. Dogs, hungry after five days of doing without, sat on porches of elevated homes supported by large poles. The surge must have made a real impression on them because hungry or not, they refused to leave their perches.

The entire community was devoid of human life, so we turned around and headed back.

Our next stop was Pleasure Island. This was where the well-to-do stay and play, so naturally we had to take a look around. Surprisingly those tall, narrow boat houses held up well and suffered only minor damage. The marina needed some work though, as the jumble of boats looked like the nautical equivalent of a junkyard. Salvaging operations were already underway and people were scurrying about.

After dark we patrolled the area along the Port Arthur-Groves boundary. More lights were seen, and through the trees we could see a building complex with some activity. Our cop curiosity aroused, we moved in to find a small hospital and staff preparing to open for business. Upon seeing us, we were invited in and treated like royalty. They were obviously concerned about security, so we swung through about every hour and a half.

Since we were in the neighborhood and Ryan was still thinking Mustangs, we made a pass around the Ford dealership again. A damaged side entrance was located and he slipped inside to snoop around. Coming back a few minutes later, he asked me to follow him in. Winding our way through debris we came upon a brand new, bright yellow Ford GT complete with a considerably hiked-up $165,000 window sticker.

Motioning me forward, we moved into a far larger room where much of the late model merchandise was parked for protection from the storm. Most of these vehicles had their ignition keys in the driver's door lock.

A car thief's paradise.

Well, make that a discriminating car thief's paradise, as I found the keys for the yellow Ford GT nearby. Visions of the original *Gone In Sixty Seconds* briefly flirted with my semi-dormant teenager imagination.

Putting this sore temptation behind us, we went back outside to find gas caps removed from some of the SUVs. But nothing else was disturbed, and remained so for as long as we were in Port Arthur.

The rest of the shift was spent prowling about and looking for trouble, but there was pitifully little found. We began tracking down every source of light we saw, and ended up meeting some nice people who were glad to see us. They offered us food, drinks, even places to stay. These are the people who make one feel more than satisfied with their choice of profession.

Yet there is a flip side to their sort, as well as to human nature itself. Something that stuck with me was no matter how bad things were, others still managed to get drunk or high. Or both, depending upon their perceived need.

One unit came across some loon out chasing the little animals, silver flecks of paint covering his nose from sniffing the stuff. They corralled the badly spaced out fellow and took him to a safe place. Considering that most of those little animals were alligators and cottonmouths, those officers did him a real favor.

In the wee hours, we were down to a half tank and began looking for some more push juice. For some reason the National Guard trucks had departed for parts unknown, not to be seen again. The new plan was to get our fuel straight from a refinery, and we were directed to a civilian tanker.

As Ryan and I filled up, we were both thinking the same thing. *'Man, this swill really stinks.'* I wondered aloud how this was going to work with multi-port fuel injection, MAF sensors, anti-knock sensors, O2 sensors and the like. Within twenty-four hours, we would find out.

After another five hours of sleep, I was up and moving again. It was becoming a routine now; shave, polish my boots, read awhile, grab some chow and attend the evening brief. On our way over Ryan and I visited with two of our brother highway patrolmen, fuming over their ailing Crown Vic. The check engine light was glowing and the Ford's engine was missing and running really rough.

They were certain the culprit was the hog urine put in the car's gas tank during their latest fill up. After smelling the stuff the night before, I was inclined to agree. Bad gas can sometimes be worse than no gas at all, and so we said hello to Problem Number Seven.

That evening we patrolled along Texas Highway 82, making for the old swing bridge crossing into Louisiana. Enroute, we saw more devastation like the day before in Sabine Pass. Lord help me, but I felt myself becoming used to the unending destruction.

Our unit eased past more forests of downed power lines, chunks and pieces of buildings of all kinds, and water vessels of different types scattered across the surrounding landscape. Upon arriving at the bridge, there were barricades and 'Road Closed' signs up, and just immediately behind them was a large highline pole that had toppled across. No one was passing through here anytime soon.

But just to make sure were two Cameron Parrish deputy sheriffs standing beside a marked Tahoe, watching our approach. They were also fishing. By far, this had to be the loneliest checkpoint of any around yet when it came to fresh fish, lonely might not be so bad after all.

We stepped out of our Ford and I yelled "Hey, Louisiana! Ya'll the end of the line, or the beginning?"

BLACK AND WHITE

A big, burly deputy laughed and responded in a rich Cajun accent. "Well Texas, I guess that depends on how you look at it!"

For the next several minutes we enjoyed their company and listened to the descriptions of horrific damage done to their side of the Sabine. If we were hit hard, they were much, much worse off. At the bridge we were about thirty-five miles from Cameron, which first took a big wallop from Katrina. But then it was waxed flat by Rita, as the town sat just east of the hurricane's eye.

The deputies described entire communities gone, nothing left but some poles and pipes sticking out of the ground. These two men had been manning this location for twenty-six hours straight with no relief, and had to stay here because the bridge was declared unsafe. No one had tried to cross as of yet, but as we all know there is one in every crowd. We wished them luck but did not offer any of our food, they were far better prepared for the long haul than we were.

Upon our return to the Port Arthur area, we started checking on National Guard posts along the Groves boundary. This shared city limit had become a point of consternation, as the Groves mayor opened up his community while Port Arthur remained in lock down. The National Guardsmen, unarmed and with little to no communications, were having a real problem with civilians overtly disregarding them.

Many of these young people came from the Dallas area, and had little to no supervision or concern from their staff NCOs and officers. Not only did they lack communications, some posts had no food or water. We gave them all we had.

One of the posts we checked frequently was located on Main Street and Texas Highway 87. There were only two guardsmen at the spot, not near the number needed for such an intersection. They reported hearing gunshots to the north and from their description, the rounds fired were from a fast-stepping handgun or centerfire rifle. After checking with other guardsmen, we speculated they came from somewhere near Main and 25th Street.

Our rough triangulation was confirmed by a Groves PD unit, who also informed us of a grocery store nearby looted three different times since noon. Whoever it was had a powerful thirst, because they were stealing nothing but beer. Ryan and I prowled the immediate neighborhood to show the flag, and for future reference.

Shortly afterwards, we observed a silver Hyundai SUV pulled in the driveway of a private residence. The vehicle's lights were on and the engine running, so we stopped to investigate.

Things here did not look kosher. Ryan pulled out the shotgun, while I unholstered my Sig and went to low cover. A quick check of the Hyundai's interior revealed an H&R .22 revolver on the front passenger seat. Opening the driver's door, I turned the ignition off and pulled the keys. Checking the handgun and finding it fully loaded, I locked both the gun as well as the keys in our trunk.

And still not a sign or a sound of anyone around.

Meanwhile, Ryan was scouting the rear of the residence. As I softly closed the trunk lid he returned, saying everything was similarly quiet in the backyard area.

Our next two concerns were an unsecured garage, flanked by the front door to the residence. With Ryan covering me, I swung wide and away from the garage and melted to the side of the main entrance. From that vantage point, I could see the front door wasn't completely closed either. Getting as low and out of the way as possible I pushed the door open, identifying myself and challenging anybody within.

A complete silence followed. I looked, listened and actually 'felt' with my back pressed against the outside wall of the house. Absolutely nothing, yet somehow, I knew there was someone inside.

I announced myself several times and heard nothing in return, yet could not shake the gut feeling about the place being occupied. Finally, I half circled back to the patrol car for a better overall view.

We were in an unfamiliar town, in an unfamiliar neighborhood, at an unfamiliar residence with an unknown number of people inside who either would not or could not respond to my commands. It didn't take me long to radio the CP and request a Groves PD unit. As we waited Ryan and I kept our eyes and ears open, and planted firmly behind cover.

Evidently it was another slow night for others on our shift. Within minutes we had five police cars as well as a DPS Motor Vehicle Theft unit, manned by two of my fellow classmates from the academy. It was good to see them after all those years, especially considering the circumstance. They were both men to be counted upon.

Having noticed a volunteer firefighter sticker on the Hyundai, I calculated the owner of the home might be known to the responding officers. Turned out they did know him, which was helpful to our situation.

After a short pow-wow, we decided a local SWAT officer and myself would make entry through the front door. Readying ourselves, he went high and I went low into a living room area. Midway through he shouts a warning of someone off to our right. Our flashlights and muzzles zeroed in on a figure lying on a fully reclined lazy boy. Immediately we started barking commands and demanding to see some hands.

Then the SWAT officer sounded off, "I know this guy, he's all right. He's the one who lives here." We moved in closer and though he might have lived there, the subject was definitely not all right. In truth, he was considerably beyond the line of falling down drunk.

The other officer began calling the subject's name in a loud voice, as we still could not see his hands. Everyone else was inside by now clearing side rooms, and after repeatedly being yelled at the drunk finally began to stir.

Someone remarked the guy probably had downed one too many sixteen-ounce stress relievers. By my own estimation, the one too many came a couple of six packs ago. The locals thanked us and we gave them the gun and keys, and started our patrol again.

About an hour later we ran into the Groves officer who told us about the looted store. With a big grin on his face, he stated he had finally caught the persistent thief.

It was another drunk. When the officer drove by he saw the guy half in and half out, trying to crawl through a broken window. He was sweaty from the heat, bloody from the broken glass and bombed out of his mind, but going back for more Budweiser.

The Groves officer laughed and closed with a "I almost never got him loaded in my unit!"

After midnight we returned to the CP for some more bottled water and snacks for the National Guard posts. In the room was a large plot board, giving the status of patrol units for the Port Arthur Police Department. At least a half dozen were out of service due to "engine missing," "surging," and "check engine light on." Problem Number Seven was becoming an epidemic, my hope was our Crown Vic had a better immune system.

The next day saw many of our fellows starting back home as fresh troops continued to pour in. Hearing this, I again volunteered both Ryan and I to stick around. The way we had it figured, we knew the general area now and were getting to know the locals. Besides, it felt like quitting with a job only partly finished.

Our offer was accepted and we headed for our racks, only to be woken up about two and a half hours later. Three female troopers came bursting through the door, having been assigned our room. They beat a hasty retreat at my somewhat rank response, and I made a makeshift sign advising there were no co-ed vacancies in Room 407.

After that little episode I slept with one eye open, wondering what might wander in next. By noon, I could not stand it anymore and started my daily chores. We were told to pack for five days and since we were now into the eighth, it was time for a little laundry business in the bathroom sink.

The next surprise was a welcomed one. Trooper Scott Warren showed up, looking for a place to stay. I had known Scott since I was a rookie and he was one of many who served as a valued mentor. His professionalism, his optimism and his sincere desire to help others were all well known. Some years back Scott retired, then decided he wasn't quite ready to do so and rejoined the Department. We quickly ushered him into our room, glad for the addition.

Dalton and I attended the evening brief, along with the others forming Sergeant Land's section. There were far more troopers than before, which explained the mad scramble for available rooms. In the mix were many younger troops who remembered me as a field instructor at the academy.

Some recalled defensive tactics, some firearms and some the driving schools I taught at. For a brief while it was like old home week, yet among a more youthful crowd. As we talked a bittersweet realization settled upon me, these outstanding young men and women were now veterans in their own right. Time waits for no one, including graying highway patrolmen stationed in Ozona.

Tonight, Sergeant Land's section would take the new people to the different checkpoints, and make certain they were properly manned. After doing so, we would begin roaming patrol again. Ryan and I took a detachment to the new Checkpoint Seventeen and then hit the road.

We made our way to Port Neches, another community adjoining both Groves and Port Arthur. The main highway from the south was still blocked by downed power lines, so we snaked our way in via back roads. Once in town we located their police station and offered our services, which were gratefully accepted. What remained of the fading daylight was spent in learning the nearby landmarks.

Our reconnaissance was interrupted by a radio transmission, advising our section to report to the command post. Something was definitely up, and we returned post haste to find out what.

Once everyone was present Sergeant Land made it simple, we were going home tonight. After having been told we would stay another three days, this change in marching orders took a moment to sink in.

Once more I offered to remain. But Land explained there were now more troops than they knew what to do with, and the supervisors were having a hard time finding enough rooms. It was only then I really began to feel tired, that needed small measure of continuing adrenaline no longer had a purpose.

I asked Ryan to find our DPS repair truck to replace the plugged tire. It was 480 miles back to Ozona, and the idea of changing a flat at night along I-10 was not an appealing one. While he was doing so, I made the other needed arrangements. On our way out, we stopped by the Port Neches PD to advise them of the change in plans. We wished each other luck and started the long drive to Crockett County.

Some hours later our Ford eased into a Denny's for a nighthawk breakfast. Sitting in the quiet of the diner I sipped on hot, black coffee while taking in the sights, sounds and smells of normalcy. It was hard to believe the contrast to how we had been living the past eight days, and I couldn't help but feel a little guilty in leaving it behind. There was still a great deal needing done on the Texas side of the Sabine, but we were no longer part of the program.

BLACK AND WHITE

After dropping off Ryan I pulled in front of our home a little past 6 am, just as Ozona was beginning to stir. Cathy was up to welcome me and helped bring in my bags. After she started her morning routine I sat on the back deck, petted the dogs and watched the sun rise. Levi and Ethan came out to join me, and we visited on what had happened in my absence. Life was fast returning to what it recently was.

Later I read through my emails in a leisurely fashion, enjoying a lazy morning and trying to decompress a bit. The black and white was unloaded and my gear stowed away until next time. My weapons were cleaned, checked and placed where they belonged. Every so often I caught a whiff of the Gulf Coast on my clothing. It was a long way from Port Arthur to Ozona, but that fleeting odor served as a pungent reminder of where I had been just last night.

For someone familiar with the film noirs of the 1940s, the name Rita brings to mind a tough, good looking dame with a bad attitude. But Hurricane Rita was much more than that, she was an awesome act of nature that marked her passing with devastation coupled to untold human miseries. Her destructive path would take years, even decades, for the Sabine River region to recover from.

As part of our Civil Disturbance Management Team for nearly an entire career, I deployed to political rallies, tornadoes, massive hail storms, court sentencings, police shootings, prison riots, presidential visits, standoffs, border duty, refugee operations and a host of other challenges.

But Rita was my last big show, so to speak. I would like to think I finished up in style.

After all, that's what I came to the party for.

THP Area 4B07 in 2006. From left to right: Trooper Danny Nunez, Corporal Donald Van Zandt, Trooper Rito Renteria, Trooper Mike Johnson, Secretary Debra Brown, Trooper Ben H. English, Trooper Steve Torres, Trooper Castulo 'Junior' Bilano, Trooper Joey Van Gundy, Trooper Norbert Ortiz, Trooper Ryan Dalton

CARL W. MAYFIELD

In the Book of Proverbs is a passage that speaks of some men being closer than a brother. When I think upon this scripture and the true meaning behind it, Carl Mayfield is one of those who comes to mind.

He was my sergeant for ten years, a feat unequaled by any other during my decades of working out of Ozona. If memory serves me correctly, during that length of time THP Sergeant Area 4B07 had fourteen sergeants total. More so, the figure is debatable. There were some who when told they were going to Ozona, declined the promotion.

Not that Ozona was really such a bad station, but in many ways it was somewhat isolated. When a new sergeant came on board and his wife asked about the nearest Walmart, the standard reply was "seventy-five miles down that road, first building on your right." She'd get kind of wild-eyed and the next thing anyone knew, we had another sergeant coming.

Often enough they came without their wife and family, which gave a fair idea of how long they were going to last themselves. Many were from the other side of Texas, along the I-35 corridor and points east, which often made for a real culture shock.

The way the job was done where they came from, versus being a highway patrolman in West Texas, could at times be seen as two completely differing styles of the same line of work. The wise ones laid back, watched what was happening day by day, and after making some mental notes gradually assumed their authority. In contradicting fashion were others who started trying to change everything at once, mainly because of a *'that's the way it was done where I come from'* mindset.

Many who wanted to be supervisors never realized how truly difficult the position was until put to the task. Being a highway patrol sergeant, and doing the job right, is the most demanding position found in the Texas Department of Public Safety, or most anyplace else.

As a first line supervisor you were not only responsible for yourself, but ten or so other men with guns and badges on. To a large degree you inherited their problems, their trials and their weaknesses, as well as their family and personal lives. If you wanted their respect and loyalty, they had to know you sincerely cared for all that as if it were your own.

Then you had the assorted ulterior reasons for promoting, the ones no one really talks about because no one wants to admit to them. For a family man, there can be a need to escape the stresses put on one's domestic life from being on the road daily.

As a road troop you work nights, weekends, holidays and can be sent across the state for weeks with a single phone call. It takes a strong woman and strong children to live that kind of life, and in knowing the next time you walk out the door might also be your last. None of them volunteered for your chosen profession. You drafted them into it, and each day they pay a certain price for having done so.

There's a time-honored truism you hear all over, but it remains supremely relevant to being a highway patrolman: *"If mama ain't happy, nobody's happy."* She's had one too many bad wreck calls, one too many drunks, one too many special emphasis programs and one too many nights with a cold, empty spot beside her in bed. Something needs to be done and this something is either quit or promote, or have a divorce.

Sometimes the reason is the result of something which happened on the road. A lingering premonition, an eye opening incident, or a close miss that honestly scares the pee-waddling out of an officer. Or much like the wife; one too many bad wrecks, or unpredictable drunks, or just too much blood on the ground for one man's soul to rest easy at night.

The third reason is one with no possible redemption, and often creates the greatest long-running disasters. It consists of those who have such a high level of arrogance and egotism as to think that working the road, in itself, is somehow beneath them.

They exist only for the chance to promote, and barely make it out of probation before setting their sights on a higher rank. Usually these types are way long in book learning and way short on common sense, and sometimes common decency. It is said the devil drives those of ambition hardest through the front gates of hell, but in this particular profession they never seem to enter alone.

In any organization one can think of, these particular types make for the greatest banes of all. They are archetype Peter Principle in living technicolor, and seem to thrive most in the halls of bureaucracies as supervisors rather than in being leaders of men.

And then you have those few, those precious few, like Carl Mayfield. If you took everything I've written for the past two pages, wadded it up and threw it out the nearest window, in through the opposite door would walk someone like Carl.

Not that he was the perfect man, none of us are and he would have been the first to say so. But he did have two qualities above all others, and that was natural leadership as well as an unswaying personal sense of honor.

Carl was raised in Haskell County north of Abilene, a true son of Texas to his very core. They say that leaders are born and not made, and with Carl this adage seldom proved truer. I have spoken with people who knew him when barely a teenager and all mentioned his ability to lead, and to set the example.

BLACK AND WHITE

Everything Carl Mayfield did, he did right. When he joined the Marine Corps fresh out of high school, he quickly became known as a Marine's Marine and ultimately earned the rank of first sergeant in the Marine Corps Reserve. There is no doubt in my mind that if he had been able to stay a bit longer, he would have made sergeant major.

Same in him being a family man. He married once and he married for life, choosing an equally strong and independent-minded woman who proved his equal more than once. Dale gave him two sons, and no father was ever prouder or loved his offspring more.

When he was assigned to Ozona as our new sergeant, his reputation preceded him. Carl graduated DPS Academy in 1984, which meant he was on the road for over ten years and in tight spots more than once. In fact, Carl earned a Director's Citation early on by talking an armed and barricaded subject into surrendering peacefully.

He never wore the ribbon for that award unless asked to do so. When you expressed interest about the circumstance, he'd say something about it really being nothing, and likely what most any other troop would have done in the same situation.

Yet someone up the chain of command happened to take notice and was sufficiently impressed to put him in for this citation. I personally knew enough of what happened to realize the result was far more than 'really being nothing.' He saved at least one life on that day.

But that was only Carl being Carl, and why he was so respected in a profession made up of men who are hard to impress, and do not give their allegiance easily.

When Carl first came to Ozona, he lived in a little travel trailer near the junior high. His wife Dale was a teacher and coach in Brownfield, and she and the boys had remained there to finish their school year.

This was when I really first came to know Carl, and to know him well. I would get a sketchy call of some sort and no matter the time of day or night, I'd look around and sure enough there would stand my new sergeant. These incidences usually occurred when there was no back up available, and it did not take me long to determine that was when he responded most often.

It was the beginning of a close friendship I shall treasure for all my remaining days.

Now, that is not to say we didn't have our spirited disagreements and differences in opinion, or every now and then a pretty good argument. These seemed to pick up their pace when I became the area corporal, and began working more closely with him.

Almost always these disagreements had to do with how the job was done, as he had one opinion and sometimes I had the other. You see, most every Texas highway patrolman I ever knew was about as independent minded as most anyone could be. They also have egos about the size of Alaska, which gives you a better idea of just how hard the job of a highway patrol sergeant is and how hard to do even passingly well.

I found it hard to argue with Carl past a certain point. After all, he was my sergeant and there was still enough of the Marine Corps in both of us to serve as a constant reminder of that.

However this went far deeper than simple sewn rank on a sleeve, it was because I genuinely liked and respected the man so much. Carl was the rarest of breeds who would argue voraciously against some stupid idea from Austin during a supervisor meeting. But once he had his say and the decision remained the same, he would do his level best to come back to our area and sell the rest of us on it. That's a tough tightrope to walk, and one of the other many reasons why being a highway patrol sergeant was such a challenging position.

When it came time to put that same stupid idea to practical application, Carl led the way. No matter how inane or silly the program, he took the point and carried the team ball forward. In short, he never asked any of his men to do anything he was not willing to do himself, and proved this by doing so time and again.

Something else made it hard to second guess Carl, as he was one of the most loyal men to his people I have ever come across. Right, wrong or indifferent; if one of his men made a mistake he did his best to support that man while still rectifying the situation. And if the man made that mistake while trying to do the right thing, Carl was nigh fearless in defending him against all comers.

The years went by and we grew closer, sharing in both good times and bad. With each of us having two sons of about the same age there was always something both of us wanted to talk about. Carl was one of those who cheered on our community's youth in every endeavor, especially in sports. He served as a role model for many a young person in Ozona, and it was always for the better.

Then 9/11 came along and the world changed again.

I mentioned before Carl was also a first sergeant in the Marine Corps Reserve. Before that fateful September morning, I would sometimes give him a hard time about the 'weekend warrior' bit. I had served active duty in the Marines for seven years.

But upon realizing we were about to go to war, I found myself trying to join one of those weekend warrior outfits. The recruiters were always happy to give me the chance, too, until they saw my date of birth. One even pushed my service record all the way to Headquarters Marine Corps yet the result was the same: too old. When Carl was activated for the invasion of Iraq, it was real hard for me to watch him go.

However, in doing so our friendship deepened in ways. We stayed in contact through writing letters, going back and forth about one thing or the other while I tried to take care of anything needed done back home. I kept every one of them, for they were not only valued personal correspondence but contained history of the war as it unfolded.

During that invasion, the Marine Corps moved faster and deeper inland than ever before in any combat operation. As the first sergeant of a motor transport unit Carl was with his young Marines and leading from the front, pushing them as hard and as far as they could possibly go. He wrote of the great pride he had in them, and how they responded in heroic fashion to the innumerable challenges faced while encapsulated within the fog of war.

And when it was all over, he wrote movingly of what he was proudest about of all. First Sergeant Carl W. Mayfield, USMCR, came back with the same number of young Marines as he had gone into battle with.

I never uttered another word about weekend warriors again.

But upon returning home Carl found himself embroiled in yet another war, and certainly not one of his choosing. Only a few days after coming back, he was rushed to Shannon Hospital for an emergency appendectomy. When the doctors opened him up, they found something else entirely.

It was stomach cancer.

I learned later he had not been feeling well during much of the time spent in Iraq, but gritted his teeth and put that all aside so he could be with his young Marines. In the meantime, the cancer grew. To this day, I wonder how the following events might have changed if the cancer had been treated early on.

However, this is only for a Higher Power to know and me to speculate upon. As far as Carl himself, he just turned to and met his newest challenge head on. All with that same warrior's heart and indefatigable spirit.

After further surgery and a long, painful bout with chemotherapy, Carl Mayfield was declared fit for duty and returned to Ozona as our highway patrol sergeant. This was about the same time as when we lost Kurt Knapp, and Carl took it hard. He had been a counselor in Kurt's academy class and was the reason for Kurt starting out as a rookie in Ozona.

For him, losing Kurt was almost like losing a son.

During the next few years Carl continued his exemplary work not only as a leader of men, but also as an always contributing member to our community. I would like to think we grew closer still during that period, even with our usual spirited disagreements behind closed doors. I was already formulating plans concerning my retirement, which included showing up in his office about every week or so, and just giving him you-know-what about some piddly thing or another.

However, man makes his plans and God laughs, and mine were made in much the same vein. Three summers after Kurt was killed the cancer was back, and Carl went under the knife again. This time the doctors found much more of the insidious scourge than anyone had bargained for. Carl returned to duty again, but this time in San Angelo to remain closer to the needed medical facilities.

Two more months and more bad news. We learned that Carl's stomach was not functioning and the cancer was spreading faster than ever. The front door for Shannon Hospital became an all-too-often revolving one for him, and he was forced to use it several times within a matter of weeks.

Throughout this awful ordeal he remained optimistic and fought as hard and as bravely as any man I have ever known. When the doctors said they could do no more than have him go home and put under hospice care, I think he considered it as just another challenge to be overcome. The ensuing battle was a tremendous one, and went far beyond the point where the doctors held out any hope.

Carl set his mind and remaining strength to making it from one holiday to the next. I did my best to stop by each day, to check on Dale and marvel at this man who seemingly had no comprehension of what the word 'quit' meant. To have gone through so much, to be in such constant pain and still rise to fight again.

It hurt so much to see him lie in that bed. But at the same time I was humbled to be in his presence, and bear personal witness as to what a man of such spirit could accomplish through sheer grit and personal willpower.

Yet Carl was never in this fight alone. You see, he was drawing upon a Faith few others actually possess. He had always been a man of such persuasions, but now as his body grew weaker that special light from within shined brighter than ever before. While most would think in terms of how long any normal man could last in such a horrendous situation, Carl Mayfield had already gone to his knees and received an incredibly powerful alliance from above.

Against all odds and all medical predictions he made it to Christmas. Then he set his mind and will on New Year's and conquered that goal too. From there his sights settled upon Easter, and watching his younger son Colby graduate from high school.

In those final days Carl and I talked for as long as he was able to do so. They had him on some really heavy-duty pain killers, and those were starting to affect his mental processes. Some days he would appear as lucid and mentally sharp as ever, giving me marching orders for taking care of this or that. I'd sally forth to address those concerns, only to learn my quest was but a fevered figment of his imagination, or had been taken care of months or even years ago.

Toward the end his hallucinations became more real and involved, as did the nightmares. There were mornings I would come by and Dale would tell me that Carl and I must have been in one heckuva firefight together. He would yell out in the middle of the night for me to give him cover, or to check if I had any spare mags. This went on for a couple of days, followed by yet another turn for the worse.

One night he began calling out for my older son Levi and I, saying some people was trying to hurt him. This was about rock bottom for me, because here was a man who never asked for help from any other. Yet when he finally reached out to someone it was me he called to, and I was not there for him.

That single thought has weighed as heavily on my heart as anything else I ever did, or failed to do.

The last time I spoke with Carl he was fading in and out of consciousness. My friend was played out, and we both realized it. We talked as he drifted back and forth until it was time for me to leave, he was so tired and weak. As his mind moved away for the last time, he began to sing softly and sweetly.

I had never heard Carl sing before. The song he sang goes like this:

> *"Jesus loves me, yes I know,*
> *For the Bible tells me so,*
> *Little ones to Him belong,*
> *They are weak but he is strong.*
> *Yes, Jesus loves me,*
> *Yes, Jesus loves me,*
> *Yes, Jesus loves me,*
> *The Bible tells me so..."*

The next morning Dale called to say that Carl had passed in the early morning hours. In my heart, I already knew.

The next few days were a blur, Carl's earthly remains were cremated and arrangements made for his funeral. So many stepped forward to help, and a few special ones come to mind as I write this.

Otis Locklear and his son Burleigh, two generations of Texas Highway Patrolmen who assisted in making arrangements with the Marine Corps, as well as providing regional support within the DPS. At the time Otis was still in the Marine Corps Reserves himself, and both Locklears had been Carl's friends for many years. To them this was not only a duty, but a matter involving personal honor.

I also think of Ruben Galindo, who was not only running our area then but making certain Carl and his family received all proper considerations and respects. Not too long ago, Ruben had been a rookie under Carl Mayfield's command. Now he was the sergeant in charge of THP 4B07.

Somehow, I found that more than fitting.

Carl's memorial ceremony was likely the biggest Ozona ever saw, or perhaps ever see again. People came from all over the state by the hundreds, and there was not a church in the county big enough for the crowd. So the service was held in the town's convention center and even at that, it was elbow to elbow and standing room only.

Dale Mayfield asked me to give the eulogy. That was one of the most difficult tasks I ever had in all those years, and also the most humbling.

In full dress blues, Otis Locklear took the crisply folded American flag from the Marine honor guard and presented our nation's near sacred symbol to Dale. That was about as hard on him as the eulogy was on me.

Carl had requested we scatter his ashes along Interstate 10 west of Ozona, so a few days later we gathered to get the job done. It was mostly the troopers from Carl's area, his family and Tommy Matthews, who came down from San Angelo to help where needed.

The plan was for Bradley and Colby, Carl's two sons, to do the honors from a rolling patrol car traveling at 35 MPH. The ashes had been placed in a .50 caliber ammunition box with a half inch hole drilled in a bottom corner, and covered with a piece of tape. Bradley was in the front passenger seat and would pull the tape, while Colby sat in the rear and shook the can slowly to scatter its contents.

It was a good plan, a simple plan and was going to be done exactly as Dale, Bradley and Colby saw fit. But there is also this guy named Murphy, who seems to always have the final say over any plan, anywhere, for any reason.

Bradley and Colby were to ride with me, in my recently issued Ford Crown Victoria. As a sergeant area we lined up our patrol units, flipped on our rollers and began gathering speed; one behind the other in the outside lane. It was a near perfect day on a late January afternoon, the sun was shining and nothing more than the slightest breeze to disturb the crisp West Texas air.

The two young men rolled down their windows. Bradley reached back to pull the tape, and Colby gently began shaking the can.

Nothing happened.

Colby started shaking harder, moving the can not only from side to side, but up and down. Both were trying so hard to remain cool and collected, and to render the deep respect they had for their father in a dignified, caring manner.

However what little remained of Carl Mayfield's earthly presence was not going down, or away, easily.

Colby began banging on the side of the ammo can while Bradley leaned halfway out the car and joined in. Now, both of these young men were full grown in anybody's book; big, muscled up lads that each went way over six feet tall. Yet the more they shook, banged and muttered under their breaths, the more determined Carl seemed to want to stay in that .50 caliber ammo can.

Their voices became louder, even a bit exasperated and the shaking and banging more insistent. Finally in near desperation, one of them unlatched the top of the can and flung the cover open.

Ashes went everywhere, including throughout the interior of that Ford as well as all over us. I couldn't help myself, I started laughing so hard I could barely hold on the steering wheel. Not at them, of course, but at the rapidly devolving position we found ourselves in.

Carl had remained true to his natural disposition until the very end. Determined, obstinate, stubborn and incredibly willful in everything he ever did. I only wished he could have done so in my long-gone Caprice slick top we used to call Ol' Rocket Sled.

He always really liked that car.

When Carl Wayne Mayfield passed, he was only forty-four. But in that far-too-short amount of years, he accomplished more good for his fellow man than most manage at double the age. He certainly had more courage and character than the average half-dozen others. And for me, he proved to be closer than the Biblical brother in Proverbs. I'll always consider myself blessed because of that.

Semper Fi, Boss. I'll see you on the other side.

*Sergeant Carl Wayne Mayfield, Texas Highway Patrol
End of Watch January 20th, 2007*

MY LAST FATAL

I was nearing fifty and had been on the road for over twenty years. The Big 5-0 was of special significance to me, as it marked the earliest age in which I could retire. The question was, did I really want to?

A man worth his salt has an innate need to be useful, to provide for his family and to the welfare of his fellow man. Fifty was awfully young to put oneself out to pasture, and I had taken care of myself both mentally as well as physically. During my annual examination, Doctor Sims would shake his head and exclaim I actually made him sick.

"Ben, I have high school star football players who aren't in your shape!" he would say. Don't know if it was exactly true, but it sure put me in a prime state of mind.

Yet there was another side to all this, and in that the odds were stacking up.

Peace officers by nature are conservative in their philosophical outlook on life. We are resistant to change, and our profession was changing rapidly due to the continuing changes within the society we served.

One day I came home griping about the latest silliness by edict from Austin, and Cathy stopped me about midway through.

"Once you hit fifty, you don't have to do this job anymore" she said. "Everything we have is paid for. Levi is doing well at Annapolis and Ethan will get his appointment, too."

"But you have to promise me one thing," she added somewhat ominously. "And that's after you retire you never put on another badge and gun again. I've done my time."

I looked up at that last remark, knowing she had never been real keen about law enforcement in general and the DPS in particular.

"You put seven years in the Marine Corps and over twenty working rural interstate, mostly by yourself. Time to count your blessings and move on."

Then she went on to say something about me not being John Wayne, not being ten foot tall, not being bulletproof and that I was getting older. All the things a man really does not want to hear from his closest friend and confidant.

Yet the worst thing was, she was right on all counts.

Of course, I could promote, and from what I had seen the DPS promote during those years I knew I could do no worse. But that idea had several shortcomings, as we most likely would have to move to a far bigger town or city and if I was moving anyplace ever again, it would be back home to the Big Bend.

Plus, the idea of sitting in some office day in and day out while driving a desk was not appealing to me in the least. That was not the reason I became a peace officer, and once you begin to promote it behooves you to be a 'company man.'

This was not me, either. In fact, I was told a few years later some DPS supervisors had actually named ulcers after me.

Imagine that.

So, there I was on a late Saturday morning, a stiff wind blowing hard from the south that occasionally sent up plumes of dust at pavement's edge. I was pondering my near future and how it may play out not only myself, but others.

It was October 13, 2007. At about 10:41 a.m. my unit radio came to life, and any thoughts of the future were replaced by the harsh realities and needs of the present.

Paula Maness was working the communications console that day. Though now a supervisor, she would still take one of her operators' shifts when requested. This was one of those days.

Paula advised me of a major accident with injuries on Interstate 10, about twelve miles east of Ozona. It wasn't so much what she said as to how she said it, a tone of voice can tell you considerably more than mere words themselves.

And in her short transmission of a dozen words or so, I knew this one was going to be bad.

Real bad.

I hit my lights and reversed direction, squeezing every bit of power I could get out of that slug of a Crown Victoria and its undersized V8. The wind was buffeting me around, but not enough to even think about lifting. Someone needed help, and they needed it now.

About a mile ahead and coming on the entrance ramp from Ozona was Deputy Ray Francis, already rolling to lend me a hand. I blew by him like he was sitting on blocks, the certified speedometer pegged on my Ford at 130 MPH. That was all she had, and I was using it for all I could.

Six minutes after receiving the call, I topped a low slope and could see the wreck below. I radioed Paula that I was 10-23, meaning I had arrived on scene. There was no reason to request assistance, I already knew she was rolling everything our little community had in my direction.

But the word 'wreck' was not even close to what I was observing before me, the site was like an old western movie where they show the wagon train after the massacre.

A trail of vehicle parts, personal belongings, road rash and debris led from the pavement to a blue Chevrolet Trailblazer, the distance some 500 feet and more in length. Other vehicles were parked haphazardly on the improved shoulder and in the median, and people on foot were running back and forth through the area. One guy was doing his best to try to move traffic to the inside lane, and away from what remained of the Trailblazer.

There were also two small groups working frantically on and around two bodies, about a hundred feet shy of the blue Chevrolet.

They were the bodies of small children.

Then I was hard on the brakes, bringing two tons plus of black and white Crown Vic to a smoking, rotor searing stop as the ABS let the tires slip and grab repeatedly.

Bailing out of the Ford, I was greeted by the unearthly sound of a woman screaming; "Help my babies, somebody please help my babies!!!"

I sprinted to the body of the nearest child, a red headed boy about nine years old. He was bleeding from the ears and nose, and had severe head trauma. CPR was being administered, and the three people who were working on him identified themselves as an active duty Marine and his wife, who was a nurse.

The third was a freshly minted border patrolman, who was also a former grunt from the Marines.

I said a quick prayer of thanks to God for the help from my old alma mater, and continued on to the second body. It was a little girl of about five years of age and obviously dead, even as a good Samaritan continued to try to give CPR.

Rising up from the dead child, I ran for the Trailblazer as quickly as my legs could carry me. The mother was still seat belted in and in fair shape physically, but near completely covered in dirt, debris and blood. She was beyond hysterical and screaming at me to please save her babies.

Scanning the interior of what was left of the devastated SUV, I saw a baby seat in the right rear passenger area and bounded around the Chevrolet to check. There was a two-year-old boy in the safety seat, still belted in.

He was dead, too.

I spent the next half hour guiding emergency personnel, calling in updates, loading both injured and dead, and trying to restore some sense of sanity to a chaotically sad situation.

In that same time frame, some of our best community volunteers turned into walking zombies on me. One of my EMTs had somehow gotten the dead baby out of the interior of the Chevrolet, still in the bloody safety seat. The EMT was carrying it around aimlessly, with that unmistakable thousand yard stare in near vacant eyes.

I called her by name and she stopped, almost as if in a trance. Walking over to her, I extended my arms out and implored gently, "Here, let me help you with that."

Without any change in expression, she slowly handed me the car seat and continued on. I carried the seat and dead infant to my patrol unit and placed it by the right rear tire. Opening the trunk, I took a blanket and draped it over both. No one else needed to see this. Not today, not ever.

Two of our EMTs quit that day, and I for one didn't blame either one bit.

As I worked the preliminary investigation, more details of this horrific tragedy became known. The mother and her three children were a military family, her husband was in the Army and had been deployed to Iraq. The night before, she received word he had been severely injured by an IED blast, and was medevacked to Brooke Army Medical Center in San Antonio.

She was enroute from Fort Bliss to be at his side when the wreck occurred.

Once the accident was cleared and certain evidence marked, I climbed in my Ford and headed back to town. Waiting for me in the DPS parking lot was Dick Hudson and one of his friends. Both were riding their motorcycles through Ozona and wanted to meet with me.

I briefly explained what caused the delay, and Dick said that Paula had filled them in earlier when she had the chance to step outside.

Then he exclaimed, "My God, man! Do you have to do this sort of thing often?"

I shrugged my shoulders as a reply. We visited for another minute or so and they decided to get back on the road. For them, it was plain to see I had more to do at that particular moment than I could say grace over.

Walking into the building, I saw Paula with her head buried in her forearms on the communications console, crying.

In the decades I had worked with her, I had never seen Paula cry before.

To this day, I believe these sort of awful events were often hardest of all on our communications personnel. After all, we troopers were out there neck deep in the action and very much a part of what was happening.

We were doing something actively, and with this also comes a certain comfort in having a modicum of control in some very bad situations. That ability to be hands on provided a viable release for not only our physical tension and angst, but also our mental as well as emotional states.

But our PCOs? They could do little more than sit in a small room, staring at a computer screen and microphone, and listen to our radio traffic while wanting so badly to be of more help. Sometimes I wondered how they did it.

Like now.

Paula and I sat down and wrote out a preliminary communications report on what occurred. While she was typing this into the system, I faced up to my next challenge: notifying next of kin.

Specifically, a young soldier wounded in battle and now lying in a hospital bed at Brooke Hospital, waiting for his family to arrive.

A flurry of phone calls ensued and soon enough I was speaking to an Army sergeant first class. I told him what had happened and that we needed to notify the father. I could hear him pause and swallow hard over the phone, as he mentally processed this heart wrenching circumstance.

Then his voice came back over the receiver. "I'll take care of it, sir." he responded firmly.

"Sergeant," I urged. "Why don't I contact DPS San Antonio and have a trooper come by to help you with this?"

"No sir, that's not necessary. He's one of my people, and this is my job" he replied.

I gave him the information needed and closed our conversation with my phone number, and a standing offer to help in any way I could.

At the end I said, "God bless, Sergeant. You're in my prayers."

"Thank you," he replied. "We are going to need them. I'll keep you posted."

And at that precise moment, I was very close to joining Paula.

The next morning, I learned the nine year old was still alive, though he had coded again enroute to San Angelo. From there he was rushed to Dallas where some of the best neurosurgeons in the country were trying to do something for him.

His head injuries were about as bad as they possibly could be. To keep his brain from swelling any more, the doctors put him in a drug induced coma. The mother was also being transferred to Dallas, and the Army was making arrangements to move her husband from San Antonio so they could be together.

I tried my best to put my mind on the investigation itself. You keep your mind occupied and hopefully things will ultimately shake themselves out. Much like that Army sergeant first class, I had a job to do.

Investigating this nightmarish kind of crash was much like eating an elephant, you try to take it one bite at a time. Likely half of the fatalities I worked during my career involved a one vehicle rollover, and I had already worked far too many of them. In those years, Interstate 10 through Crockett County was said to be the fifth deadliest in the nation for miles traveled.

Meanwhile, the accompanying speed limits did nothing but continue to increase through the decades; from 55 to 65, then 70, 75 and finally 80 MPH.

Speed in itself does not necessarily cause more accidents. But when something does go wrong, that speed makes the ensuing wreck far more lethal. This relationship brings to mind an old public safety announcement from years back, where an officer would face the camera and say he had never unbuckled a dead person.

When the speed limit went to 75 MPH, I started unbuckling dead people. Most of these wrecks involved SUVs, pickup trucks, minivans and so-called crossovers. These styles of vehicles are not as well suited for highway speeds as passenger cars, as they have a higher center of gravity and thus by their very nature are more unstable.

This cause and effect was all simple physics, and the laws of physics are irrefutable in such scenarios. Isaac Newton proved so over three hundred years ago.

My investigation revealed yet another case for the above, along with other contributing factors such as weather conditions, lack of rest and faulty evasive action by the driver.

At the moment of loss of control, the Trailblazer was running in the outside lane of the interstate at the posted speed limit of 80 MPH. As I mentioned before, gusts of wind from the south were reaching at least 25 MPH, making for a somewhat unpredictable crosswind.

The mother was drowsy, having little sleep from the night before. She was also driving straight through, stopping only for gas when needed. Even with driving part of the trip in darkness and with the time consumed in leaving El Paso proper, she was still averaging over 65 MPH.

As the Trailblazer came out of a low, somewhat long right-of-way cut that protected the vehicle from the offending crosswind, it was hit again by the high gusts. Once fully exposed, the effect eased the vehicle into the inner lane and on to the north edge of the roadway.

Now suddenly alert, the driver realized what was happening and panicked, jerking the steering wheel hard right and jamming on the brakes. This was exactly the wrong kind of response for this type of vehicle traveling at high speed.

The Trailblazer went into a pronounced yaw, the left front corner of the blue Chevrolet leading. It slid off the south edge of the pavement and began overturning in a series of wild flips, rolls and somersaults. There was ample physical evidence for four complete rotations, and in actuality there was at least six due to the centrifugal forces involved.

The five-year-old girl and nine-year-old boy were both ejected during these vicious upendings, before the vehicle finally came to rest on all four wheels. The path of the SUV was littered with window glass and pieces of the vehicle. It suffered so much structural damage that much of the roof caved in, which caused the instantaneous death of the infant in the restrained child safety seat.

Inside the vehicle blood and human gore was splashed and smeared on the seats, door panels, dash, floorboards and overhead areas. The outside of the Trailblazer displayed splatterings of the same.

Both rear springs were dislodged and the right rear shock absorber was snapped in two. The front suspension was twisted and buckled under, and the steering linkage was completely severed from the steering shaft. Every door had been jammed shut and all four tires were deflated.

BLACK AND WHITE

This was just part of the damage incurred by a late model SUV with the latest safety features of its period, while traveling at the legal posted limit of 80 MPH. For whoever may be reading these lines, keep that in mind next time you sit behind the steering wheel of a motor vehicle.

I spent most of next day's shift either at the accident scene or in the wrecking yard, piecing together what happened over those five fatal seconds. Yet this was only the beginning of what had to be done.

The days continued to go by, and true to his word the sergeant first class kept me updated on what was left of that family. The mother was released from the hospital after treatment for a neck injury and assorted cuts, bruises and abrasions.

Due to his head trauma and the other wounds suffered in combat, the father had memory loss and was speaking with a pronounced stutter. Most likely he would never be one hundred percent again physically.

Ten days after the fatal crash, mother and father left their surviving son's side to attend the funeral of their other two children in Arkansas. I cannot begin to imagine what they must have felt like, having to leave one child at death's door to bury two others.

On the following Thursday I received another advisory from the Army SFC, who was now assigned as the family's official point of contact. The son was not supposed to make it through the night, and was not showing any indication of brain activity.

Yet I still prayed, as something mighty had kept him alive this long. On the morning of the wreck, I honestly did not think he'd make it to the hospital. Many others were doing the same, and we prayed not only for the boy but also for his greatly suffering parents.

The wreck caught the attention of the mass media, and I found myself handling phone calls from radio and television stations, newspapers and magazines nationwide. The interviews were sometimes a half hour long, then condensed into a paragraph or two, and they still usually managed to get something wrong.

The power of the press, I suppose. This was a longstanding situation throughout my career, and not one single time did any reporter get the story completely straight save for our local newspaper. I figured that had to do with taking an extra bit of care when writing the story, it is different when you know and live among those whom you are reporting upon.

Meanwhile, I received word from the Border Patrol concerning their rookie agent at the scene. He had been nominated for a special award due to his actions, and his supervisors wanted to visit with me.

This was one interview I did not mind giving. Every volunteer who helped out that morning deserved some sort of recognition.

More days passed and the sergeant first class discharged his duties in commendable fashion, including in keeping me posted. The boy was still alive, though just barely. He was on a ventilator and his kidneys had failed, so they were starting dialysis.

The news continued to get worse. His hands and feet turned black, and were swollen to about the size of small melons. As I understood it, the extremities were not getting enough oxygenated blood due to the ventilator doing his breathing for him. There was serious talk about having to amputate.

With each update the situation became grimmer, and at times utterly heartbreaking. From the descriptions given by the SFC, my gut would wad up and a great weight would sink into my heart. I had two sons myself, not that much older than this dying nine-year-old. His mother and father were enduring agonies of the spirit that no one could ever hope, or ever want, to understand.

Stalwart to the end, the sergeant called on the following Sunday night. With grief that could only be intensely personal, he said the son had passed away the afternoon before, exactly three weeks from the date of the accident.

Though by now I was expecting this awful result, the news still came as a blow. In practice I am often a lousy Christian, but still a man of Faith who still believed in miracles, and had witnessed more than one. Where there is life, there is hope.

Yet part of Faith is in being able to accept God's Will and move on, even when it hurt.

It was hurting now. Three weeks and three dead children, and two parents who had gone through their own personal hell on earth that would be a part of them for the rest of their days.

All they had now were each other and their own Faith. The SFC said they were believers, and I had come to respect his opinion during our conversations. He was a good man, and though I have never met him in person I hope someday I shall.

Just to shake his hand and commend him for sorrowful deeds well done.

On Tuesday, November 13, I finished the final report for my investigation. This summation would be submitted to the sitting grand jury as it involved unattended deaths. Thus ended my official duties, or so I thought. However and yet once again, I would be proven wrong.

A critical incident debriefing was put on by a state agency whose representatives came to Ozona, but I did not choose to attend. There were other commitments, and in my opinion the debriefing should have occurred at least a week earlier and scheduled during evening hours.

Most of those folks involved from our little community were volunteers, and many worked day jobs precluding their presence. Thing was, many of them needed to be there for their own inner struggles over what had happened.

Subsequently, we lost some good people in those vital positions and they are always so hard to replace.

And I knew for certain I was done. God never gives us more than we can handle, but He will conduct a gut check every now and then. Retirement was a question that had been plainly answered for me.

In a little over nine more months, I would put away my badge and gun for the final time. In between would be other bad wrecks, other special operations, other challenges and other tragic deaths. To each I gave my all, knowing my finish line was just ahead.

Like Willie Dale used to say, there was a big wheel in life that went around and around. Sometimes you're on the bottom, and sometimes on top. God willing, I was stepping out while on top.

One final part of this sad story still needs telling. I mentioned before I was wrong when thinking my official duties were done concerning this case. Some time after the final report was filed, I was called into the sergeant's office.

"Ben," Sgt. Galindo said, "they want you to file charges on the mother for the deaths of those three children."

Now I had known Ruben Galindo since he was a deputy sheriff in Kimble County. A reservist in the Air Force, Ruben had gone through the academy as a recruit while I was instructing, and later became a rookie in our area.

And now he was my sergeant and as solid as they come, and I knew these orders weren't originating from him. I had explained at length in my investigation packet how the two older children were buckled in when leaving El Paso, and were covered with a blanket for warmth.

Somewhere along the way they unbuckled themselves, either for something otherwise out of reach or to sleep more comfortably. Both had a habit of doing so, and this was verified through friends, relatives and neighbors.

Both were sitting directly behind their mother, there was no way she could have seen their safety belts were not secured.

Furthermore, why in the world would she go through all the trouble of properly securing the two year old infant, and not make certain the other children were secured before starting out?

There is not one of us who would not have done the same, given like circumstance. Yes there was the long distance, the drowsiness, the weather and not stopping for a needed break. But who among us could have done any better, given what that poor woman was dealing with?

"There but for the Grace of God goeth I," states the old proverb. No truer words were ever written.

And just what could be done legally to this heart-wrenchingly piteous figure of mother and wife, which had not already been done?

My reply was blunt, and I meant every single word.

"Sarge, you can tell whoever said that to file those charges themselves. And when they do, I'm going before that grand jury as the investigating officer and make them look like the biggest ass in West Texas."

No charges were ever filed.

But I didn't think too much about that promotion option anymore, either.

Though both years and decades have passed since that awful time, I still think about the young soldier and his wife. Two people living their lives as honorably and meaningfully as anyone could, yet swept away by a raging sea of near incomprehensible horrors, pain and grief.

Throughout these recollections, I have endeavored to keep the innocent anonymous as many have already suffered so much. One should learn from the past, but not kept in perpetual captivity there.

But I will say this, the mother's first name was Monalisa. For all likely intents and purposes, the same as in the song made famous by Nat King Cole.

And I find myself wondering, did a time ever come again when this Monalisa smiled once more?

Dear Lord, I surely hope so.

FRED FIERRO

Of all the officers I worked with during my career, Fred Fierro was the one I did so the longest. He was there the first day I went on duty in Ozona as a rookie highway patrolman, and for the next twenty-two years we shared many an adventure, a few close calls, more than a few laughs, some tears and a grin or two along the way.

With Fred around, you had to grin every now and then. His good humor and like spirit were near infectious, he was the one who usually seemed to see the silver lining in the darkest of clouds. That sort of outlook is sorely needed in our line of work, for there are times you have only two choices; laugh or cry about it.

Though born in Stanton as a Fourth of July baby, Fred's immediate family moved to Ozona early on. I say 'immediate family' because if you started counting heads for his extended one, they were present in force not only in Crockett County but across most of West Texas and northern Mexico.

It was almost a standing joke when saying he was going someplace to see a cousin, as that could be anywhere from Ciudad Chihuahua up to the Panhandle and about as much a spread to either side. Fred was never lacking for blood kin.

After graduating high school in Ozona, he tried college but found the academic life not to his liking. He knocked around the country as part of a surveying crew for a while, before returning home and trying his hand with the Crockett County Sheriff's Office.

That was where Fred Fierro found his calling.

For the next quarter of a century Fred moved through the ranks as jailor, then a juvenile officer, a patrol deputy, a captain and ultimately the chief deputy. Along the way he proved himself to be a man of heart, and one who cared a great deal about his community and the citizens who lived there. This was especially so in regard to the young people of Ozona.

Fred was one of those special kind of peace officers who seemed to know everyone; their background, their sometimes intricate familial ties, where they lived, where they worked, even what kind of vehicle they drove. I suppose coming from such a large family and being a local himself helped in that, but he was also genuinely interested and concerned about those around him. People, all people, were his passion.

Not that his situation didn't cause him personal troubles at times, as well as heartache. Having to enforce the law on his many relatives and friends was hard on him, especially in those cases where a serious crime was committed. In this regard Fred was much like our constable, Bear Borrego..

Bear was from a large local family too, and often faced those same difficult choices and no win situations. But they did their job as best as most men could, and suffered through whatever slings and arrows that came along for doing so.

I admired this particular quality in both.

During his decades with the sheriff's office Fred worked for three sheriffs, including long-time Crockett County Sheriff Billy Mills. It was Billy who gave Fred his chance as a jailor and then a deputy. Fred near worshipped the ground Billy walked on, which would be understandable to many because of the sheriff giving Fred his start.

Yet in reality that bond went far deeper than just a job offering, for Fred and Billy were much the same in their shared outlook in being an officer. It was a sense of caring for others, and maintaining a personal balance between the law and justice. It did not matter if it was the town drunk, a rowdy teenager, a passing hitchhiker, a stranded truckdriver, a petty thief or someone just down on their luck; they saw each in turn as a human being first.

I often thought officers such as these actually gave the most of all, due to who they were inside. That kind of caring does not come easy, especially as the years and decades of disappointments and tragedies pile upon that special place where a man resides in spirit. This ultimately causes health problems in which they, as well as many of their fellows, find their lives drastically shortened.

So it was with Billy. After suffering a massive heart attack while still in office, he lived for only about two years following retirement. With him died not only some of the irreplaceable ties that bind a community together, but an entire era in West Texas law enforcement.

In the intervening decades following Billy's passing, Fred stayed true to his mentor's teachings about what a rural community peace officer should be. In one way it was fairly easy as Fred's natural disposition leaned that direction, even more so than what Billy's had.

I honestly believe we will never know how many people, young and old, locals and complete strangers, deserving or otherwise, that Fred helped in some way and never said a word about the gesture. He was a humble, giving man in so many manners.

But a giving heart cannot go forever and there is more than one kind of injury brought on by a career filled with stress, strain, brutal inhumanities and expectations in others left unrealized. For Sheriff Billy Mills, that fatal injury to health was physical.

For Chief Deputy Fred Fierro this mortal wound manifested in his mind, deep down in the psyche where no one suspected such an insidiously despondent torment to lurk. They say the saddest performer in any circus is often the clown, who puts on such a brave, happy face for the adoring crowds while literally breaking in two inside.

BLACK AND WHITE

Fred was no clown, but his brave and happy facade finally broke into tiny pieces early one Monday morning while at his residence. His wife Petra heard the fatal shot, and rushed into the bedroom to find that Fred Fierro had surrendered to the private torment he had been suffering from.

The news devastated our little town, and reverberated across miles and miles of open spaces and into the hearts of others far away. Fred had a lot of friends, and his well known compassion for his fellow man made those reverberations all the louder and longer lasting.

Mike Johnson, Bruce James and myself were supposed to pull out for Van Horn the next morning, as part of a mostly dog and pony show called Border Star. With our local sheriff's office down to just over half strength, and the tragic pall of great personal loss settling on them as well as the rest of Ozona, I figured my higher ups would hold us back to give our brother officers a breather.

Yet I was wrong again, and realized once more how much the Peter Principle had infested our own organization, and that jackasses do not always come with long ears. The next morning the three of us set out dutifully for Van Horn and a near useless border operation, while our own south county line was situated only forty miles from Mexico.

When Fred's funeral date was set, I raised enough of a personal stink to be allowed to drive back and attend. However those same higher ups were not going to allow Bruce to go, until we pointed out he was an honorary pall bearer.

Mike Johnson had to stay in Van Horn.

When I rolled into the cemetery, Junior Bilano was waiting. Junior started out as a highway patrolman in Fort Stockton, at about the same time when I was a sophomore in high school. He had gone on to serve in Sanderson for several years before transferring to Ozona. Good natured and one who found humor in the darndest things, our mutual friend Trooper Keith Olive had christened him with the nickname of 'Critter.'

With Junior, it more or less fit in agreeable fashion.

"I knew it, I knew it!" he exclaimed. "I told the sergeant they couldn't keep you from coming." Junior paused and cocked his head quizzically before adding, "How much trouble are you in this time?"

I smiled faintly, good old Junior. I went on to explain the brass had actually given their acquiescence, but would not let Mike come. In turn, Junior brought me up to speed on what was happening around town. Fred's useless death was casting a dark pall on the small community of Ozona.

The funeral itself was a somber one, sad beyond written description. People who before never said more than two words to me wanted to talk, seeking to bring some rhyme or reason to such a senseless tragedy.

At graveside with my wife, I looked around to those who stood with me. Fred's family, friends, pillars of the community and church going folks mixed with those who walked a different path in life. Some I had arrested more than once, some Fred had more than once, and a few who spent some time in prison because of it. We were all here, all coming together for something none of us really wanted to be a part of.

Yet we still came to mourn the loss of someone who meant so much to each of us. That need overcame everything else which divided, both before as well as after.

At the close of the service I slowly made my way to my waiting black and white, stopping every few feet to visit momentarily with those who sought me out. Driving to our home, I visited with Cathy while grabbing a bite to eat and then hit the road again for Van Horn.

It was a long, quiet drive, and life went on. But without Fred Fierro.

I have written these lines as a remembrance for Fred. However, the reason for doing so also has a greater purpose. It is to remind others, specifically those who wear the badge, of the many terrors that haunt a man's soul and how they can overwhelm you, if even for a moment.

A moment that can prove to be fatal.

It is my firmest belief that if Fred Fierro could have ever imagined the hurt, despair and numbing pain he would bring to so many others, he would not have pulled that trigger. Fred loved people and would have never intentionally brought so much grief to anyone, especially those he cared most for.

Those would include his wife Petra, his other family members and so many who believed in and admired him. It would also include his fellow peace officers like Texas Ranger Brooks Long, who after drinking coffee with Fred at the Cafe Next Door almost daily, was the man tasked to handle the investigation into Fred's suicide.

No one can begin to imagine what it feels like to see a friend lying lifeless with a self-inflicted bullet hole in his head, unless you've walked that dark, awful path yourself.

And maybe in this terrible reality is the one good thing coming out of such an obscenely hurtful event. To recognize we are all human and all vulnerable, and to be on constant watch for that vulnerability not only in our brothers and sisters, but in ourselves.

I failed completely in making such an observation about Fred, too sure of the brave, happy face to ever question what went on behind the façade. That fact will be on my conscience for the rest of my life, and I know there are many others who deal with the same guilt from this same failing daily.

Readers, do not let this happen to you.

*Chief Deputy Fred Vela Fierro, Crockett County Sheriff's Office
End of Watch March 28th, 2008*

PAT SIROIS

As I look back on my life, there is so very much to be thankful for. Home, health, family, security and worldly possessions of which I never dreamed of as a small boy. I drink from my saucer because my cup of personal blessings runneth over.

Chief among these is I live not only in a nation that exemplifies the virtues of personal liberties and freedoms, as well as their attending responsibilities, but also in a state that holds true to those same essential tenets as vigorously as any other geographical location on earth.

Texas was birthed in the spirit and blood of heroes, and nurtured from troubled infancy by the continuing sacrifices of same. Some of these larger-than-life figures were in actuality not born to this land, but as the old saying goes "got to Texas as quick as they could."

And this multi-generational migration of brave and serving souls continues on to this day.

Another of those personal blessings plays part and parcel to the one addressed above, personified by the men I have come to know throughout life's many journeys. These outsized blessings presented themselves in varied forms of different backgrounds and personalities, and of all colors, creeds, ages and sizes.

However, each one did possess a common denominator. They were of the sort who always seems to be in the shortest supply when trouble comes, and the proverbial wolf is either on the roof or at the door.

One of these was Patrick Sirois.

I first met Pat while on patrol late one night on Interstate 10, a couple miles west of Ozona. The reason was an official one, he was running a wee bit over the posted speed limit. I vividly remember the First Air Cav sticker plastered on his vehicle's rear window, along with a bold logo reading 'UNITED STATES ARMY.' A long whip antenna, suitable for a mobile radio ham operator, jutted toward the night sky.

Somewhere in those memories I can also recall thinking this could prove to be an interesting traffic stop. Boy, was I ever right about that.

When I asked the driver to step to the rear of his car a small, wiry gent about my age came bounding out with a large grin and a special sort of twinkle in his eye. His face was well used and his nose outsized when compared to the rest of his features. You could tell it had been broken in the past, and most likely more than once.

This fellow literally exuded energy and enthusiasm, a trait I would learn as infectious to nearly anyone else in his presence. He identified himself as

First Sergeant Patrick Sirois, US Army, and handed me his driver license, military identification and concealed carry card. It did not take me long to decide I needed to get to know the gent better.

As he had not been driving much over the posted speed limit and was in the military, I issued a written warning and had him sign the paper copy. Thus completing my professional duties, we began visiting alongside the road.

What started out as a five minute traffic stop quickly became a half hour in length, and then some. I learned he was attending the Army Sergeant Major Academy at Fort Bliss and traveling back and forth from Fort Hood. Originally from Connecticut, my new acquaintance had joined the Army after a difficult time as a teenager trying to fit in someplace. As he quipped that night, "I had already tried everything else, so I thought I might as well try the Army."

The decision proved to be a good fit for all concerned. Like so many of us, he had found a home in the military as well as a refined sense of higher purpose. Pat had basically grown up in the Army, it was his family and he was wholly dedicated to the institution, as well as the people who made up its ranks.

Now at the age of thirty-nine, he was preparing for the highest enlisted rank this institution possessed. I do not impress easily, but he was an impressive soldier whom I found myself liking, as well as respecting, almost immediately.

During our conversation he mentioned his interest in becoming a peace officer after his retirement from the Army, and that he wanted to stay in Texas. The Lone Star state was his home now, and where he wanted to spend the rest of his days.

We talked about his future a bit more and I gave him my card, saying to come to Ozona sometime and ride with me for a better feel of the job. As he accelerated into the darkness, he gave a big wave out the open driver's window and I went back to my assigned duties. Little did I know this would be the start of a memorable friendship with a truly memorable man.

It did not take very long for my phone to ring. Pat was on the other end of the line, reminding me of our meeting and of my offer for a ride along. Of course I was honored to have him go on patrol with me, and Mrs. English made it crystal clear that he would stay with us and not in some motel room.

And so it went. The now Command Sergeant Major Sirois spent time in our home at every given opportunity for the next few years. Whenever he showed up, it was like a combination three ringed circus and wild west show come to town. Pat always seemed to have about ten different things going on, with around two dozen options on each one and a hundred stories to tell on top of those.

When I think of Pat Sirois, the adjective 'intense' naturally follows. Whatever he was involved in he was giving it one hundred percent, and with an insatiable desire for knowledge and experience, often simply for knowledge and experience's sake. For him life was not simply something you passed through, but rather a finite time to cram an infinite amount of living in between. I sometimes found myself wondering if he ever slept.

I mentioned before his infectious enthusiasm, you had to see this in action to really believe it. My two sons, Levi and Ethan, were about eight and ten years old and followed him around like two little puppy dogs.

Pat would regale them with stories of his decades in the Army, of places he had seen in South Korea and Europe. He spoke of his escapades during combat operations in Bosnia, trekking across the empty deserts of Kuwait by the dark of the moon and of many other far flung places he had been to.

They would hang on to his every word, totally enthralled by the man and what he had to say. He left a lasting impression and though both now fully grown with years of experience as military officers, either will still tell you he was one of the most unforgettable people they ever met.

Pat's innate likeability and impressiveness carried over into other relationships with my fellow highway patrolmen. Carl Mayfield was my sergeant during those years, and as good a man as I ever stood shoulder to shoulder with. Carl was also a first sergeant in the Marine Corps Reserve, and would be activated shortly for the upcoming invasion of Iraq. He and Pat hit it off from the start, partly due to their respective ranks and positions, but mostly because they were of the same cut from the same whole cloth.

Our young rookie, Kurt Knapp, also quickly became acquainted with Pat and would take him on patrol when I was either off duty or unavailable. The two together were a sight to behold; the tall, baby faced Kurt who never got in much of a hurry and the short, ball-of-fire Pat who seemed ready to explode at any moment with uncontrollable energy. Lasting friendships were born that would only grow stronger with the passage of time.

We often kidded about Pat having a 'trouble magnet' in his front pocket, because when he showed up weird things invariably started happening. On one occasion he hadn't been in our office for more than ten minutes when we received a call about a commercial bus wreck about twenty miles out, the only such incident in Crockett County that anyone could remember.

All four of us rolled in two different units on that one; Carl, Pat, Kurt as well as myself. When we arrived no one was really hurt, but it took us hours to get the necessary information from all the passengers riding inside that Greyhound. If you are familiar with some of the clientele found on those buses, you can probably understand why.

I have already mentioned in a prior chapter when the four of us ended up in my Chevrolet Caprice, so Carl could do a check ride on Kurt. Our hapless rookie not only had his sergeant advising him on this or that, but also two back seat drivers named Sirois and English. I still chuckle about the startled responses from motorists we pulled over that afternoon, three men in Texas

BLACK AND WHITE

Highway Patrol uniforms and one guy in civvies who was grinning continually.

Then we had the forced landing of a single engined aircraft on U.S. 190. We showed up and the plane was there, but no one else was. Turns out the pilot and passenger had experienced engine trouble and picked this desolate stretch of two lane blacktop for an impromptu airstrip. With no one around to help, they pushed the plane against a fence line and began walking, ultimately hitching a ride into Iraan some 40 miles away. We almost never figured that one out.

On another afternoon we received a call of a wreck near the Pecos River Bridge. I was driving Ol' Rocket Sled, an LT1-powered Caprice slick top that could outrun a fast teletype. We headed west with my foot in the fuel injection system, going hell bent for election as fast as that big Chevy could carry us.

After about twenty miles, the engine simply sputtered and died. We coasted for over a mile, me scanning the gauges and trying to figure out what happened while Pat kept asking me questions for which I had no answers. Then he started laughing, which made it all the worse as cars we had just blown by now did the same to the ailing Chevy. We had not reached a complete stop when I popped the inside hood release and we bailed out to take a look.

It did not take me long to find the culprit, somehow the coil wire had come loose and was dangling uselessly near the front of the intake manifold. I slipped it back on and we jumped into the Caprice again; leaving dirt, gravel, dead weeds and streaks of Goodyear Eagle GT+4 rubber as we rocketed off the shoulder.

I made several comments about that proverbial magnet of Pat's as we pushed through 140 MPH, then cut a quick eye over to him. He was leaned back, obviously relaxed and enjoying himself hugely with that irrepressible grin on his face.

Later on, I was issued a black and white Camaro LS1 to ply my trade in. When Pat heard that, he showed up expressively for the purpose of taking a ride in that little misshapen god of speed. As soon as we went on patrol, things started happening. On my very first traffic stop, the right rear tire went flat for an unknown reason that completely confounded me.

These cars were severely limited in trunk space with no room for a spare due to the amount of issued gear, so I had to radio a sheriff's unit to get an air tank to us. We limped into the Circle Bar Truck Stop with me commenting again about that particular magnet. The tire was repaired and we were back on interstate again, just in time to spot a BMW M3 trying to break the land speed record. I reversed course across the median and laid the hammer down.

We were nearing 160 miles an hour when I cut another quick eye over to Pat. He was sitting there just like he had been in the Caprice, leaned back with that grin on his face. Most people with any inkling of sanity would have been trying to dig a hole in the front passenger floor. After our ride together Pat promptly went out and bought a Camaro SS, the civilian version closest to the Code B4C pursuit unit I drove.

This was vintage Pat Sirois, candle lit at both ends and loving it.

A little further in time, Pat retired and joined the newly formed Department of Defense civilian police force at Fort Hood. Not being able to keep himself constrained to only one pistol-packing job, he also signed on as a reserve officer for the nearby Nolanville Police Department. Again this was so typical of him, habitually trying to cram two pounds into a one pound bag.

But Pat was not coming through Crockett County much anymore, so I did not see him as often. We kept in contact via email but he was a lousy correspondent and I only heard from him occasionally, and usually with the sparsity of words that would do justice to a telegraph operator.

There were only two real exceptions to this, when Carl Mayfield died after a bitter battle with cancer and Kurt was killed on patrol. Pat was there for me both times, knowing instinctively how much I was hurting inside. He wrote words of condolence I will always appreciate, and shall never forget.

The last time I heard from Pat was after the Fort Hood shootings. As an officer he responded to this horrendous act of mass murder and betrayal, as well as the ensuing aftermath. I could tell it had really gotten to him, Pat Sirois was retired from the Army but it was still his family and his people, and always would be. When you hurt one of them, he took on this pain as his own. Retired or not, in his heart Patrick Sirois was still a Command Sergeant Major of the finest army in existence.

We talked on the phone that night for hours, sharing both grief and laughter. Pat said he wanted to come visit and work it all out, and just reminisce about the old days. I agreed, I was now retired myself and it sounded like something worth doing.

The two of us never had the chance. On the following Thanksgiving Eve at around 7:45 pm, Pat and his fiancée were traveling on Highway U.S. 69 near Eufaula, Oklahoma. Pat observed a stranded motorist, a young man in a pickup truck and trailer alongside the opposing lanes. He could have just driven on or placed a phone call to report it, but that was not Pat's way.

He stopped his car, put on a reflective vest and walked over to see if he could help. An oncoming vehicle with a distracted driver did not notice the disabled truck and trailer until too late. At the same time Pat snapped on what was about to happen, yelled a warning and shoved the young man clear.

But by doing so, Pat was not able to get clear himself. My friend was pinned in the ensuing high speed crash between the trailer and guardrail, and died while enroute to the Eufaula hospital from massive internal injuries. His body was escorted to the Texas state line by a detail of Oklahoma Highway Patrolmen as a gesture of respect.

I know not a man who made up that particular honor guard, but I owe each for doing so all the same.

Command Sergeant Patrick Roger Sirois was buried with full military, as well as police honors at the Central Texas State Veterans Cemetery just south of Killeen. Nearly a thousand police officers, active duty military, veterans, community leaders and citizens attended his funeral.

I was among them, trying my best to be there for him as he had been for me when Carl and Kurt passed on. A United States Honor Flag, one of those which flew above the ruins of the World Trade Center following 9/11, was on display during his memorial service.

Standing there among so many strangers, I attempted to steel my thoughts as Pat's many honors were recited. The Bronze Star, the Legion of Merit, the Drill Sergeant Badge and a host of other military medals and honors had been bestowed upon him.

Just prior to his death, Pat was named Officer of the Year by the Nolanville Police Department, the first reserve officer ever to receive this award. Later he would be recognized by our state legislature as the 2010 recipient of the Texas Law Enforcement Achievement Award for Valor.

Those are big, deep footprints for a short fella from Connecticut.

Patrick Sirois was a hero, and this requiem is for him. I still count my blessings for knowing Pat, as well as so many other remarkable men the Lord has sent my direction. May God keep him close, and on a bit of high ground that will remind him of Texas.

After all, he got here as soon as he could…

Officer Patrick Sirois, Fort Hood, Texas Police Department
Reserve Officer Nolanville, Texas Police Department
End of Watch November 23d, 2010

RETIREMENT, OR SOMETHING LIKE THAT

The Ozona Stockman
August 2008:

To My Fellow Citizens of Crockett County,
   I would like to take this opportunity to thank you for the faith, support, prayers, and yes, deserved criticism on occasion which you have bestowed upon me during my many years as a peace officer in Crockett County.
   It has been my distinct honor and privilege to serve in this community, and live among you in Ozona. You have opened your hearts and homes to my family, and treated them as one of your own in all matters great and small. I will always be grateful to you for that; no peace officer could ever ask for more.
   As I move on to a new challenge here in Crockett County, I will continue to try to serve you and your young people as best as I know how. You deserve at least that much, as Ozona surely is the place 'out in the West, where the air is pure, the climate agreeable, and the people friendly--- The best place on Earth to call home.'
   May God bless each and every one of you, and may God bless America,

Ben H. English
Senior Trooper, Texas Highway Patrol (ret.)

   So read the note published in our local newspaper upon my retirement. My last day in uniform was one day shy of my fiftieth birthday. The actual date of retirement would be the last day of the month.
   But though I had hung up my gun and badge, this did not mean I was done serving my community. Once my retirement plans became known school board members, principals, teachers, parents and local citizens called or came by, imploring me to try my hand at teaching school.
   It was almost as if I was the subject of some sort of conspiracy.
   When first approached I had no desire to work for anyone else ever again. I had done so since I was thirteen years old, and had the social security statements to prove so. My mind was full of other plans, including my longtime hobby of working on old cars, making far more trips into the backcountry of the lower Big Bend, and finally getting serious about becoming a writer.

Other jobs had already been offered but I turned them down one and all. This was especially true for the ones concerning badges, as Cathy lived up to her part of our agreement and now fully expected me to keep mine.

However, she was as a high school teacher herself and admitted I could be of real service on the campus. I suppose it was her estimation, along with so many others, which started me thinking in that direction really hard.

Plus there was the matter of an unpaid personal debt still needing attended to, one going back nearly thirty-five years. During high school after my parents divorced, I was in sore need of guidance and a strong hand. It was a teacher who stepped forward and saw to this necessity.

He was a tough, gruff World War II veteran who had gone to see the elephant on more than one occasion. Frank Baker had been a Darby's Ranger, an ambulance driver, a hunting guide in Alaska and a diver along the Great Barrier Reef of Australia. Once a football coach he was then head of the social studies department at Fort Stockton High School, and my world history teacher.

We students called him 'Dad,' but for some blessed reason this was proven to me most of all. Without his steadying influence, there remains a doubt in my mind if I would have graduated at all.

One time I decided to play hooky but Mom heard of what I was up to. She did not call the police or anyone else, she called Dad Baker at the high school. Somehow he managed to find a substitute that morning and came looking for me. With his typical bloodhound kind of tenacity, he found me too.

When he did he had some serious words for my consumption, including to not ever make him go looking for Bennie English again. There were other words, strong words, about what he expected from me no matter what my home situation might be. I took this conversation to heart, and tried to straighten up my act as much as any punk seventeen-year-old kid could. One sure thing though, Dad Baker never had to go looking for me again.

That was also the year he had his first heart attack. As they were wheeling out of his classroom, he grabbed hold of Steve Williams and said "You are Bennie's friend, keep an eye on him because he's right on the bubble."

A lot had happened in my life since then, and there was many a life's lesson in between. Dad Baker made certain I started that special journey on the right foot.

Yet something from the past remained unresolved, calling out to my conscience. I had never properly thanked him for all he did for me, the old army ranger finally succumbed to another heart attack while I was overseas. After equal applications of both thought and prayer, my decision was to accept the teaching job.

I met with Superintendent Abe Gott and Principal Dan Webb to hash things out. According to them, my honors at Angelo State and subsequent instructor billets in the DPS were qualification enough to teach. I would do so on a part time basis, developing a criminal justice program for our local high school as I saw fit.

There was no written contract, we just shook hands after talking through the necessary details. I wore my uniform for the final time on a Thursday, and appeared before my first morning class the following Monday in a coat and tie.

So began two of my most memorable and satisfying years ever in any workplace. I was afforded the precious opportunity to work with young people whom I never would have been able to reach as an officer, until likely too late.

Some came from families in which I arrested close relatives, including on felonies leading to prison time. Some already had flunked one year and others were on that same bubble as I, all those years before. Far too many were craving for care and concern, because they were not getting anything like that at home.

I vividly remember trying to explain to them the purpose of the course early on. All was well until my use of words like 'honor,' 'integrity,' and 'selflessness.' Looking around, I observed far too many blank looks on far too many young faces.

In truth they were not actively turning me off, they just simply did not have a clue as to what I was talking about.

Since we had such a broad, empty canvas to work with, we started at the beginning. I wanted them to understand when a man or woman swears an oath and puts on a badge, they were no longer just another Joe or Jane Smuckateloe from back on the block.

Four thousand years of Western civilization now stood with them, and an oath to uphold the law was something far more than a collection of pretty words haphazardly strung together. That badge and accompanying oath were near sacred, far too many others had paid the ultimate price in keeping both in such a state of reverence.

A few had been personal friends of mine.

We started with the Code of Hammurabi, then on to Mosaic Law, Roman Law, the Magna Carta, English Common Law, Blackstone's Commentaries, the Declaration of Independence and the Constitution of the United States, along with the all-important attending Bill of Rights.

There were vocabulary tests, weekly tests, quotation memorizations and inquiries each week as to how they were doing in their other classes. A guide and squad leaders were appointed, and then alternated each six weeks based upon effort and merit.

Throughout the school year we had fire drills, active shooter drills, lost child drills, hazmat spill drills and how to respond as a class to each possible scenario. We had confidence exercises, street awareness briefs and learned basic maintenance for an automobile.

There were teaching blocs for ethics, public speaking and practical application of the WIN principle, as in 'What's Important Now.' Classes would watch a weekly episode of the old television series 'Adam 12,' then write a 250 word police report as to what occurred.

And they not only learned, but did so enthusiastically. In those two years I never had a parent or guardian complain, and never sent a single student to the principal's office.

However, we did do a lot of pushups together. It's sort of hard to cop an attitude with someone old enough to be your grandfather, yet who can still have you shaking like a wet dog in a freezer while he serenely continues to call cadence in his coat and tie.

Respect is not given, it is earned and it goes up and down as well as both ways.

That was decades ago and those young students have gone on to start their own families, and make their own marks in life. A sizeable number went into the military or became part of the justice system themselves.

Every one of them has a special place in my heart, and I am so very proud of who and what they turned out to be. Though many of my various labors have since born tremendous fruit, along with some recognition and even minor repute, none will ever be as rewarding as those two years spent teaching in a small West Texas high school.

Dad Baker, I hope you consider my longstanding debt as being paid in full.

And that I did some sort of good, somewhere along the way.

EPILOGUE: REFLECTIONS UPON LESSONS AND IRONIES

One of my favorite quotes concerning the changeless march of time was by C.S. Lewis. The great Christian author and philosopher once wrote: "The Future... something which everyone reaches at the rate of sixty minutes an hour, whatever he does, whoever he is."

And so it is with me, the end of this coming August will mark my fourteenth year since retirement from the Texas Department of Public Safety. In that intervening time an assortment of happenstances have both entered and exited my life. The entrances have been many, but most all welcome. The exits have often left a great ache in my heart.

Sometimes this deep pain is personal, sometimes shared with others of like background and nature. Some of these losses involve some of the special people in my stories.

Four years ago, friend and retired Texas Ranger Danny Rhea slipped his mortal bounds and headed for the undiscovered country. Though he left Ozona many years before, his service to the state of Texas continued in stellar fashion to the very day of his own retirement.

Following being stationed in Crockett County, Danny transferred to Sulphur Springs. Always the inveterate hunter and fisherman, he found his peace in both pursuits among the fertile fields and waterways of that part of east Texas.

But when duty called, Ranger Rhea answered. In early January of 1998, a mentally deranged individual appeared in the local DPS office, claiming to have a bomb. Everyone evacuated the building save for Danny and two troopers, who spent over an hour attempting in every way possible to reason with someone who had no reason.

Then the tense situation took a far more ominous note when the subject produced a nine millimeter pistol, and pointed the weapon at one of the troopers. Ranger Rhea fired exactly one round, fatally wounding the subject and stopping this mortal threat to a fellow officer. For his actions Danny received the Texas Medal of Valor, only one of five Texas Rangers to do so since 1935.

After retirement he and his wife Sue moved back to San Angelo, and Danny piddled around with one project or hobby after another while enjoying his grandkids. But the man who had met every difficult task in life so successfully was about to encounter yet another, and this would be his biggest battle of all.

A debilitating disease took over his body and this powerful, larger than life man was gradually reduced to a walker while suffering acute, unrelenting pain. One sad day I was notified of his passing by his son Devin, once one of my smallbore rifle shooters and someone I looked upon as almost one of my own.

At Danny's funeral, I was humbled to be asked to sit with the family. It was a somber day for a lot of us.

Danny Vaughn Rhea, Sergeant, Texas Rangers

Other friends and mentors were to follow. Six months later, Emmit Moore passed away in Pecos at the way too young age of fifty-seven. A man of great personal honor and conviction, Emmit was one of the first black troopers in the Department and was sent to Reeves County as a young rookie.

Most everyone in DPS Headquarters Austin held their breath, but they need not had been concerned. Emmit with his eternal optimism, sense of wit, good-naturedness and outgoing personality soon had the town and county in his back pocket. And for anyone who persisted in trying to push him into a corner, Trooper Emmit Moore was always more than ready to accommodate them.

Emmit not only served the community of Pecos, both he and his wife Louise became an integral part of the locale. She was the juvenile probation officer there for twenty-four years, and the two of them made a force to be reckoned with. Throughout the decades their consuming passion was the welfare of area youth, and in helping bring a future worth having to those young lives.

Emmit became an enduring symbol of the law in that part of West Texas, known far and wide and for all the right reasons. He served our Department with distinction for thirty years, then four years as a Reeves County Sheriff's Deputy. Louise went on to be a teacher for seven years, as well as a county commissioner.

But the man with a heart as big as the land he served began having complications with that same outsized organ, including a heart attack. There were several surgical procedures, all sorts of medications, bypasses and finally a transplant itself.

Emmit remained supreme in both good humor as well as personal courage through all of this. He never gave up, his personal situation never keeping him from wanting to help others and in bettering his community.

When Emmit died, he and Louise were working on a program to provide quality STEM education to youth in underserved rural areas of West Texas. Among his many interests, Emmit was always enthralled with science.

Trooper Emmit Charles Moore, Jr. Texas Highway Patrol

These were the sort of men, among so many others of the same brand, who spurred on my writing of this book. Again, it was not something I wanted to do near as much as needed to. My peers, those who I both served with and admired reminded me of this solemn responsibility, and the necessity of rekindling the memory of those who gave their all.

But the bringing forth again of these recollections and events sometimes had attending high price tags, as well as inflationary costs with the passing of so many years. I was about a quarter of the way through this book when I realized that subconsciously, my writing style had changed. It was completely different in many ways from any of my prior four books.

Yet it did not take long to identify this new-found style, for in reality it was an old one. You see, I had used it many times before in my life. In the most emotional passages, the ones that had been buried for so long, my prose reverted back to the strictly detached manner of an offense report or investigation packet.

One could call it the Joe Friday Syndrome, as in "just the facts, ma'am."

And I knew why, too. It served as a ready-made defense mechanism, to keep those long dormant emotions of horror, helplessness, despair and occasionally a killing anger held at arm's length. The old saying of fighting the way you train has precedence here. I was going back to long-established habits to accomplish what needed done, but without having to live through it all once more.

However, you can never completely do so as those memories lie there patiently waiting, like a primed snare waits for the unwary to trip the release. You pick up a yellowing fatality folder, feeling somewhat awkward and disconcerted as you do not even recall the name on the jacket. Someone died, and you can't remember anything about it.

Then you open the file and within reading the first line you are there again. Hearing the traffic going by, the wails of pain and inconsolable grief, the feeling of sleet pellets stinging your face as the cold wind blows up under your felt hat, and the searing sights of devastation and sudden death.

The date says it was over thirty years ago, but in your mind it is now and with the opening of each of those files, the memories play the scene like an old 8mm film projector you can't find the off switch to.

Following my retirement, it was five years before I could hear a siren and see an emergency vehicle go by, and not get an adrenalin flow. I have not talked to anyone of like background who would not admit to the same.

Other times the sensation is something far more ominous, even vile. Not too long ago I was walking past a house where a murder recently occurred. My senses caught a far too familiar scent from those years, something pungently ugly that smells like nothing else on this earth.

It was the odor of death.

Instantly my mind snapped backwards through the fabric of time, and to our old Ozona DPS office. Norbert Ortiz is trying to explain something to a new sergeant, who possessed hardly any time on the road before promoting.

"Ben," Norbert calls out to me. "Come here!"

I step into the room and into the middle of a somewhat heated dispute. Norbert has turned in a fatality packet and in the box marked 'Unusual Odors,' he had written "the smell of death."

Now Norbert was not simply referring to the smell of a decaying human body, but was trying to describe what might be better termed as some sort of ethereal presence that sometimes near overwhelms the normal five senses. To put it in terms best associated for the uninitiated, it would be an odor.

The new sergeant says there is no such thing, but I agree with Norbert.

His lack of essential knowledge was not the new sergeant's fault, it was the fault of a promotional process that allowed such oversights. In the end, we manage to persuade him of the validity in Norbert's experienced observation.

The new sergeant had an open mind, some don't. Ultimately, he would learn all too well about what we were trying to convey.

In the career of a peace officer, you are exposed to so many rare lessons in life, as well as ironies. Looking back there were so many poignant, even heartbreaking ones in my own. I saw my field training officer, the man who warned me most often about watching vehicles coming from behind, killed by a truck that struck his unit from the rear.

I saw one of my rookies, likely one of the most careful and conscientious of any while behind the wheel of a patrol car, killed when he neglected to see oncoming traffic as he was crossing an interstate median.

I saw a friend, one of the most professional, alert and tactically proficient troopers I personally ever knew, murdered by seventeen-year-old generations-long loser with a World War One revolver over a minor traffic accident.

I saw a friend, who to every outside eye appeared to be as happy-go-lucky and full of life as ever, take a pistol one morning and blow his brains out while lying in utter despair on his own bed.

Finally, I saw a friend, closer than a brother, do everything right in his life in honoring country, profession, community and family die of a stomach cancer first diagnosed as a ruptured appendix. He neither drank nor smoked, trained as hard physically as any, yet still succumbed to this insidious killer at the age of forty-four.

It killed him just as surely as any bullet ever could, and I still believe that his absolute commitment to so many others gave this cancer an upper hand early on.

People who do not know any better talk about 'cop humor' as if it was a bad thing. In truth it can be the only thing helping you hold on to whatever sanity you might have left, at that particular moment.

For at that precise tick of the eternal clock, you can either laugh or cry about all that is going on around you. When you laugh, you find the emotional release to carry on.

When you cry, the world around starts to fall apart. You cannot let that happen as you are the guy with the gun and the badge. If you lose it, everybody loses it.

My story is not unusual among my comrades in arms, we did the same job and faced the same challenges. I just happened to be one who sat down and wrote about a few of our shared experiences.

Far more importantly, I also wrote about the lives of others who gave their all.

As I sit finishing this final chapter, our mass media is full of sensationalist stories of so-called police brutality, and the strident calls from self-serving, near comically pompous politicians to defund our law enforcement agencies. I find this a supremely sad irony in itself, because at the same time violent crime in general and assaults on police officers in particular are increasing percentage-wise in numbers that are simply appalling.

The sheer hypocrisy in this is conscience numbing. To hand pick and sensationalize a single story where all the facts are not even known, while ignoring so many others who are literally dying in planned ambushes on the mean streets across our nation.

Their only fault? Fealty and faithfulness to a sworn oath involving service and protection of others.

Meanwhile, our country is enveloped in a noxious fog best described as the balkanization of America. Differences in our populace are pried at, hammered upon and magnified to create great clefts of separation running deep and wide in every direction.

History tells us repeatedly to beware of those who have such a penchant for destroying, as very seldom do they have any inclination to build anything truly worthwhile. Yet these sorts have become so prolific in our society as to become a rotting pestilence within our midst. They are, in effect, the infectious carriers of anarchy, destruction and death.

You know I never saw an officer, an EMT, a fireman or an ER crew ask anyone what their politics were, and then refuse to care for them because of their answer. The color of skin pigment, the last name, the amount of money in a bank account, none of that mattered. All that mattered was someone needed help, and they had the skills as well as the burning desire to do so.

Yes, they are only human and internally flawed and prejudiced as any other. But their true nature, their crowning glory in mortal life, is their ability to rise above those flaws and prejudices when called upon. In a world of hungry, destructive wolves, they stand as the sheepdog who serves and protects the flock.

I close this book with one more story, one more tragic example of the losses we as a people incur most every day.

About a year ago I was enjoying retirement in one of my favorite pastimes, prowling the backcountry of the lower Big Bend. Upon my return, I learned of the ambush-style slaying of Trooper Chad Walker. Upon hearing he was alive but in critical condition that gnawing, miserable feeling in my gut began to grow once more.

A short time later came the news. He was gone.

BLACK AND WHITE

Now I did not know this young man personally, I retired sometime before he even went through recruit school. But I know his kind, the rarest of all who instinctively run to the first sign of trouble, rather than away from it. I have been at graveside for far too many of his fellows, and the hurt is never completely apart from who and what I am deep inside.

Upon hearing he had passed on, all that came back in near tidal wave proportions. Worse still because I knew that I was not the only one feeling such a singular sort of sorrow and grief. For his death was not only a loss for his friends, family, neighbors, co-workers, community and society as a whole, but in the timeless struggle between right and wrong, and good and evil.

And right and good lost out.

I keep telling myself God has a plan, and all will be set right in His Eternal Glory. My Bible tells me this and I try to keep the flame of Faith lit, as well as a seeking prayer on my lips.

But it still hurts enough to bring tears to my eyes, like the scars of battles from long ago ripped open again without warning.

Like so many others I have known, the time came far too early for Chad Walker to go rest high on the mountain. Each fought the good fight as best as they knew how, and their reward is to rest with other souls of like spirit.

Trooper Walker is now in a better place far away from where his journey began, and his like-minded kind were the first to greet him.

In the James Michener classic about naval aviators during the Korean War entitled *The Bridges At Toko-Ri*, one of the main characters poses a question that should haunt each and every one of us.

"Where do we get such men?"

Much like those carrier pilots, these men and women behind the badge launch every day when going to work. Their sworn duty is to uphold the laws of their state as well as our nation, to venture forth into the mouth of the cat and to confront every manner of man's depravity to his fellow man.

They try their best to right the wrongs, protect the helpless and serve their community and society while enduring not only the battles without, but the battles within.

Then they go home to loved ones and family, and do their best to act like it was just another day at the office. Their next day at the office begins with another launch tomorrow, or with a phone call, or being in the right place at the wrong time somewhere in between.

Thank you, Lord, for giving them to us.

Thank you, Lord, for the generous blessing of allowing me their company for a while.

And thank you Lord, for the lessons of life that continue on…

Trooper Ben H. English, THP (Ret.) and 'The Beast' (Still on Active Duty)

ABOUT THE AUTHOR

Ben H. English is an eighth-generation Texan who was raised in the Big Bend Country of the Lone Star State. He attended schools in Presidio, Marfa and later, a one room school house in Terlingua. During this time his family had several ranching and business interests in the area, including the historic Lajitas Trading Post which was run by his grandparents.

Mr. English served seven years in the US Marine Corps and upon returning to civilian life, graduated college with honors. He joined the Texas Highway Patrol in 1986, where he served until his retirement in late 2008. He spent the following two years working part time as a Criminal Justice teacher at Ozona High School.

Mr. English has spent much of his life prowling about in the lower Big Bend. His first book, Yonderings, detailed just some of those journeys and was published by Texas Christian University Press.

Presently, Mr. English and his wife live in Alpine, Texas so they can be closer to the land they both love so much. To this day, he likes nothing better than grabbing a pack and some canteens, and heading off in a direction he has never been before.

THANK YOU FOR READING!

If you enjoyed this book, we would appreciate your customer review on your book seller's website or on Goodreads.

Also, we would like for you to know that you can find more great books like this one at www.CreativeTexts.com

www.ingramcontent.com/pod-product-compliance
Lightning Source LLC
Chambersburg PA
CBHW071234070526
44583CB00017B/2179